*–and I worked at
the writer's trade*

# –AND I WORKED AT THE WRITER'S TRADE

## Chapters of Literary History, 1918–1978

## MALCOLM COWLEY

THE VIKING PRESS  NEW YORK

First published in 1978 by The Viking Press
625 Madison Avenue, New York, N.Y. 10022
Published simultaneously in Canada by
Penguin Books Canada Limited

LIBRARY OF CONGRESS CATALOGING IN PUBLICATION DATA
Cowley, Malcolm, 1898–
—And I worked at the writer's trade.
Includes index.
1.   American literature—20th century
—History and criticism—Addresses, essays, lectures.
2.   Authors, American—20th century
—Biography—Addresses, essays, lectures.
I.   Title.
PS221.C646          810'.9'005          77–28713
ISBN 0–670–12291–2

Printed in the United States of America
Set in Linotype Fairfield

ACKNOWLEDGMENTS
Farrar, Straus & Giroux, Inc.: From "Several Voices Out of a Cloud" from
*The Blue Estuaries* by Louise Bogan, Copyright © 1938, 1968 by Louise
Bogan. Reprinted by permission.

Gale Research Company: "Georgia Boy," which appeared in *Pages*, Copyright © Gale Research Company, 1976.

Harcourt Brace Jovanovich, Inc. and Faber and Faber Ltd.: From "The Love
Song of J. Alfred Prufrock" by T. S. Eliot, from *Collected Poems 1909–1962*.
Reprinted by permission.

Oxford University Press: From *Collected Poems* by Conrad Aiken, Copyright
© 1953, 1970 by Conrad Aiken. Reprinted by permission of Oxford University Press, Inc.

Random House, Inc.: From "In Memory of W. B. Yeats" from *Collected
Poems* by W. H. Auden, edited by Edward Mendelson, Copyright 1940 and
renewed 1968 by W. H. Auden. Reprinted by permission of Random House,
Inc. From "Anecdote of the Jar" from *The Collected Poems of Wallace
Stevens*, Copyright 1923 and renewed 1951 by Wallace Stevens. Reprinted
by permission of Alfred A. Knopf, Inc.

Southern Illinois University Press: From the introduction to *Malcolm
Cowley, a Checklist of His Writings, 1916–1973* by Diane U. Eisenberg,
Copyright © Southern Illinois University Press, 1975; from the Afterword
to *Yesterday's Burdens* by Robert M. Coates, Copyright © Southern Illinois
University Press, 1975.

The Viking Press: From the Introduction to *Writers at Work: The Paris
Review Interviews*, First Series, Copyright © 1958 by Paris Review, Inc.
Reprinted by permission.

*For Peter and Ebie Blume / Neighbors and friends since always*

# Contents

# A Foreword

These are chapters of literary history written at intervals over the last twenty years, though dealing with a longer period. I call them chapters, rather than essays, because they tell parts of a continued story and because each of them presents what I have learned about a particular situation or problem in the lives of American writers since the First World War. I was one of the writers, beset with the same problems as others, so the book tells part of my own story too.

What has most impressed me over the years is the change in ideals of life and letters, and of the language itself, produced by the appearance of each new age group. Is there a pattern to be discerned in those changes, a sort of inner logic, or are they purely the result of external circumstances? That question regarding age groups, or literary generations, is a recurrent theme in these chapters, but there are other themes as well. One is the waves of enthusiasm that sweep over the literary community, as notably during the 1930s and the 1960s. Another is the mechanics of literary reputations: Why have some writers of talent been persistently neglected? Might it be partly the result of their choosing not to be celebrities? What is the effect on an author's work of the image he constructs of himself and presents to the public? What are the institutions that advance or impede his work, the types of apprenticeship, the official recognitions? Finally there is the author himself as he has moved through those situations with his own little bundle of beliefs and has tried to meet his own standards.

The author has to confess that, in these later years, he has felt increasingly alone and beleaguered. He is, after all, a humanist by instinct, one who believes that literature should deal with persons (though it may also deal with animals, objects, or forces that exist as persons for the reader). He believes in the reciprocal connection between artists and their audience. He believes that literature comes out of life—where else could it come from?—and that, if successful in its own terms, it goes back into life by changing the consciousness of its readers. All these are primer-book notions, but, during the past few years, they have been less universally accepted. It seems to the author—it seems to me—that much of our fiction, much of our poetry, and a substantial body of our criticism have become more and more unpeopled, unliving, and even inhuman. But fashions will change, as they always do.

A word about the sequence of chapters. The book starts, as is proper, with a discussion of literary generations; it tries to define their nature and describe some of their conflicts as these affected the course of American writing. A second chapter treats an example of such a conflict in the battle over Hemingway's posthumous reputation. Beginning with the third chapter, the sequence is roughly chronological—not by date of writing, which is the author's private affair, but by subject matter. That is, we move from Harvard in 1918 to Greenwich Village and Paris in the 1920s, and thence to the mood of the literary world in the Depression years. The later chapters continue with more recent situations down to the youth rebellion of the 1960s and the revival, in the 1970s, of a modified religion of art. Once I set out to write, but never finished, a history of American letters in the twentieth century. Most of the chapters that follow might have found a place in it.

M.C.

*Sherman, Connecticut*
*January 1978*

# I "AND JESSE BEGAT ..."
# A Note on Literary Generations

1 ✍ Almost anyone who has dreamed about writing a history of American literature, or indeed of any national literature, has noticed one circumstance that marks the appearance of remembered writers. They do not come forward singly, at random intervals of time; instead they appear in clusters or constellations that are surrounded by comparatively empty years. Take for one example the record of American authors born during the nineteenth century. If we set down a list of famous names with dates of birth beside them, we shall find that they arrange themselves in a number of clusters, six by my reckoning, with the men and women who compose each cluster so close in age that they might have gone to school together if they had lived in the same neighborhoods.

Let me run over the familiar list.

The first cluster, or age group, not the least distinguished, is composed of authors born during the first ten years of the century: Emerson (1803), Hawthorne (1804), Simms (1806)—the group was not confined to New England—Longfellow and Whittier (1807), Poe and Holmes (1809), Margaret Fuller (1810), and perhaps we might add the belated name of Harriet Beecher Stowe (1811). Of this group Emerson and Hawthorne were the leaders and spokesmen, soon to become the eponymous heroes.

After some nameless years, a second cluster takes shape, this time composed of Thoreau (1817), Melville, Whitman, and Lowell, all born in 1819, and Parkman (1823). When Van Wyck Brooks was writing his five-volume history of the literary life in America, he chose the eponymous heroes by calling one volume *The Times of Melville and Whitman.*

Again there follow some relatively nameless years—though Emily Dickinson was born in 1830—until a new cluster starts with Mark Twain in 1835. The other names here are Bret Harte (1836), Howells (1837), Henry Adams (1838), Ambrose Bierce and William James (1842), and Henry James (1843), with the oldest and youngest of these remembered as the two heroes. One might remark, not incidentally, that a number of admired painters—Whistler (1834), John La Farge (1835), Winslow Homer (1836), and Thomas Eakins (1844)—were born in almost the same span of years.

For the first three literary clusters, the median years of birth are respectively 1807, 1820, and 1839. By projection there should have been another group of writers born in the neighborhood of 1855, and indeed one finds a few distinguished names, but not enough of them to form a cluster. The names that occur to me are those of Sarah Orne Jewett (1849), Lafcadio Hearn (born abroad in 1850), and Kate Chopin (1851). If we should also mention some of their less distinguished coevals—as I don't propose to do—we should see that the local-color school, once dominant in American fiction, was largely composed of writers born shortly before 1855. The local colorists still have their place in literary records, but most of them have disappeared from the public memory.

Edith Wharton (1862) was more or less isolated in time (as Dickinson had been in her different fashion). The next real cluster, the fourth in our synopticon, is that of the years from 1869 to 1876. It includes Robinson, Masters, Moody, and Tarkington, all born in 1869, Frank Norris (1870), Stephen Crane and Dreiser (1871). No famous author was born in 1872, the median year for the group, but then come Willa Cather (1873), Gertrude Stein, Amy Lowell, Ellen Glasgow, and Robert Frost (all 1874), Sherwood Anderson and Jack London (1876). Of this group I should judge that Dreiser and Frost have become the eponymous heroes.

A fifth cluster is composed of writers born between 1879 and 1889. Here I shan't mention all the famous names, but the cluster includes Wallace Stevens (1879), H. L. Mencken (1880), William Carlos Williams (1883), Van Wyck Brooks and Randolph Bourne (1886), Marianne Moore (1887), Eugene O'Neill and T. S. Eliot (1888), and Conrad Aiken (1889). Perhaps the central year for this cluster is 1885, which marked the birth of Sinclair Lewis, Ring Lardner, and Ezra Pound.

The sixth and last cluster of American writers born during the nineteenth century is what Gertrude Stein called the Lost Generation: Fitzgerald, Faulkner, Hemingway, Wilder, Wilson, Hart Crane, Thomas Wolfe, and their many gifted coevals, all born between 1894 and 1900. In those years nature seemed in such a hurry to produce writers of talent that Hemingway and Hart Crane were born on the same day—July 21, 1899—four months before Allen Tate and three months after Vladimir Nabokov.

If we bear such clusters in mind—and they have occurred in every large nation—the history of literature assumes a different aspect. No longer does it seem to be a plain dotted with separate obelisks and sloping gently upward toward the present. Instead—to adapt a figure from Ortega y Gasset—it becomes a rugged landscape crossed at intervals by mountain ranges. Talented writers cluster in the valleys between the ranges, where they often have as neighbors talented artists, composers, social thinkers, and scientists of the same age, besides a larger community of those willing to listen. In each of the valleys, moreover, all the inhabitants have a common fund of memories, aspirations, antipathies, and a shared feeling of what it means to live in the world. Starting with similar problems, as all of them do, they come to vastly different conclusions, but seem to express them in the same tone of voice, which can be distinguished from the voices of those in neighboring valleys. In spite of their rivalries, often intense; in spite of shifting alliances and broken friendships, they tend to think of themselves as "we" and of other age groups as "they," strangers and potential enemies.

And what about those authors who live high in the mountains, separated by years from the older or younger groups competing for the same body of readers? Usually they do not live out their lives alone; instead they follow a path that leads downward toward one or another of the market towns. Emily Dickinson, born in 1830, did live alone, but she belongs in many ways with the Melville-Whitman cluster of writers a decade older. Edith Wharton, born in 1862, went forward to join the writers a decade younger. Sometimes the top of the mountain is a zigzag. Thus, Edna St. Vincent Millay and Archibald MacLeish were born in the same year, 1892, but Millay wrote in the style of an older group while MacLeish is closer to the Lost Generation. In each case the groups are identified not only by dates but also by shared feelings and something close to a common language.

Such observations about the way that remembered writers —and great men in other fields—tend to appear in clusters have been made by European scholars since the age of Louis XIV. Others were made even in classical times, as has been shown by citations from Tacitus and from Velleius Paterculus, a Roman historian of the first century. Velleius explained the phenomenon by what we should call a behavior pattern: "Talent is stimulated by emulation," he said. "In some cases envy, in others admiration, impels it to surpass." Modern scholars have found an explanation in historical events, or in economics, or in simple biology. It was Michelet, in the *Histoire de la Révolution,* who stressed the biological theme. After puzzling over the question why so many great Frenchmen were born in the two years 1768 and 1769, he wrote:

"Those admirable children were conceived, produced at a moment when the century, raised in moral stature by the genius of Rousseau, was recovering hope and faith. In the dawning day of a new religion, women awakened. The result was a more than human generation."

What Michelet seems to be saying is that the awakened women were more passionate in those two years and hence produced more talented children. There has been no support for his contention in recent biology. Today we take for granted that the innate capabilities of children born in a given year are about the same as those of children born in any other year. But why, then, do so many persons of the same age distinguish themselves as writers (or artists or scientists)? Why is a brilliant class in college followed so often by a succession of lackluster classes? "Talent breeds talent," we hear people say without any suspicion, on their part or ours, that they are paraphrasing Velleius. Henry James offers a longer paraphrase in an often-quoted passage of his little book on Hawthorne:

> The best things come, as a general thing, from the talents that are members of a group; every man works better when he has companions working in the same line, and yielding the stimulus of suggestion, comparison, emulation. Great things of course have been done by solitary workers; but they have usually been done with double the pains they would have cost if they had been done in more genial circumstances.

I suspect that James lays too much stress on the vocal exchange of judgments and the mere rubbing of elbows. There can be literary constellations whose members seldom or never meet. Faulkner, to mention one example, never met Hemingway and they exchanged very few letters, two or three at the most, yet both men expressed a spirit that prevailed at the time. In 1946 Faulkner's editor at Random House suggested that Hemingway might write an introduction to a new edition of *The Sound and the Fury*. Faulkner quite sensibly rejected the notion; he said, "It's like asking one race horse in the middle of a race to broadcast a blurb on another horse in the same running field." In the middle of the race for fame, Faulkner and Hemingway read each other's work with close attention. "The stimulus of suggestion, comparison, emulation" can be derived from books as well as from companions, especially if the books are written by rivals of one's own age and are addressed to the same audience, also of one's age. We can think of a generation, in this sense, as collaborating on the same many-volumed work. Emerson said in one of his notebooks:

> As a vast, solid phalanx the generation comes on, they have the same features and their pattern is new in the world. All wear the same expression, but it is this which they do not detect in each other. It is the one life which ponders in the philosophers, which drudges in the laborers, which basks in the poets, which dilates in the love of the women.

2 ✍ In various European countries—Germany, France, Italy, Spain—scholars have advanced rather elaborate theories about the nature and term in years of literary generations. One reason why the scholars differ among themselves is that they have used the word "generation" in different contexts, sometimes biological (or familial), sometimes biographical, and sometimes as a facet of cultural history. To be specific—

Biologically a generation is simply the "begat" of the Bible: "And Jesse begat David the king," as we read in the first chapter of Matthew; "and David the king begat Solomon of her that had been the wife of Urias; and Solomon begat Roboam"—begat, begat, and the list continues until it is summarized in verse 17: "So all the generations from Abraham to David are fourteen generations; and from David until the carrying away into Babylon are fourteen generations; and from the carrying away into Babylon unto Christ are fourteen generations." We have no dates for Abraham, but King David was born in the neighborhood of 1020 years before Christ, and that would make the subsequent generations some thirty-six years in average length. They are, in other words, a little longer than the biological generations of the modern world, which differ in span from country to country and from one era to another, but which might average thirty-two or -three years from parents to children.

Biographically a generation is something different; it is the term of years during which a writer works effectively at his profession. The term varies widely among American writers, from less than ten years in the case of Stephen Crane to sixty or more for patriarchs such as Whittier and Howells. If there is an average for writers with an audience to sustain them, it might be thirty-five or forty years, so that it does not quite correspond with the average length of a biological generation.

In terms of cultural history, the word "generation" has still another meaning and a different time value. Here the word is applied to clusters or constellations of writers, with their coevals in the other arts, and we have seen that these appear at uneven intervals. When I listed six clusters of American writers born during the nineteenth century and gave median years for each, the interval between those dates was as short as thirteen years in two cases and was more than thirty years in another (though here I suggested that an expected cluster had failed to appear, or had failed to make itself remembered). It is to be noted, moreover, that listing clusters and assigning writers to each involves a number of judgments on which critics are certain to disagree. Everything in this field is inexact, but one might venture that the average interval between clusters—often called literary generations—is roughly half the span of a biological generation.

Some theorists incline toward one meaning of the word, some toward another, while some try to harmonize all three. The effort has led to a sort of numbers game played with the length of generations. Giuseppe Ferrari, to mention a nineteenth-century political philosopher, sets the length at exactly thirty-one years and three months. He says that four generations together form a grand cycle of 125 years, in accordance with what he calls "the arithmetic of history." At another extreme is the critic Albert Thibaudet, who started with actual clusters of French writers and set the interval between them at eleven years. He added that thirty-three years, or three such intervals, would be the average productive life of a writer, and that three such lives would span a century. Toward the end of his own life, he wrote a history of French literature since 1789 and found in practice that he could not follow his numerical scheme. History, it would appear, has a poor head for arithmetic.

José Ortega y Gasset (1883–1955) is the most systematic of all those who have tried to formulate a generational theory. Generations come forward, he says, at intervals of fifteen years, and each of them is marked by what he calls a new form of "vital sensitivity" that it tries to impose on the world. Ortega uses the same quindecimal system in proposing a pattern of man's years on earth: from one to fifteen, childhood; from fifteen to thirty, youth; from thirty to forty-five, initiation; from forty-five to sixty, dominance; and from sixty to seventy-five, old age. The old men, he says, are "outside of life"; yet Ortega himself regained a dominant position in Spanish intellectual life when he came back to Madrid at sixty-six, long after the civil war, and he retained it until his death six years later. Human lives and careers have predetermined limits, but they refuse to follow a strict numerical pattern.

For all his attachment to fifteen as a magic number, Ortega contributed more to the theory of generations than any other scholar. He says that each of them is "a complete way of life that imprints itself indelibly on the individual"; and it is also—he writes in *The Modern Theme* (1933)—"a variety of the human race in the strict sense that is given to that word by naturalists." Again he says, "Age is not a date, but a zone of dates, and not only those born in the same year, but also those born within a zone of dates are of the same age vitally and historically. A generation is a zone of fifteen years during which a certain form of life was predominant." Three active generations always coexist— if we omit old age and childhood—and each of them tries to impose its form of life on the others. It is this conflict of generations that leads to the movements of historical evolution.

In this country Ortega has had no effect on popular thinking about the patterns of history. Most of the widely accepted patterns are based on decades rather than generations, for the simple reason that decades are numerically convenient and easy to find epithets for: the Gay Nineties, the Roaring Twenties, the Depression Thirties. But since changes in life style occur at irregular intervals, usually longer than ten years, decades on the calendar become a confusing element.

They are all the more confusing because, in this country, we have had no generational philosophers, but only social observers and men of letters with their usually random insights into the problem. Jefferson, for example, calculated the interval between generations as eighteen years and eight months. He felt that each new generation was justified in rejecting the past and choosing its own lines of development. I have quoted from Henry James and Emerson, and I might also quote from Scott Fitzgerald, who was anything but a systematic thinker. Nevertheless he brooded over the special nature of his own generation—"my contemporaries," as he called them affectionately—and at one point he attempted a definition that would apply to other age groups as well. That was in a disordered but suggestive article "My Generation," which he wrote in the late 1930s, though it remained unpublished until it appeared in the October 1968 issue of *Esquire*. There he said in part:

> . . . by a generation I mean that reaction against the fathers which seems to occur about three times in a century. It is distinguished by a set of ideas [a narrower term than Ortega's "vital sensitivity"] inherited in modified form from the madmen and the outlaws of the generation before; if it is a real generation it has its own leaders and spokesmen, and it draws into its orbit those born just before it and just after, whose ideas are less clear-cut and defiant.

That is a clear working definition, but one that needs to be amplified. I should like to combine Fitzgerald with Ortega— not a difficult feat, since they are talking about the same things— and offer a sort of generational paradigm.

**3** ✍ I might start by saying that a new cluster of writers—not to mention those in the other arts—does indeed appear every fifteen years or so, as Ortega is right in saying, even if there is nothing magical about the numeral 15. Ortega calls each of the clusters a generation, but they might better be called age groups or half generations, to distinguish their span from the thirty-odd years that separate parents and children. Here and elsewhere I think that the conflict with Fitzgerald is more in words than in meaning. "There have been generations," Ortega says, "who felt there was a perfect similarity between their inheritance [of ideas] and their own private possessions. The consequence, then, is that ages of accumulation arise." But Ortega's scheme also includes "ages of elimination and dispute," and these are what Fitzgerald has in mind when he speaks of a "reaction against the fathers." I think Fitzgerald is right in holding that such ages—"real generations," as he calls them—have occurred about three times in a century, that is, at intervals of thirty years or more. In our century the Love Generation of the 1960s was the first real successor to the Lost Generation of the 1920s.

Before a simple age group becomes a generation in Fitzgerald's sense of the word, it has to satisfy all the preconditions he listed and one or two others. First and I should say most important, it has to possess its own sense of life, something that might be defined as an intricate web of perceptions, judgments, feelings, and aspirations shared by its members. That sense of life—a phrase I prefer to Ortega's "vital sensitivity" and Fitzgerald's "set of ideas"—goes back to early childhood. Usually it starts with notions acquired from one's parents, but it is vastly extended by other notions acquired at school, on playgrounds, and in recent years by watching television. The generation plays the same games, hums the same tunes, wears the same sort of clothes, reads the same books as it grows older, and chooses much the same models for emulation. By the age of twenty its lines of development have been established. "It is as though when I was twenty," the novelist François Mauriac told an interviewer, "a door within me had closed forever on that which was going to become the material of my work."

Before that time, as a rule, the generation finds that it has rejected most of the notions acquired from its parents. It may return to them later, but most often in devious fashions and after a long delay. That rejection of the parents is the second precondition to be satisfied. Of course it has to be noted that some degree of rejection is almost universal in Western culture. The Freudians attribute it to the Oedipus complex, that convenient structure for explaining almost everything, but one notes that some manifestations of rejection in the literary life are very hard to connect with childhood sexuality. What distinguishes a real generation is its thoroughness and even violence in casting aside parental or merely prevailing notions. "Don't trust anyone over thirty," the students said at Berkeley in 1964 (and are those former students to be trusted now?). From my own college years I can remember climbing the steps of Widener Library, alone on a bright spring morning, while murmuring to myself, "Everything they told me in school, everything I heard in church, was a lie." It did not seem to me even then that this was more than a partial truth. What I judged to be lies was a group of notions about temperance, chastity, success, progress, and Divine Providence that had been proffered by my elders with a shade of inner doubt, perhaps, that a child was sure to detect. Rejecting them gave me confidence and moral comfort. Under my breath I was proclaiming solidarity with an age that was still to come.

As a third precondition, the generation has to have precursors. Often these are writers cast aside by the preceding generation—"the madmen and the outlaws," Fitzgerald calls them —but young men and women are attracted by their bold ideas, which give an intellectual structure to their own rebellion.

The generation must participate in, or at least be witness to, historic events that will furnish its members with a common fund of experience. This fourth precondition is a comparatively simple one to meet, since there appears to be no lack of wars, depressions, persecutions, public enthusiasms, and movements that seize the imaginations of generous-hearted persons, then sweep through a country or the whole Western world. Ortega makes a wise observation about such convulsions. In their effects, he says, and even in their essence, they are different for each of the five age groups that coexist at every moment. Thus, Hemingway's World War II was not the same as that of Norman Mailer or his coevals, and Mailer's war was not the same as that of Donald Barthelme, who was still a boy when it ended. The shared memories, however, have all the deeper effect for being confined to a single group.

A fifth precondition: the generation must have what Fitzgerald called "its own leaders and spokesmen." Obviously he was not thinking of political leaders. I suggest that what he had vaguely in mind were members of the age group who proclaimed or exemplified new standards of conduct, a distinctive life style that was soon adopted by others of the group. Hemingway was such a leader during his Paris days, though later most of his followers were younger than himself. Among spokesmen, in proper terms, for the Lost Generation, Fitzgerald himself was the earliest. At the end of his first novel, *This Side of Paradise,* he offered a sort of manifesto to his coevals. "Here was a new generation," he said, ". . . dedicated more than the last to the fear of poverty and the worship of success; grown up to find all Gods dead, all wars fought, all faiths in man shaken." Then he turns back to his hero: "Amory, sorry for them, was still not sorry for himself—art, politics, religion, whatever his medium should be, he knew he was safe now, free from all hysteria—he could accept what was acceptable, roam, grow, rebel, sleep deep through many nights. . . ."

As innocent as that program seems today, in 1920 there were thousands of young persons eager to identify themselves with Amory Blaine, or to dream of having him as suitor (not yet as lover; that was to come a few years later). There were thousands eager to roam, grow, rebel, and win success by taking extravagant risks, which they did not regard as risks because they felt "safe now," with fate on their side. The existence of an audience ready to accept an author's feelings as their own is a final precondition of what Fitzgerald calls "a real generation." To quote again from Ortega: "A generation is not a handful of outstanding men," that is, of leaders and spokesmen, "nor simply a mass of men; it resembles a new integration of the social body, with its select minority and its gross multitude, launched upon the orbit of existence with a predestined vital trajectory."

**4** ✍ After this new quotation from Ortega, it becomes necessary once again to reconcile his quindecimal scheme with Fitzgerald's notion that a real generation comes forward "about three times in a century." Two of Ortega's generations are roughly equivalent to one of Fitzgerald's. Might it be possible that Ortega's "ages of accumulation"—perhaps "acceptance" would be a better word—occur in rhythmical alternation with his "ages of elimination and dispute"? The "silent generation" of the 1950s, followed as it was by the youth rebellion of the 1960s, would be a case in point. Might the two age groups be taken together as a complete generation, one extending from 1945, a fixed date, to some year in the middle 1970s and hence corresponding roughly to the thirty-year span of a biological generation? "And Jesse begat David the king."

That there is a real alternation of moods in successive age groups is a fact attested by many episodes in literary history. The swing of the pendulum, however, is probably between other extremes than simple acceptance or rejection. Louis Cazamian, especially in the history of English literature that he wrote with Emile Legouis (1924), holds that the swing is between romanticism (feeling, imagination, yielding to instinct, soaring into dreams) and classicism (logic, acceptance of reality, the search for perfection). He also holds that the English spirit is essentially romantic and hence that romantic periods have been the great ones for English literature. Later Cazamian discovered, or thought he discovered, the same oscillation in France, with the difference that the French spirit was held to be essentially classical. Critics noted that he had to be somewhat arbitrary with names, dates, and masterpieces in order to fit them into his pattern.

Still another pattern might be discerned in the moods that prevail among successive age groups. Here, with apologies, I quote from something I wrote on the mood of the 1930s and its fruits in literature.[1]

> Writers of any new age group [I said] try to avoid the mistakes and enthusiasms of the group that preceded them. As the groups follow each other at intervals of ten or fifteen years, there seems to be an alternation of expansive and contractive moods, of interests turned outward to social problems and of those turned inward to dilemmas of the author; it suggests an immensely slow heartbeat rhythm of diastole and systole. The cycle may take thirty years or more to complete, something close to the span of a biological generation, with the result that periods separated by thirty years often bear some resemblance to each other. Thus, the 1950s were like the 1920s in being a contractive or systolic period devoted to the quest for personal fulfillment; "identity" was a watchword of the time, as "experience" had been a watchword of the 1920s. The 1930s, on the other hand, were like the early 1900s in being a diastolic period that admired breadth, observation, and social purpose.

I should have added that during systolic or contractive periods the emphasis is more on literary form in the old, loose sense of the word—that is, on structure, texture, and sequence —whereas the diastolic periods show more interest in new material, some of it confessional, as well as in political crusades and revolutionary feeling. There is some resemblance here to Louis Cazamian's pattern of classicism followed by romanticism; the diastolic periods, as I called them, are clearly more romantic.

Either sort of period can become what Fitzgerald called a real generation, but only if it meets with the various preconditions I tried to summarize. The unmet requirement is sometimes

---

1. See in this volume "The 1930s: Faith and Works."

that of possessing leaders and spokesmen. This lack was evident in the American 1930s, when young writers in the John Reed Clubs kept apostrophizing the masses, but couldn't speak for them. In England, however, the new men of the 1930s did have leaders of talent, notably Auden, and they became a real generation. More often the missing element is the audience, as happened with the new American writers of the 1890s; they went down to defeat because the public was either indifferent or implacably hostile. The 1950s were another and rather more complicated example of the missing audience. Many young men had come back from the war with limited ambitions; they wanted to be secure and modestly successful in a corporate society. As regards public taste, the period was one of accumulation, acceptance, and men in gray flannel suits (almost always with rebellious impulses that they concealed as private matters). The age did have rebellious spokesmen, including Ginsberg and Kerouac, but these were regarded as "the madmen and the outlaws," and they had to wait until the 1960s before they found a generation willing to listen.

In the literary world, an immediate cause of the alternation from one extreme to the other is disappointment with the works produced by writers of the previous era (not to mention the simple need to be different). The famous "reaction against the fathers" is more likely to be a sibling rivalry, that is, a revolt against one's older brothers in art. The young writer of twenty-five affirms his own worth by disparaging writers of forty. If the forty-year-olds have expressed the notions of a systolic era—if they have aimed at individual fulfillment and the creation of masterpieces— then the next age is certain to expatiate on the intolerable loneliness of self-centered artists and on their social irrelevance. That reaction is to be noted during the 1960s, another diastolic or expansive period that in some ways repeated the 1930s. "If there is one sweeping statement that can be made about the children of the last decade," Jeff Greenfield wrote in *The New York Times Magazine*, "it is that the generation of World War II was saying 'no' to the atomized lives their parents had so feverishly sought. The one most cherished value of their counterculture... was its insistence on sharing, community, a rejection of the retreat into private satisfaction.... Spontaneous gathering was the ethic. Don't plan it, don't think about it, do it....

"As a state of mind," Greenfield adds, "it was a pleasant fantasy. As a way of life, it was doomed to disaster." One must reflect, however, that every age group is doomed to disaster, or at least to defeat in terms of its aspirations, when these are measured against its actual way of life. Some groups are defeated sooner than others, for more predictable reasons, but each in the end reveals some fatal overemphasis, some flaw in calculation, some failure to cope with historical events; or else it will be destroyed by the simple passage of time.

> *The rabbits are eaten by foxes.*
> *The foxes die of the mange.*

There comes a morning when the survivors grope among the wreckage, as after a tidal wave, and learn that their world has been swept away with, among other things, its web of literary relations, its editors, its magazines, its responsive audience, its rewards and penalties for being honest, and its fine gradations of respect. A fortunate generation, in literature, is one whose defeat is palliated by a few lasting achievements and perhaps by the memory of great purposes and good times.

5 ✍ It must be obvious by now that I have been feeling my way toward a method in literary history. There was a time when I suspected that works of this category might be impossible to write. No matter that so-called histories of American literature existed by the dozen; that many of them were useful in the classroom, or for reference, and that a few—most notably Brooks's *Makers and Finders*—were even rewarding to the reader. I said to myself that *Makers and Finders* was a history not so much of literature as of the literary life in its various geographical centers, while the other books were weakened or destroyed as unified

works by a contradiction in terms. If they deal with literature proper, they are concerned with separate artifacts, each of these unique, unchangeable, and *given*. How can they move from one work of art to many, that is, from critical analysis to synthesis, from being or stasis to becoming? If, on the other hand, they deal primarily with history, they have to find some unifying principle or structure: some division into historical periods (with the assignment of books to each), some incorporation of authors into social or intellectual movements, or else some overriding myth. Whatever principle they find, it almost always distorts and simplifies what they have to say about separate works of art and diminishes the value of these by making them merely representative.

I said to myself that there might be no way out of the problem. Of course the scholar—or a posse of scholars—might combine history and literature in one or more volumes by devoting alternate chapters to each. Roughly that is the method followed by Robert E. Spiller and his many collaborators in their *Literary History of the United States* (1948), three volumes I am happy to own. But the result in this case of combining two disciplines is not so much a unified work as an encyclopedia with its articles arranged in chronological order.

Might the generational method serve as a means of resolving the contradictions? It would provide a unifying principle, one that has the advantage of being based on ascertainable facts— "the numbers of roads, the names of rivers, the numbers of regiments and the dates"—instead of depending on abstractions such as Romanticism, Populism, the Death Wish, or American Innocence. It would start from the principle that each age group tries to express a new sense of life, and it would trace the manifestations of this new consciousness or "vital sensitivity." Those manifestations are to be found in separate works of art, and hence the method invites full treatment of these, including studies of their imagery, rhythm, and structure as well as of their messages, and not omitting their discrepancies with the age. On the historical side, the method would reveal some real connections among works by separate authors, if these belonged to the same age groups, and a real progression (not progress) from one group to another.

Those notions about the generational method, though reached independently, are by no means original. In France the method has been rather widely applied by scholars, sometimes with more success than was achieved by Albert Thibaudet. One notes René Jasinski's two-volume *Histoire de la Littérature Française* (1947), organized on what is chiefly a generational scheme. I owe a special debt to Henri Peyre for *Les Générations Littéraires* (1948), a book that should be brought up to date and published in English. It offers a brief history of the generational method, compares it favorably with other ways of presenting the literary past, and undertakes a chronological survey of European generations (or age groups) born during the period from 1490 to 1910. Peyre says that there have been twenty-eight of these, appearing at intervals that would average fifteen years over the centuries, but mostly at ten-year intervals since 1800.

I am not aware that anyone except Peyre himself, quite briefly, has worked out a similar scheme for the literature of the American Republic. It would not be advisable to carry back such a scheme to colonial times, for the simple reason that these *were* colonial and, in large part, reflected English literary fashions after a lapse of years. But the situation changed with the first cluster of writers born in the 1800s—or earlier, perhaps, with Irving, Cooper, Bryant, and Prescott, all born between 1783 and 1796— so that the generational method would cast light on almost everything written during the nineteenth century. In twentieth-century literature it would have even greater value as helping us to recognize patterns in the confusion of the times.

There as elsewhere, however, the method would have to be applied with concessions and qualifications, since the difference between age groups is never so absolute as Ortega held it to be (or as I suggested in an emotional moment). The generational layers merge into one another and are intersected at right angles by many vertical lines of force; "traditions," we call them as a way of suggesting their lastingness. Within the general framework of American society and literature, some of the traditions are connected with such lasting institutions as government, churches, universities, or the literary profession. Others can be grouped into four general types.

One type consists of traditions based on moods or movements such as classicism, romanticism, realism, Platonism (also called Transcendentalism), naturalism, symbolism. . . . But when do these represent permanent forms or directions of the human spirit, and when should they be treated as historical movements with recorded dates? There is an ambiguity here that has led to scholarly misinterpretations.

A second type includes the traditions connected with regions, social classes, or racial inheritance. Most of these keep changing with the times and some of them disappear. In our own century we have seen the revival in modified form of a Southern tradition and the appearance in American literature of several ethnic traditions, notably Jewish, Black, and Amerindian. The last two have recovered a past—something the Jews had never lost —and are busy shaping their future.

A third type of tradition is simply the literary genres: tragedy, pastoral, the novel, the confession, and others that seem to have lives of their own. They grow, decline, vanish for a time, then reappear in altered forms.

A fourth type is marked by lines that radiate from heroes of Western culture on the order of Dante, Cervantes, Shakespeare. Such lines have shown little respect for centuries or national frontiers. One remembers that Fielding, though he represented a new age in England, placed himself in one of the lines when he formally stated that his *Joseph Andrews* was "writ in the manner of Cervantes." Another line is best represented in American fiction by *Moby Dick* and *Absalom, Absalom!* Different as these are from each other, they are both Shakespearean not only by virtue of their intention and their obsessed heroes but also partly in their language, which sometimes lapses or soars into blank verse.

Among all those transgenerational forces—another term for traditions in general—not one can be neglected in discussing an author whose work it helped to shape. But neither should we neglect another aspect of the problem: that the forces are to some extent transformed as they reappear in the consciousness of each new age group. Each group has its own reading of Shakespeare, if it reads him at all. Each elects its own ancestors, usually from the second or third rank of cultural heroes. Donne, Swift, Skelton, Smollett, Kierkegaard, Kafka: we have seen them each seated for a time in the grandfather's chair. The generational method casts a good deal of light on the decline and resurgence of posthumous reputations. It helps us to identify the various age groups that adhered to such movements as romanticism, realism, symbolism, while attaching, as the groups did, a new significance to each of those terms. It serves to mark the changes in national, regional, and ethnic traditions. To be an American, a Southerner, a Midwesterner, a Jew, or a Black no longer means what it did for those who were young in the 1920s—as note, to give one example, the difference between writers of the Harlem Renaissance and the young Black poets of the 1970s.

In all those fields of study, the generational method has a heuristic value, as Henri Peyre insists; that is, it helps us to find connections and distinctions, and sometimes to find authors who have been unwisely forgotten. One distinction it enforces is between books that are merely contemporary with each other and books produced by the same generation; the word here is coeval. Although *An American Tragedy* and *The Great Gatsby* both appeared in 1925, Dreiser was older than Fitzgerald by a quarter of a century and their works belong to different eras. But *Manhattan Transfer* and *In Our Time*, which also appeared in 1925, that fruitful year, are truly coeval because, with *Gatsby*, they were written by members of the same age group. In that matter of connections, the method helps to reveal similarities in spirit between literary works and coeval productions in the other arts (not to mention science and public affairs). Best of all, the method permits literary history to become something else than a contradiction in terms; something more than a toying with abstractions or a mere catalogue of books and authors. It makes such history not a science, God forbid, but a definite, vastly complicated, and rewarding area for literary exploration.

# II MR. PAPA
# AND THE
# PARRICIDES

⚓ "Great men die twice," Paul Valéry said, "once as men and once as great." Their second death, in the public mind, may be no more than a forgetting, but in other cases it becomes a noisy spectacle that makes one think of a very old tree assaulted by a band of savages. The tree is the great man's reputation, which has hidden the sky and prevented lesser reputations from growing in its shade. Now it must be destroyed, by tribal necessity, but the tribesmen have only stone axes that shatter against the enormous trunk. So they start by hacking off roots and branches one by one, then wait for the weakened tree to crash in the first gale.

That process of severing roots and lopping off branches is known in the critical world as "reassessment." If the critic is also a teacher, he is likely to speak of "establishing a canon," which means choosing the works that his students will be required to read and more or less abolishing the others. For many years I have been taking notes on a classical example of that operation, as performed by critics of a younger age group on the works of Ernest Hemingway.

The earlier notes became an article published in the June 1967 number of *Esquire* and here reprinted without substantial revision. I have followed the critical record of the Hemingway case in later years, and it shows an effort by some critics, notably Alfred Kazin and Scott Donaldson, to reach a fairer estimate of his work. It also provides fresh evidence as regards the conflict of age groups, but it does not seem to affect my earlier conclusions.

1 ⚗ "At the time of his death in 1961," says one critic, John Thompson, who teaches English at the State University of New York at Stony Brook, Hemingway "was probably the best-known writer in the world, and one of the most popular. But his writing no longer exerted an influence on literature, and serious critics usually disposed of his work as being of minor interest compared to that of writers like Fitzgerald and Faulkner, whom he had once completely overshadowed.

"Such questions as may arise about his writing today," Mr. Thompson continues in the tone of a Supreme Court justice reading an almost unanimous opinion, "are only manifestations of the slow and uneven filtering down of accepted opinion, or of the uneven rates at which the glamour of his settings evaporates in different minds. Nearly everyone agrees now on the order of quality in the canon of his work. *The Sun Also Rises* and many of his short stories are absolutely first-rate, surpassed in scope by other novelists of his time but unsurpassed by anyone in their perfection." Nothing else that Hemingway wrote is really worth the trouble of rereading. "Thus, while he is still recognized clearly enough as an artist of occasional success," the critic concludes in *The New York Review,* "his work no longer seems to contain promises for others, and his books are not much regarded by writers anymore."

I envy the assurance with which Mr. Thompson, never speaking in the first person, repeats what he thinks that other people think who he thinks are serious critics. He might not regard Vance Bourjaily as one of them, since Bourjaily makes the critical *gaffe* of speaking for himself and in any case is not a critic primarily. His profession is writing novels, and he owes a substantial debt to Hemingway, as do other writers of talent in his World War II generation. In an article contributed to *The New York Times Book Review,* Bourjaily acknowledges the debt, but he also engages in what seems to be the inevitable business of drawing up a canon. "As a reader," he says, "and claiming to speak for other readers, I suppose I rank the works quite simply according to the frequency with which it seems to me that I would now enjoy rereading a given one. By this test, *The Sun Also Rises* is incomparably the best novel; I reread it every fourth or fifth year. There are between fifteen and twenty short stories, mostly early but including 'Macomber' and 'Kilimanjaro,' which I read as often and feel to be of the same extraordinary merit. *A Farewell to Arms* is somewhat below these, but not far—perhaps on a seven-year or eight-year cycle. I suspect that *Green Hills of Africa,* which I discovered quite recently, will come in next."

From other books Mr. Bourjaily recalls "a few moving things," but he does not propose to reread them. Thus, even in his favorable report, the Hemingway canon is reduced to fifteen or twenty short stories, most of them early, the first two novels, and a travel book. But all the Hemingway critics are engaged in critical canoneering, and most of them carry it to a greater extreme —as does, for example, Stanley Edgar Hyman, who says in *The New Leader,* "... at his best Hemingway left us, in *The Sun Also Rises* and a handful of short stories, authentic masterpieces, small-scale but immortal." How many stories make a handful? Certainly fewer than the fifteen or twenty that Vance Bourjaily delights in rereading. Robert Emmet Long, writing in *The North American Review,* wants to shorten the list of canonical works to a few of those produced in the early or vintage years. "Almost all of his best work," Mr. Long says, "was done while he was still in his twenties.... *The Sun Also Rises, A Farewell to Arms* and half a dozen short stories present Hemingway at his best." Having added a novel to Mr. Hyman's version of the canon, Mr. Long subtracts from it three or four stories—unless "half a dozen" and "a handful" are synonyms.

Leslie Fiedler places the same emphasis on the early work, which he admires for a curious reason, as Hemingway's celebration of "the bleak truth it had been given him to know." That truth was "death and the void," or so we learn from Fiedler's *Waiting for the End* (1964), where we are also told that "after the first two novels and the early stories, he was able only to echo, in the end parody, himself." Other critics want to reject even those first two novels. "The fact is Hemingway is a short-story writer and not a novelist," Dwight Macdonald says in *Against the American Grain* (1963). "He has little understanding of the subject matter of the novel: character, social setting, politics, money matters, human relations, all the prose of life.... In a novel he gets lost, wandering aimlessly in a circle as lost people are said to do, and the alive parts are really short stories, such as the lynching of the Fascists and the blowing up of the bridge in *For Whom the Bell Tolls*."

I shall resist the temptation to argue with Mr. Macdonald, though it would be easy to cite passages from Hemingway's novels that reveal his understanding of character, social setting, politics, money matters, human relations, and—if only by implication, since he does not burden the story with extraneous material—all the prose of life. It would be still easier to show that instead of getting lost in a novel he marches ahead in a straight-line narrative that appears to be simple, but is actually a difficult type of writing, since it avoids the tricks by which novelists are enabled to impart or withhold information at their own convenience. Those citations and proofs, however, can wait for another occasion. At present what interests me is that Mr. Macdonald's judgment, however debatable, seems to have been accepted by segments of the academic world. I remember the comment made by a professor of American literature on an anthology I was helping to revise. "Why not include Hemingway's two or three best stories," he said, "and omit any reference to his novels? Hemingway is beginning to be taught chiefly as a short-story writer." "Pretty soon," I said to myself, "they will have him chipped down to 'Big Two-Hearted River.'" The next step would be to chip that story down to a single paragraph, presented by critics as the only true essence of his work, from which they could infer the rest of it much in the fashion that paleontologists reconstruct the skeleton of an extinct animal from a single bone. Perhaps it would be the paragraph that reads:

> He watched them holding themselves with their noses into the current, many trout in deep, fast moving water, slightly distorted as he watched far down through the glassy convex surface of the pool, its surface pushing and swelling smooth against the resistance of the log-driven piles of the bridge. At the bottom of the pool were the big trout. Nick did not see them at first. Then he saw them at the bottom of the pool, big trout looking to hold themselves on the gravel bottom in a varying mist of gravel and sand, raised in spurts by the current.

The echo of that paragraph has sounded first loudly, then faintly but still discernibly, through fifty years of American prose. But would the critics choose another paragraph for fear of having to confess that they had never seen the big trout? I respect most of those whose judgments I have quoted and some of them are my friends, but in the present connection they evoke a mental picture I should like to forget. This time the picture is not of a tree being felled, but of a dead lion surrounded by a pack of jackals. At first they gather round him cautiously, ready to take flight at any sign of life, and then, gaining courage from one another, they rush in to tear the flesh from the bones. I suppose the bones are the critical canon, but they will not remain undisturbed; soon the hyenas will come to crack them for their marrow. There will be nothing left but a white skull on the wide African plain, and hunters will say as they look at it, "Why, it wasn't such a big lion after all."

But Hemingway for much of his life was our biggest lion. In the midst of those posthumous assaults on his reputation, I should like to interject a few remarks about the lasting values in his work and about the whole business of setting up a critical canon.

2↙ It seems to me a snobbish business essentially. Each critic is tempted to display his superior discrimination by excluding a little more than other critics excluded. The process is exactly similar to the one by which drinkers some years ago used to display their superior taste by insisting on less and less vermouth in their martinis: the man who ordered eight parts of gin to one of vermouth was obviously twice as high in the social-drinking scale as the man who was satisfied with four parts to one. Just so in the critical scale: Vance Bourjaily, who admits to liking two Hemingway novels and fifteen or twenty stories, is only half as discriminating as Stanley Hyman, who praises only one novel and "a handful" of stories—would it be a single or a double handful? —while Hyman in turn must bow to Dwight Macdonald, who retains a few stories but completely excludes the novels. They can each be assigned a rank, but it has nothing to do with their sense of literary values.

There are other reasons for distrusting the process of critical canoneering when it is applied to an author of any standing. Of course it has the practical justification that students can't be expected to read everything; the instructor has to make choices. But when he chooses a book for them to read, he shouldn't imply, except in special cases, that nothing else by the same author is worth their attention. The special cases are those of one-book authors, a genus that has some famous members; Hemingway isn't one of them. Some of his books are immensely better than others. Some I should surrender without regret, as notably *Across the River and into the Trees*; perhaps that is the only one. *Green Hills of Africa* and *To Have and Have Not* fall short of their mark, each for a different reason, but both contain passages I should hate to relinquish.

*For Whom the Bell Tolls* does not belong among those partial failures. It seems to me the most complex and powerful of Hemingway's works, as it is certainly the longest. Often it is dismissed by critics as if they had reached a tacit agreement, but that appears to be the result of circumstances quite apart from its literary value. One circumstance is its popular success; critics always distrust a novel that has had an enormous sale—in this case eight hundred thousand hardbound copies in the first few years—after being announced as a masterpiece by the daily reviewers. *For Whom the Bell Tolls* has suffered from the additional handicaps of dealing with the Spanish Civil War, a subject that many critics wanted to forget, and of dealing with it in a fashion that offended most of the political factions: Fascists, Stalinists, Trotskyites, pacifists, Spanish patriots on both sides, almost the whole spectrum. As time passed the book was so bitterly condemned on political grounds that critics did not feel they had to read it with close attention. Nothing they said against it was likely to be challenged, even if their judgments were based on obvious misinterpretations.

Take for example Dwight Macdonald's judgment, already quoted, that "the alive parts are really short stories, such as the lynching of the Fascists and the blowing up of the bridge in *For Whom the Bell Tolls*." His notion that the parts would be better if separated from the whole is not supported by the text. Conceivably the lynching of the Fascists might stand alone, but it is an essential shadow in the picture that Hemingway has been presenting all through the novel. The blowing up of the bridge, with Robert Jordan's death as recounted in the last forty pages of the novel, clearly depends for its power on the tensions that have been created in the preceding four hundred pages. It is no more a short story than the fifth act of *Hamlet* is a one-act play.

There is more to be said about Jordan's fight at the

bridge. In addition to being the end of a novel, it is also last in a series of events that had continued through several books. Most of Hemingway's early heroes are aspects of the same person, whether we call him Nick Adams or Frederic Henry or Jake Barnes, and of course he reappears in Robert Jordan. The hero's adventures began in Michigan, but they reached their first climax in *A Farewell to Arms,* when, falsely charged with being a spy, he deserted from the Italian army (and also, in a sense, from organized society). The fight at the bridge might be read as a sequel to that earlier climax, which had taken place at another bridge; this time the hero accepts the fate from which, in *A Farewell to Arms,* he had escaped by plunging into a flooded river. Hemingway's books are interconnected in several fashions; the connections are what many critics miss by their canoneering. Though a story in itself may be an authentic masterpiece, small-scale but immortal—to quote Stanley Hyman—the scale is magnified when we read it with other stories, which in turn are enhanced in value by the novels. Almost everything is part of the same pattern.

In the background of the pattern are death, loneliness, and the void, but these are not Hemingway's subject—Leslie Fiedler to the contrary—except in two or three of the early vignettes and in a few stories written during the thirties. In "A Clean, Well-Lighted Place," for example, the old waiter says, "What did he fear? It was not fear or dread. It was a nothing that he knew too well." But although the old waiter seems to speak from the depths of nihilism, he suggests a remedy against that feeling of nothingness: it is for the lonely man to sit all night in a bright, pleasant café where he will be surrounded with order and decorum. That appears to be an essential statement, and we can see more clearly in other stories that Hemingway's real subject is the barriers that can be erected against fear and loneliness and the void.

Decorum in the broadest sense, in which it becomes the discipline of one's calling and the further discipline required of every human being if he is to live as a man, not collapse into a jelly of emotions, is the strongest of those barriers. "Be a man, my son," a priest in one of the early vignettes says to Sam Cardinella when he loses control of his sphincter muscle as he is being strapped for the gallows. Sam is the specter of fear that seems more repulsive to Hemingway than death itself. To maintain discipline in the face of death requires a strict control of the imagination, lest it get to racing "like a flywheel with the weight gone," as Robert Jordan says in *For Whom the Bell Tolls*. It also requires complete attention to every action in its proper sequence, as if that single action, at the moment, were the whole of life. Meanwhile the sequence of actions is being reported in a disciplined style that is in harmony with the subject matter and that also becomes a means of suggesting—while at the same time warding off—fears that are not directly expressed.

Besides imposing a discipline, the implied or actual presence of death in Hemingway's fiction has compensations that are also part of his subject. This feature of his work, not often discussed, is one that I found easy to recognize from a memory of youth; there must be many others with a similar memory. In my case it goes back to Paris in the early summer of 1917. I was on leave from driving a munitions truck for the French army, not a proud occupation in those days when one's friends were enlisting in various flying corps and getting killed with astonishing dispatch. In the Lafayette Escadrille, for example, the average expectancy of life was something less than three months. I decided on that June morning to enlist in American aviation, knowing that I should make an incompetent pilot and should certainly be killed with greater dispatch than the others; nevertheless the decision was made. Suddenly everything changed for me. The chestnut trees in the Champs-Elysées seemed greener, their blossoms pinker, the girls on the sidewalk more beautiful, and the sky an unprecedented shade of blue, as if my senses had been sharpened and my capacity for enjoyment vastly increased by the imminence of death. Humming a silly wartime song, stumbling at the curb, smiling to passersby, I went to a restaurant and ordered what seemed to me the best meal I had ever eaten, washed down with a bottle of miraculous wine.

The experience had no sequel in life, since I was rejected by the army doctors, but much later it helped me to recognize a lasting quality in Hemingway's prose. It is life-conscious and death-conscious at the same time; one feeling is linked with the other. Because, at moments in his writing, death seems to hover in the air like an obscene bird—or moves silently in pairs, on bicycles, like French policemen, or has a hyena's wide snout and prowls outside his tent as in "The Snows of Kilimanjaro"—because of this wordless presence, the author himself seems doubly alive, with all his senses more acute than those of ordinary persons. He sniffs the morning air like a hunting dog. He feels and transmits to the reader a special cleanness and freshness in the physical world in a way that has not been equaled by any other novelist of our time. It is a quality one finds in many poems of the Middle Ages, also written by men whose enjoyment of nature was sharpened by their feeling that death lay in ambush at the turn of the road.

Landscapes, the sea, the weather, fishing for trout or marlin, the taste of food, drinking round a campfire (or almost anywhere), killing big animals, and making love: those are the magical things in Hemingway. The ideas are interesting too, even though merely implied, for he was always more of an intellectual than he pretended to be; but he was most at ease in describing natural scenes and activities. He made everything palpable, so that a landscape was suggested by hills to be climbed with aching muscles or by the feel of hemlock needles under bare feet, all remembered with a sense of precarious joy. His readers envied the joy while disregarding the nightmares that lurked in the shadows. Young men of three or four successive age groups were eager to go where he went and have a share in his pleasures, with the result that, in his favored localities, he became an economic force of measurable importance. As I wrote of him in *A Second Flowering*, "Yes, he brought the fishermen to Key West and Bimini, and bands of hunters to the high African plains, and American college students by hundreds, then by thousands, to the yearly festival at Pamplona. Ski resorts in Tyrol and Idaho, bullfights all over Spain, restaurants in Venice, Milan, Paris, Havana: he had good times at all of them, he told with gusto what they had to offer, and the crowds came streaming after."

That side of his career is not what interests me. Many writers were inclined to resent it, on the ground that there was no place in it for books and bookmen. Not sharing that resentment, I still find that Hemingway the writer paid a high price for his activities as a sportsman and war correspondent. His real excuse for engaging in them, implicit in everything he wrote, was that he liked them. That was not the same as his public excuse, which was that they furnished him with material. "In going where you have to go, and doing what you have to do, and seeing what you have to see," he said in his preface to *The Fifth Column and the First Forty-nine Stories,* "you dull and blunt the instrument you write with. But I would rather have it bent and dulled and know I had to put it on the grindstone again and hammer it into shape and put a whetstone to it, and know that I had something to write about, than to have it bright and shining and nothing to say, or smooth and well-oiled in the closet, but unused."

It is the old doctrine of experience at any cost that held an important place in the mind of the 1920s. Hemingway carried it farther than others. Long before the end, and in fact before World War II, he had gathered more material than he could ever put into his writing. In "The Snows of Kilimanjaro" (1936), he deliberately threw away material for a dozen stories, each of which was reduced to one or two paragraphs of the dying hero's recollections, as if both hero and author were trying to get rid of compulsive memories. As for "the instrument you write with" —if Hemingway meant his head—it was scarred and battered like a punch-drunk boxer's head in a dozen serious accidents, from one of which, the second airplane crash in Africa, he never recovered. That was our loss, but we should remember that in all those costly adventures there was something on the other side of the ledger too, not for literature, but for the world. The public career was in itself an artistic creation. By the enormous zest with which he studied the rules of every game, including those of love and war and the chase, he made our world more dramatic than it would have been without him.

3 ✍ But the work is what interests me, not the career, and that is why I am disturbed by the later sapping and pruning of his literary reputation. Does nothing survive of the work but a few short stories? Why not toss them out with the novels and finally reduce the Hemingway canon to a blank page? As yet that gesture of total rejection has not been made by any reputable critic. Even Dwight Macdonald, who comes nearest to making it, still finds a few things he would like to save. There were, however, premonitory hints of the gesture in a few newspaper reviews of *A Moveable Feast*, in 1964, mixed in with favorable comments by others. "... aging boy that he became," Glendy Culligan said in *The Washington Post*, "Hemingway was finally surpassed by his own imitators." I wonder what books by which imitators she had in mind. The anonymous reviewer for *The Harrisburg Patriot News* wanted to dismiss Hemingway's readers along with the books and their author (again that conflict of age groups). "The reputation he built up studiously," the reviewer said, "will linger among the middle-aged generation that naturally clings to the illusions of youth."

What this cry from Harrisburg, Pennsylvania, suggests— when taken with other evidence—is the broader scope of the operation that had seemed to be directed against Hemingway and no one else. He isn't the only victim; he isn't even the first. Thomas Wolfe has already gone down under repeated assaults— for which there was more excuse in his case—and Dos Passos, though not stoned to death, has been loaded with the sins of the literary community and driven into the desert. Of course the ultimate goal of the operation is the whole age group of which Hemingway was a member. A few of his coevals have escaped the attacks, notably Faulkner and Fitzgerald and Edmund Wilson, but it is not hard to foresee that their turn is coming.[1] What we

---

1. That prophecy, made in 1967, was a safe one to offer. Ten years later the editors of *Esquire* wrote to various novelists and critics asking the question, "Which American writers of this century do you consider the most over- and underrated?" The answers were printed under the title

are witnessing is a crucial stage in an event that has been delayed beyond expectations, that is, the ritual murder of the literary fathers.

To cast some light on that ceremony revived from prehistoric times, I might quote a famous passage from the last chapter of *Totem and Taboo*. Freud introduces the passage by recalling Darwin's notion that the first form of human society may have been a primal horde in which a violent, jealous father kept all the females for himself and drove away his growing sons. The notion has never been confirmed by anthropologists, but Freud accepts it as the basis for a more dramatic picture of his own:

> One day [he says] the expelled brothers joined forces, slew and ate the father, and thus put an end to the father horde. Together they dared and accomplished what would have remained impossible for them singly.... Of course these cannibalistic savages ate their victim. The violent primal father had surely been the envied and feared model for each of the brothers. Now they accomplished their identification with him by devouring him and each acquired a part of his strength.

Freud goes on to explain that the original parricide, or *Vatermord*, was the original sin and hence was the beginning of religion. I shall not follow him into those further conjectures. All I wanted to suggest is that a ritual murder of the fathers has become a custom in the literary world.[2] Each new generation or

---

"American Writers: Who's Up, Who's Down?" (*Esquire*, August 1977). To speak in general terms, Faulkner, Fitzgerald, and Wilson were cast into outer darkness along with Mr. Papa.

2. Elsewhere I speculate that the ritual murder is less likely to be a parricide than a fratricide. That is, the favorite victims of a new age group are likely to be representatives of the preceding age group, persons too young to be their parents. Hemingway is an exception here; he was a man of the 1920s; but he was also an idol of the 1950s and hence something to be destroyed with other idols of the time. As regards Freud's myth of the primal *Vatermord*, it has more power as a metaphor than as a verifiable pattern of behavior.

age group provides admired, then feared and envied models for the generation that follows. The new men and women, however, have their own sense of life, which they are bent on expressing in their own fashion, and therefore they have to break free from the models. Often they do so by denying that the models have any virtues, by rejecting their works one after another, and, in effect, by killing them as men of letters. Of course they eat them too, in the sense of absorbing what they can from the slaughtered parents.

For a new generation of parricides, Hemingway becomes an especially tempting victim, partly because he had been so abundantly paternal. All the hard-boiled novelists of the 1930s, with most of the proletarian novelists, were his sons in one way or another, and so too were almost all the war novelists of the 1940s. He had been extremely kind to them in the beginning, so long as they did not threaten his pre-eminence, but later, when they promised to become rivals, he expelled them one by one from the primal horde. No wonder that many of the sons joined forces against him. Hemingway, in fact, had offered them a model of filial ingratitude in his early career, since his third book, *The Torrents of Spring,* was a ritual murder of Sherwood Anderson, from whom he had learned valuable lessons. The young men might argue that they were paying him back a death for a death.

If I deplore the continued attacks on Hemingway's reputation, it is not because I think that the critics are guilty of more than the customary measure of ingratitude. It is not for personal reasons, because I want to defend my own generation or the man who for thirty years and more embodied many of its perceptions (notwithstanding his defects of character), and it is not because I think the attacks will be successful in the end. With the necessary subtractions made, Hemingway's work as a whole is so clearly permanent that, even if his reputation were destroyed for the moment, and the work buried, it would be exhumed after a hundred years, as Melville's was. My protest is simply in defense of American literature. This is vastly richer now than it was when Hemingway started writing, but it is not yet so rich that it can afford to disown and devalue one of its lasting treasures.

# III THE NEW ENGLAND VOICE

1 ✒ In the matter of reputation, S. Foster Damon was as different from Hemingway as any two authors can be. Although he produced a considerable body of work, he never had to be destroyed by his successors or forgotten by the public, since he was never sufficiently known. His influence, less broad than intensive, was exerted chiefly on his friends.

I was one of the friends for fifty years. He disapproved of my first marriage and we saw less of each other after 1919, but still we kept in touch. At the end of a letter written the day after Thanksgiving, 1966, I asked Foster a question. "Did you introduce me to Laforgue," I said, "or was I already Laforguing when I used to come out to Newton and drink tea in your room, in the spring of 1918? I remember your copy of *Tender Buttons,* but there is so much I forget." Foster waited a month, then answered frugally on a New Year's card. "Mal—" he said, using a nickname that everyone else has forgotten. "Yes, I remember showing you the poems of Jules Laforgue. We went over them together. Happy New Year to you both!"

So Laforgue was one more of my debts to Foster.

I have tried to make a list of the others. They include the early works of Ezra Pound, especially *Ripostes,* the poems of Stephen Crane, and the prose of Herman Melville, who as late as 1918 was an unknown writer in this country: I don't know where Foster had found his copy of *Moby Dick.* He was a specialist in hard-to-find books by unknown authors. Blake, of course, was not forgotten; almost everyone had read *Songs of Innocence* and *Songs of Experience;* but it was Foster who introduced me to the poems in the Rossetti and Pickering Manuscripts and to *The Marriage of Heaven and Hell.* He couldn't persuade me to follow him into the later prophetic books, and there were other gifts he offered that I was unwilling to accept: Gertrude Stein and Thomas Holley Chivers, for example, whom I always placed in the same category of might-be-interesting-to-others. His gift to me of Amy Lowell was not of her poems, on which I reserved judgment, but of her vivid and overwhelming personality; it was Foster who had her invite me to Sevenels, her big house in Brookline. I forget how many times we went there together to read our poems aloud and then to be praised and scolded by Miss Lowell as we puffed away at her Manila cigars.

Many others have owed the same sort of debts to Foster, who was "invariably an opener of doors," as the composer Virgil Thomson remarks in his autobiography. The remark comes after some memories that greatly resemble my own. Thomson says:

> I came to know S. Foster Damon, slender, pale poet with a blond mustache, at that time [1921] instructing in English A while preparing privately, since Harvard would have none of it, the book that was to open up the language of William Blake. Foster was a composer as well as a poet and a scholar —also a close associate of Amy Lowell, whose biographer he became in the 1930s. I do not remember how I first knew him; but I do remember long walks and talks; and I remember

his bringing me music and books that he thought I ought to know. Some of these, such as the critical writings of T. S. Eliot and the Irish tales of James Stephens, I found merely informative or charming. Others changed my life. Among these last were the piano works of Erik Satie, a pile of them four inches high, and a thin small volume called *Tender Buttons,* by Gertrude Stein. I returned these favors by introducing him to peyote, which we would take together, sometimes with another poet and English A instructor, Robert Hillyer. Foster has often re-appeared in my life and almost always with gifts in hand.

Among those who have acknowledged the gifts was E. E. Cummings, a close friend of Foster's when both were undergraduates. We read in his *i: six nonlectures* that "S. Foster Damon . . . opened my eyes and ears not merely to Domenico Theotocopuli [El Greco] and William Blake, but to all ultra (at that moment) modern music and poetry and painting." Cummings told his biographer, Charles Norman, "Practically everything I know about painting and poetry came to me through Damon." I wonder how many other poets might have ground for making a similar acknowledgment. Also I wonder, after more than fifty years, how it was that Foster opened so many doors for others while inveterately standing in the shadows to let them pass.

2🖋 Poets abounded at Harvard, and would-be poets, when I went there in the fall of 1915. Foster was the ancient among them, for he belonged to the class of '14 and was starting his second year as a graduate student. I saw him for the first time at a meeting of the Harvard Poetry Society, which had just been organized. The poets were seated round a huge table in the dimly lighted sanctum of *The Harvard Monthly.* Pale in the lamplight, with straight ryestraw-colored hair, Foster read some poems that were chaste in form, but rather less chaste in sentiment. The reading was almost apologetic, with a notable lack of drama. When Foster came to a line that was shocking, for those days, his flat New England Seaboard voice would become flatter and more noncommittal. Still there were a few gasps of indignation. I don't remember whether I spoke to him after the meeting— that would have been a presumptuous act for a freshman—or whether we were introduced on some later occasion. But it seems to me, as I go poking among my memories, that more than once in my sophomore year, when poems of mine were beginning to be printed in *The Advocate,* we went into Boston together to drink seidels of dark beer at Jake Wirth's German saloon. One of my new literary friends warned me against Foster's pernicious influence.

It was in 1918 that I saw more of him than in any other year. In February I had come back to Harvard after six months as assistant driver of a munitions truck for the French Army, and another month with two Pittsburgh friends, Jimmy Light and his wife Sue Jenkins, who had moved on to Greenwich Village, where Jimmy was soon to become a director of the Provincetown Players. Foster, still in Cambridge, was continuing his graduate studies after trying to enlist in the army. Many times he appeared at my door with a green baize bag full of books. He would open the bag, select a book, and read aloud a passage that had struck his fancy; then we would talk about the usually forgotten or disparaged author. Once he had me visit the family's big suburban house in Newton for the weekend, and once or twice he took me to the rooms above the Western Club, where he lived with Philip Hillyer Smith, now my neighbor in Connecticut, and a group of noisy seniors. Smith tells me that Foster used to prowl up and down the study, smoking a long-stemmed German porcelain pipe, then dart to the table and write either a line of verse or a bar of music—or perhaps a sentence about Blake's prophetic books; one could never be sure which it would be.

At that time his poetry was better known than his scholarship, as a result of his appearance the previous year in

*Eight Harvard Poets,* a volume that included the best of his early work along with that of Cummings, Dos Passos, Robert Hillyer, and others. I don't know what he saw in an awkward and acne'd boy of nineteen with country manners; it must have been our interest in poetry that brought us together. We were both enlisted in another war that raged simultaneously with the war in Europe: this one between the Ancients and the Moderns in poetry. Of course we were on the Modern side, and I ridiculed the Ancients for believing—or so I said—that poetry should express the daydreams of a twelve-year-old girl in words of one syllable. Foster attacked them for artlessness and timidity.

In April of 1918 I was, to my amazement, elected president of *The Harvard Advocate.* It was not a tribute to my brilliance, as I thought for a dizzy moment, but simply a recognition of the fact that I planned to wait a few months before going into the army. Most of my former colleagues on the editorial board were already in uniform. To keep the paper alive in their absence, I enlisted the help of such friends as Foster and John Brooks Wheelwright, that tall, quizzical, High Church Anglican poet, whose sister Louise was later to become Foster's wife. Also I struck a blow for the Moderns by inviting Amy Lowell to read her new poems at an *Advocate* smoker on May 2. In his biography of Miss Lowell, Foster quotes her as saying, "I was, as usual, smuggled into an upper chamber, and kept quiet with cigars"— which I had been careful to provide—"while they heckled me in true undergraduate fashion." Miss Lowell, wreathed in smoke, crushed the hecklers as if with bolts from a fat thundercloud. But she made no answer of record to Jack Wheelwright's quite earnest question: "What do you do when you want to write a poem and haven't anything to write about?"

In June Foster and I took a walking trip that ended in a shack on a hilltop near the village of Candor, New York. A Greenwich Village friend had told me about the shack, for which we paid in advance a month's rent of three dollars. On our first evening there, over a supper of trout and wild strawberries (with bread and milk from a farm in the valley), we began talking about the *Spectra* hoax. It had lately been a front-page story in several newspapers: "Poet Unmasks Huge Joke on World of Art." The joke was a widely reviewed book called *Spectra* (1916) that presented the work of a new literary school purportedly founded by two Pittsburgh poets: Emanuel Morgan, just home from Paris, and a tempestuous Hungarian beauty, Anne Knish. In reality Morgan was Witter Bynner, who had at last revealed the imposture, and Knish was his friend Arthur Davison Ficke, another lyric poet of moderate skill and immense conservatism. Foster and I agreed that the joke was not only a good one but also a victory for the Ancients. It was time, we told each other, for the Moderns to stage a counterattack. Why couldn't we hoax the hoaxers?

On the following day, June 15, we produced almost the entire *opus poeticum* of Earl Roppel, later to be known as "the plowboy poet of Tioga Country" and "the bard of the rushing Catatonk." We also composed a letter to Bynner that served to introduce the poems. We said in part, or had Earl Roppel say, "I got your book out of the free library at Owego and read it all through that night and I like it very much though I do not understand it all. It gives you such a picture of life. Now, Mr. Bynner, what I want to say is this: I write some and I feel I write different from most. . . . And now I am drafted and have to leave next week. This seems to cut off all that my life has been. Before I go I would like to have the opinion of someone I feel knows what poetry is on my poems which enclosed please find."

I had supplied the name Earl Roppel and most of his country background. In writing his poems we tried to adumbrate the utterly inane, but our particular purpose was to burlesque what we thought was the false innocence of lyric poets like Bynner. We each wrote about half of the poems, by count, though I have to admit that Foster's were better than mine; he showed a gift for mischievous parody that he should have cultivated in his later career. A good example of his work was the precious quatrain "Moon Light," to which he appended a note for Bynner: "This one I wrote after reading your book."

*Last night when I was in our surrey,*
*Driving home with my best girl,*
*I saw the moon run down the fence-row*
*Like a fat squirrel.*

Soon after the birth of our plowboy poet, Kenneth Burke arrived at the hilltop shack with a stubbornly chaste young woman from Ohio (later she went to Paris and became an admired photographer). We saw a sample of her handwriting and thought it had exactly the unformed, ingenuous look that Earl Roppel's might have had. After providing ourselves with a ruled school tablet, we persuaded her to copy out the poems and the letter to Bynner. Then, thinking that the joke was too good to drop after a week—and forgetting our primary purpose of striking a blow for the Moderns—we made a few changes in the letter and had her copy it out for Amy Lowell (with an additional poem that Foster had written as a pastiche of Miss Lowell's style: "O Venice! Masks! Stilettos!"). Revised once again, the letter and the poems were also copied for my friend Conrad Aiken, but then we had to stop; the young woman from Ohio was complaining that she had no time to enjoy the countryside. I was enjoying it hugely; every morning I set out with a can of worms and every afternoon I came back with a string of trout. Foster would match them with a sonnet and a lard bucket half full of wild strawberries. In the evening we argued about God knows what, Kenneth and I laughing boisterously, Foster chuckling, while our amanuensis toiled away at our only table, under the only lamp.

A few days later we scattered from the shack on a hilltop: I was taking a summer course in military science (mostly sham battles and bayonet drill), Foster had an assignment from the Red Cross, and Kenneth was going to work in a shipyard. We left word with the postmaster in Candor that letters for Earl Roppel should be forwarded to Kenneth's address in Greenwich Village. The letters were slow in reaching us. First to arrive by that roundabout course was the one from Conrad Aiken; it expressed a measured appreciation of young Roppel's poetic gift and advised him to read Keats and Tennyson. Aiken also sent him an inscribed copy of Palgrave's *Golden Treasury*, which I have kept to this day. Amy Lowell was less restrained in her enthusiasm. She offered to submit some of Roppel's verse to *Poetry* and felt sure that it would be printed. "He has the modern spirit," she told Foster when he next came out to dinner at Sevenels. "I don't know where he got it, but he has it."

No letter arrived from Bynner, and for a long time we thought that our joke had missed its principal target. Two years later, however, I wrote a short article about the plowboy poet, and Bynner, when he read it, was sporting enough to tell me the whole story. He had been teaching at the University of California when he received Earl Roppel's little sheaf of verses. He had shown them to his colleagues in the English department at Berkeley, who had agreed with him that even Robert Burns might have admired their simplicity and freshness. Of course he had written to Roppel—more than once, as a matter of fact—and he had offered to help him publish a volume of poems, but the letters had been returned from an address in New York City (Kenneth had moved) with a note on the envelopes: "No such person." At Berkeley Professor Arthur Farwell of the music department had seized upon one of the poems (Foster's masterpiece of parody) and had set it to a stirring tune. It was sung before a huge audience in San Francisco by a chorus of three thousand trained voices. Professor Farwell told the newspapers that "Sun-set" (as Foster had entitled it) was the best patriotic song-poem in America:

> *Flag of our country, strong and true,*
> *The sky is rosy with your bars;*
> *But as they fade it turns to blue*
> *And radiant with your stars.*
>
> *And as I watch the setting sun,*
> *I call to God apart,*
> *"Give me the soul of Washington,*
> *And give me Lincoln's heart!"*

Meanwhile Bynner had written a letter of inquiry to the public library at Owego, ten miles from Candor. The librarian answered that nobody named Earl Roppel had ever been there to borrow books. Bynner began to suspect that someone had duped him: "Could it be Edna Millay?" he asked his friends. Others in the Bay Area maintained their faith in the plowboy poet. In his amusing book *The Spectra Hoax* (1961), William Jay Smith quotes from an article that appeared after the Armistice in *The San Francisco Bulletin*. The author was Zoë Burns, and she said: "Ever since I read the story and some of the work of Witter Bynner's lost poet, I've been wondering about the lad who had such a freshly interesting outlook on life from the narrow confines of a little New York hamlet and to whom the great dreams came thronging while he plowed the fields.... And I'm wondering if the war took that fresh fine almost-girlish sweetness out of him and made him bitter as it has so many of our youths." (Foster and I had worked hard to parody that twelve-year-old-girlish tone.) "Was the heart of him smitten by the thunder of war?" Miss Burns continued. "And the melody of his spirit silenced by its horrors? Was perchance his very life blown out like a candle in the blast?" Of course she was correct in her surmise that Earl Roppel had been a wartime casualty; he died because his only begetters had been separated by military service. Still, he had enjoyed his moment of glory, which might have been Foster's moment too, if he could have been there to accept the applause. In the next fifty years S. Foster Damon was to receive many honors, if not a tithe of those he rightly earned. Harvard never acknowledged him. Nothing he signed with his own name was ever to be sung by a chorus of three thousand trained voices.

3 ✍ Thinking back on Foster's bogus anthem and how it was glorified as the work of another poet, I felt that it might have served as a portent of his career. Always he displayed (or con-

cealed) a talent for being unrecognized and, in relation to the public taste, untimely. In that age of celebrities, the 1920s, he remained the obscure and usually unacknowledged background of celebrities. His first scholarly work, *William Blake: His Philosophy and Symbols* (1924), was an illustration of that singular gift. It was written too soon and it opened too many doors, with the result that Harvard did not accept it "in partial fulfillment," as the phrase used to run, "of the requirements for the degree of doctor of philosophy." It was to inspire many doctoral dissertations. All the subsequent Blake scholars have made use of it; some have written successful books that depended on it; but meanwhile Foster's book, which had appeared in an edition of only a thousand copies, was to remain out of print for twenty years or more.

That early example of his talent for anonymity was to be followed by others. He next wrote what is still the only extended study of Thomas Holley Chivers (1809–58). The book appeared in 1930 and, so far as I remember, attracted no attention whatever. In that first year of the Depression, nobody was interested in the question whether Poe had copied Chivers in some of his poems—or had it been Chivers who copied Poe? The Depression continued year after year, always breeding new crises, and Foster continued to stand aloof from the issues it raised. His new undertaking was a biography of Amy Lowell, an authoritative record of all the picturesque, outrageous, or illuminating episodes in her Napoleonic career. In 1935, when the book was published, the literary world had turned away from Miss Lowell and everything she stood for.

Foster's next published work was for once more timely; it was a facsimile collection, with editorial notes, of a hundred American popular songs from the years before the Civil War. It appeared in 1936, at a moment when American history was becoming a popular subject, and composers were to use Foster's book as a source of background music for some highly successful motion pictures. But the book itself had a limited sale, and again Foster received little credit as a pioneer. He was busy for several years with other projects, including plays and a very long narrative poem that nobody wanted to publish. In 1952 I gave a lecture at Brown, where Foster had been teaching since 1927. After having breakfast with the Damons, I sent him a perturbed letter:

"Dear Foster: I'm addressing the letter to you because, in addition to its serving as a bread-and-butter, or buttered-toast, letter to you and Louise, it also has to touch on the great question of your unpublished manuscripts. They worry me. I don't know any writer of our time who has had so little recognition for what he has done. . . ."

The letter continued with what I hoped were some practical suggestions for publication. Having the professional point of view, I was given to making practical suggestions—except in regard to my own work—but in this case they had no practical results. Foster told me at the time—or was it a little later?—that he had set to work on a complete edition of Chivers' prose and poetry. "Chivers, Chivers," I said to myself in despair. Only the first of three projected volumes was published (1957), in the midst of a silence that shattered one's ears.

But Foster's masterpiece of anonymity was the last book of poems he wrote, *Nightmare Cemetery* (1964). He had published two much earlier collections, and they had earned him some of the usual honors, including the presidency of the New England Poetry Society and its Golden Rose. *Astrolabe* (1927) was the more impressive of the early volumes, by virtue of two rather long mystical poems, both with the same title, "Apocalypse"; they seemed to promise further visions and experiments. The promise was not fulfilled by the poems in *Tilted Moons* (1929), which were mostly decorative and indebted to Foster's reading, with pervasive echoes of Verlaine and Laforgue. Except for that long narrative, I doubt whether he wrote many poems in the next twenty or thirty years. In his late sixties, however, he struck a new vein and worked on it until he had completed *Nightmare Cemetery*, a double sequence of seventy-three sonnets that is, among other things, a remarkable technical achievement.

That is not its principal claim to being remembered, but still the virtuosity should not be overlooked. The work includes examples, and good ones, of orthodox Petrarchan and Shakespearean sonnets, with other examples of almost every possible variation, new and old, from those two basic patterns. Foster does omit a few. Thus, he gives us a sonnet in hexameter, but none in tetrameter or trimeter, none in "sprung rhythm," and none in syllabic verse. Those metrical experiments, however, are hardly missed in the diversity of stanzaic forms he offers. To list a few, there are sonnets in which the conventional octave and sestet are replaced by two seven-line stanzas. There are two double sonnets. There is one sonnet in rhyming couplets, one in rhyming tercets, and one in *terza rima*. There is a sonnet in five stanzas of two, three, four, three, and two lines respectively; of course they add up to fourteen. All but two of the sonnets are of that conventional length, but there is also a thirteen-line sonnet with a complicated rhyme scheme and an extended sonnet in which one line, the twelfth, bursts indignantly into six lines, all rhyming in "-ation." In still another sonnet, the word "myself" replaces the rhyme in each of eight lines:

> *Yes, even the scenery (not too bad): myself.*
> *And you, the disgusted audience,—myself.*

It is a statement of philosophical idealism carried to the point of solipsism, as with many New England poets of the last century. In Foster's case, however, the dependence of the outer cosmos on the inner cosmos is expressed not only in a variety of measures but also in a candid, self-deprecatory fashion (the world is a play written by "myself," he says, but "badly written") and in a tone of voice sustained from the first sonnet to the last. He must have felt, and rightly, that the book was immensely better than anything he had written in his early years.

And what did he do to bring *Nightmare Cemetery* to public attention? Did he submit the separate poems to a hierarchy of magazines, beginning with most prestigious and running down the scale (but not too far, since printing them in the littler magazines would be a tactical error)? Did he read them for radio programs or make those personal appearances on the poetry circuit that are now so easy to arrange? After those preliminary steps, did he keep sending the manuscript to big trade publishers until he found an editor with taste enough to admire it and authority enough to get it accepted? And then did he write to famous colleagues who might be persuaded to review the book or at least to furnish a few adulatory words for the jacket? Those are the usual shifts to which poets are driven by their thirst for glory and their recognition that poetry is not a popular art. I doubt whether they even occurred to Foster, burdened as he was with New England shyness and seventy years of accumulated ignorance about the technique of becoming a famous poet. Perhaps "incapacity" would be a better word. In 1918 he had known what steps to take in order to create the reputation of Earl Roppel, but neither then nor later had he been able to regard his own reputation in the same impersonal way, as a problem in literary mechanics. At any rate, he chose the most effective means of not recapturing an audience. He had the book published, if one can use the word, by friends at the Rhode Island School of Design, in an edition of two hundred numbered and expensive copies. Then, having sent out a few dozen copies for review and some others as gifts to friends, he simply waited for recognition.

Two years later he was still waiting. He said in a mildly querulous letter (October 13, 1966), "*Not one* of the copies of my *Cemetery* sent to poetry and other literary magazines so much as got listed in 'Books Received.' And of course no reviews. I guess that one peek showed my poems to be sonnets, and sonnets are not worth noticing any more."

Sonnets are out of fashion, but there was another reason for the universal oversight. Foster had presented *Nightmare Cemetery* under a pseudonym—Samuel Nomad—and with a prefatory note that read: "All the characters in this book are entirely imaginary including the author." He must have regarded the pseudonym and the note as a transparent literary device, since, as he explained in another letter, the author's identity is revealed in the thirteenth line of the sonnet on page ten: "the clumsy letters of my name reversed." Samuel Nomad and S. (for Samuel) Foster Damon: any reader could see the connection. But where were the readers? Foster did not realize that hardly anyone, these days, would even open a book by a pseudonymous author half-

published in a small edition by a school of design. Hardly anyone, that is, took the peek that would have shown the poems
to be sonnets, let alone reading as far as the thirteenth line of
the sonnet on page ten. In the glut and gurry of contemporary
writing, there are too many nominated poets wailing for attention. Hardly any editor thinks of assigning a completely unknown
book for review.

Or did the author realize all this and was he obeying his
instinct for self-obliteration?

What *Nightmare Cemetery* needed and still needs is the
sort of adventurous reader that Foster was in his Harvard years.
But is there such a reader today?—I mean with Foster's knight-
errantry in riding to the rescue of neglected books as if they were
maidens immured in a donjon keep. Some of those books had
languished so long unread that they had become the equivalent
of maiden great-aunts before he freed them from dusty shelves
and displayed them to his friends. "Look at this, Estlin (or Jack,
or Virgil)," he would say a little proudly, as if he had returned
from a knightly quest with Sleeping Beauty riding on his crup-
per. But who will go questing after *Nightmare Cemetery?*

If Samuel Nomad were a person and if his book had
been written fifty years ago—as in some ways it might have been,
for it does not propose to be timely—I can imagine what Foster
might have said about it, after producing it from that enormous
green baize bag. "Look at this, Mal," he would have begun in his
flat voice, but with an edge of excitement: "here's something
I found today. The author calls it a Halloween prank, but it's a
grisly and labored one, a double sequence of sonnets about death.
Is it great poetry? No, it doesn't even try to be, and yet it belongs
in a great line: Emerson, Jones Very, Emily Dickinson, all the
New England metaphysicals. Yes, and let's add Edward Rowland
Sill and E. A. Robinson for a touch of pessimism. Here's why it
impresses me: it's at the very end of the line."

I would open the book and read a sonnet. "This one
doesn't sound like Emerson," I would say.

"Oh, you mean the one where Nomad compares his own
death to pulling the chain and going down the toilet? That

sonnet will prove my point as well as another. It's pure New England in its self-absorption—the wrong word; it makes me think of toilet paper—and in its identification of the self with the universe. But it's Emerson upside down, Emerson turned pessimist and raging cynic, Emerson's great tides of universal Being transformed into 'the gulp of the celestial watercloset.' I tell you, it's the end of the line."

Foster would snatch the book from my hand and go pacing up and down the room. "This Nomad fellow," he would say, "is evidently an old man telling what he thinks is the shameful truth about himself. He isn't a celebrity, he isn't popular and outgoing, and he faces what he calls 'the time when I am slowly, horribly, killed.' His dim hope of an afterlife depends on finding readers for his poetry, yet some deep compulsion makes him insult them and drive them away. He can make jokes about his shameful truths or dress them in Halloween masks from a children's party, but he hasn't time left to be bothered with telling lies. He hasn't time to be decorative in his language or to grope for figures of speech; one metaphor set forth in simple words, sometimes in slang, is all he finds room for in one sonnet. Listen:

" 'Life is the big neighborhood party, me lad,
    to which you weren't invited. And so what.

" 'walk in as though you owned the place—be brash
    and grab the prettiest girl and make her dance.

" '(This is one party that you cannot crash.)
    —So, go home; climb into bed and try to sleep.
(The cold, deep bed and your long, long last sleep.)'

"He writes for the ear, not the eye," Foster would comment, "and the only liberties he allows himself are in rhyme and stanza and especially in meter. There he delights in asperities and rugosities. His iambic pentameters are sprinkled with trochees; there are two in the first line I read, besides one anapest, and the line about the cold, deep bed has three spondees. Reading such lines makes me think of New Hampshire fields that are strewn with boulders. The soil runs thin as the blood runs thin; Nomad is the last of a great line. Sometimes his voice wheezes like the hand-pumped organ in an old meetinghouse; it is the voice of New England, and yet his own voice unmistakably. Because of it his book exists in itself when so many books are the mere facsimiles of others. Listen for a last time."

Foster would page through the book and, in his own unmistakable voice, would read me six lines of "Epitaph":

> *I tried to write my name: that much seemed needed.*
> *And I have failed if it has found a place*
> *only beneath the title. But I succeeded*
> *if in this verbal wilderness and valley*
> *sometimes you hear a voice you cannot place*
> *that speaks your own name softly, authentically.*

It seems to me that Samuel Nomad, or rather S. Foster Damon in his last book of poems, has succeeded in that self-absorbed but self-effaced and wholly authentic fashion.

A FOOTNOTE: There was to be one more published book of poetry, *The Moulton Tragedy* (1970), but this had existed in manuscript since the beginning of World War II. It is "a heroic poem with lyrics," and it is based on the legend of a New England Faust, Jonathan Moulton, who drove a Yankee bargain with the Devil. *The Moulton Tragedy* is technically brilliant like the sonnets, it is full of local history, and it has eerie moments that continue Foster's lifelong interest in the occult. It appeared when narrative poetry was even less in fashion than the sonnet. By that time Foster had suffered a stroke, and he was probably unable to read the reviews, which, as always, were as far and few as the lands where the Jumblies live.

Foster died on Christmas Day 1971 (he had been born in 1893, on Washington's Birthday). A book of his *Selected Poems* was published in 1974 by Abattoir Editions (University of Nebraska at Omaha). Besides being handsomely printed, the book is well edited and introduced by Donald E. Stanford, but I wish it could have been much longer. *Nightmare Cemetery* still serves as Foster's epitaph.

# IV –AND I WORKED AT THE WRITER'S TRADE

1 ✍ From the last of Foster Damon's books, let me turn back to my own beginnings in the writer's trade. I got started in the trade strictly from hunger, as people used to say in excusing their delinquencies. In the spring of 1919 I was twenty years old, I was hungry in Greenwich Village, and I was living in sin without paying the rent for our room. One of the possibly helpful persons I went to see was a former boy friend of my girl friend. Clarence Britten was his name, and he was literary editor of *The Dial*, then a political fortnightly that had moved from Chicago to New York under the somewhat reluctant patronage of an eccentric millionaire. Britten looked at me curiously as he invited me into his office. He asked after Peggy, made one or two abrupt gestures, then pushed half a dozen novels across his desk. "Try reviewing these," he said, "but don't give them more than a

hundred words apiece." If and when the reviews were published, they would each bring me a dollar.

Six times one dollar seemed a happy prospect for the following month, but meanwhile there was the problem of buying food for dinner that evening. Later I wrote in *Exile's Return*, with you's standing for I's,

> So you would carry the books to a bench in Union Square and page through them hastily, making notes—in two or three hours you would be finished with the whole armful and you would take them to a secondhand bookstore on Fourth Avenue, where the proprietor paid a flat rate of thirty-five cents for each review copy; you thought it was more than the novels were worth. With exactly $2.10 in your pocket you would buy bread and butter and lamb chops and Bull Durham for cigarettes and order a bag of coal; then at home you would broil the lamb chops over the grate because the landlady had neglected to pay her gas bill, just as you had neglected to pay the rent. You were all good friends and she would be invited to share the feast. Next morning you would write the reviews, then start on the search for a few dollars more.

The search led me to other editorial offices, for I was now definitely apprenticed to the trade of putting words on paper. On reading Diane Eisenberg's checklist of my published writings[1] compiled after she had grubbed among back files with more patience than most of the writings deserve, I find that each of the early items helps to evoke a way of life now vanished together with the magazines that made it barely possible. Mrs. Eisenberg does not list those brief reviews in the fortnightly *Dial*—for how could she identify the deservedly anonymous?—but one of her entries for the summer of the same year records my first signed appearance in a magazine that paid for contributions:

---

1. *Malcolm Cowley: A Checklist of His Writings, 1916–1973*, by Diane U. Eisenberg (Carbondale, Ill.: Southern Illinois University Press, 1973).

F5 "Through Yellow Glasses." *New Republic* XIX (July 23, 1919): 401.

*Victorious,* by Reginald Wright Kauffman.

As I read those cabbalistic words, I can see myself walking in cracked shoes under the Ninth Avenue Elevated. It is a late-spring afternoon and the sun is projecting a pattern of crossties on the pavement. Under my arm I carry a square brown notebook in which the first dozen pages are filled with clippings of my published work: not only those first unsigned reviews in *The Dial* but earlier signed ones in *The Harvard Advocate* and a long poem that has just appeared in *The Little Review.* I am hurrying to the offices of *The New Republic,* where Francis Hackett, the literary editor, has agreed over the telephone to give me a few moments.

Hackett, a big, red-faced Irishman looking like Jupiter in pince-nez glasses, is seated behind a pile of books at a scarred enormous desk that will be my desk ten years later (though the possibility does not then enter my mind). He glances at my little collection of press clippings, reads the brief notices from *The Dial,* then calls to his assistant, "Miss Updike, perhaps you can find a book for this young man." Taking off his pince-nez, he gives me a lordly smile of dismissal. Miss Updike looks at my cracked shoes, then picks out a novel by Reginald Wright Kauffman that she thinks might be worth five hundred words—or ten dollars, I calculate, at *The New Republic*'s two cents a word. She gives me the book as if she were pouring a saucer of milk for a starved kitten.

End of the memory, and almost the end of my first attempt to keep two persons alive by free-lance book reviewing. It was yielding us hardly more than one meal a day, and the meals were usually deficient in proteins and carbohydrates. I dreamed about the hilltop cabin upstate where I had lived with Foster Damon and Kenneth Burke on trout and wild strawberries (with bread and milk, all we could eat). One morning I was crossing Sheridan Square after no breakfast when the sidewalk suddenly came up and hit me in the face. I didn't lose consciousness for more than a moment. Less frightened than surprised, I picked myself up and walked carefully into a lunchroom to spend my last dime for a stale bun and a cup of coffee. As I sat at the counter feeling not at all hungry and more than usually clearheaded, I surrendered, for a time, my pride in living on the underside of society and my dream of being a free artisan working at his typewriter as if it were a cottage loom.

> When I was a bachelor I lived by myself,
>   And I worked at the weaver's trade,
>   And the only, only thing I did that was wrong
>     Was to woo a fair young maid.

My fair maid was older than I and more experienced, with many good friends in the Village who were now tired of lending her money. I had shielded her from the foggy, foggy dew, but, though she never complained, I had been remiss in providing bread and cigarettes and pretties. For me there was always that exasperating wait between writing a review and getting paid for it. "Anything else?" the counterman asked in an ominous voice. I started home, still walking with care and knowing now that a job would have to be found. A few days later I found it, too, by answering want ads and accepting a miserable salary. At least there would be enough to keep the two of us fed.

In the fall I went back to college, where I had a scholarship of sorts and could borrow a little money from the dean's office (there was none from home). I planned to earn a degree by taking six courses in one semester, a heavier load than any Harvard student is now permitted to stagger under. To make things more difficult, I was married by then and Peggy was in frail health. Nevertheless, in the intervals between studying and nursing, I managed to do some writing for publication, as I am reminded by other items in Mrs. Eisenberg's checklist. Mary Updike, God bless her, remembered the starved kitten and sent me at least two packages of books for review. I must have been the only undergraduate who was a fairly regular contributor to *The New Republic*.

Still another entry for the same period records the beginning of what was to be a long and close collaboration:

F9 "The Woman of Ihornden." *Dial* LXVIII (February 1920): 259–62.

*A Challenge to Sirius* and *The Four Roads,* by Sheila Kaye-Smith.

Clarence Britten, out of kindness to me or to Peggy, I don't know which, had decided that I ought to do a signed piece for *The Dial.* As an occasion for it, he sent me two novels by Sheila Kaye-Smith, an English novelist then held in some estimation. The review was accepted soon after I went back to college, but weeks passed and it did not appear. Meanwhile Britten had lost his job. *The Dial* had been sold by its eccentric angel and purchased by two other millionaires, Scofield Thayer and Sibley Watson, both recently out of Harvard. They planned to transform the fortnightly *Dial* into the most distinguished monthly magazine of the arts that had appeared in this country. For the purchase price of I don't know how much, they had acquired the name, a modest list of subscribers, and a barrel, so called—it was really a small box—full of accepted but unpublished manuscripts. Having read their way through the barrel, they decided that nothing in it was worthy to appear in a magazine of the highest literary standards—nothing, that is, except my piece on Sheila Kaye-Smith, which would serve as the only link between the old and the new. It appeared in the second or February issue of the monthly *Dial,* just as I was packing to leave Harvard with my precariously earned degree.

Leave I must, but I had no destination except, vaguely, New York. Two days before we planned to go, if I could pay for our railroad tickets, there were footsteps on the stairs and a knock at the door of our attic room. A young man, a stranger, gave me an envelope and said, "Mr. Copeland told me not to wait for an answer." Inside the envelope was a ten-dollar bill folded in a note from Charles Townsend Copeland—"Copey," as everyone called him—my favorite English instructor. "I thought you could use this," Copey had written in his big sloping hand. The ten dollars paid our fare to Grand Central, in those days of cheaper transportation, with enough left over for a taxi to the house in Greenwich Village where our former landlady had offered to put us up for a few days. We rode there holding hands through streets still heaped with grimy snow from a storm two weeks before.

Our prospects were as bleak as the Manhattan streets, but we felt more cheerful now that Peggy had partly recovered her health. She began to circulate once more among Village friends, and one of them found us three rooms on the top floor of a tenement, reached by climbing five flights of stairs that smelled of Italian cooking. A check arrived in the nick of time— like every other check that did arrive—and paid the first month's rent of sixteen dollars. Our bed was borrowed, our chairs were begged, and my writing table was bought for next to nothing at a Salvation Army store. Soon I was writing every day—poems mostly, but also any sort of prose for which a market could be found at a penny a word; only *The New Republic* and the monthly *Dial* were more generous. Mrs. Eisenberg's checklist testifies to many afternoons spent tramping from one editorial office to another.

As I look back on those years, it seems to me that I must have had a somewhat special cast of mind. I wanted to be a writer, but not a celebrated writer appearing in glossy magazines. I wanted to live obscurely, limit my needs, and preserve my freedom to write something new and perfect at some moment in the future; that was the dream of producing a masterpiece that obsessed the young writers of my age group. While waiting for the moment I was willing to do hackwork, a meager source of income, as I had learned, but one that I judged to be permissible if the work was honestly performed. Always I tried to make it better work than I was paid for doing, with the result that my little commissioned pieces had qualities not to be found in my life at the time: punctuality, for example, and neatness and logic. Editors liked them because they could be sent to the printer without revision.

Editors are sometimes excessively kind to very young writers, especially if these are talkative or show any sign of promise. With special gratitude I remember Henry Seidel Canby and his assistant Amy Loveman. I first dropped in on them when Dr. Canby was starting a new weekly supplement, *The Literary Review of the New York Evening Post;* workmen were still installing partitions in what were to be their offices. Miss Loveman listened through the din of hammers while I gave her a lecture on contemporary French poetry. Once or twice she smiled maternally, and she let me carry away two books for unsigned reviews. Later that spring Dr. Canby invited me into his by then completed sanctum; we talked about trout fishing and he reproved me for using worms. Then he suggested that I take, each week, half a dozen books that *The Literary Review* was planning to discard. I should page through them and, if I found that one or two deserved attention, I should write the reviews. For this I was to be paid ten dollars a week. I accepted the arrangement, which made me, at the time, the only salaried book reviewer in New York.

Of course I was writing for other journals as well and, in one way or another, I managed to get along. When checks were slow in arriving, I played penny ante on Saturday nights, cards held close to my chest, and could count on winning ten dollars if the game lasted till morning. For two weeks I was a stagehand at the Provincetown Players and earned twenty dollars a week. Why, I was prosperous, and independent too, and when I was offered a regular job by *Sweet's Architectural Catalogue* I came near turning it down. But finally I accepted it, and held it for a year, until I was given a fellowship to a French university by the American Field Service, with which I had served during the war. Peggy and I got ready to go abroad.

2 ⬧ Reading over this account of a literary apprenticeship, I find that it often mentions very small sums of money. There is good reason for the mention, considering that money is the central problem of a young writer's life, or of his staying alive. True as the statement is today, it was even more true in the 1920s, when there were fewer sources of literary livelihood. Universities didn't

then invite young novelists or critics to join their English staffs or young poets to give paid readings. There were very few literary prizes; there were no subsidies by foundations. Fellowships to foreign universities, like the one I had lately been given, were scarce and meager and hard to come by. More dependence had to be placed on the small sums paid for contributions by magazines of limited circulation. The smaller one's gross income, the more important each little payment became and the more pride one took in earning it.

The poverty of young American writers during the prosperous 1920s was of course a central reason for their exodus to Europe. There were other reasons too, as notably Prohibition, puritanism, and the triumph of business over art in American society, from which young writers felt no less alienated than their successors fifty years later; but there was chiefly the promise of cheaper living in Europe. It was not a false promise, as can be seen from my own experience in the years 1921–23. My fellowship was for twelve thousand francs, or one thousand dollars at what was then the rate of exchange. It was renewed for the following year, but was worth a little less in dollars, since the franc had fallen. I also earned a little money by writing for American periodicals, but not more than five hundred dollars for each of the years. On a total income for the two-year period of less than three thousand dollars, I paid for our passage to France, lived there in rather more comfort than at home, traveled a little, and had just enough left for our return passage to New York. As regards the writing I did for American periodicals while in France, there are several examples in Mrs. Eisenberg's checklist, but I shall mention only one:

> G9 "Henri Barbusse." *Bookman* LVI (October 1922): 180–182.
>
> Barbusse became famous overnight with *Under Fire,* a literarily and politically provocative novel.

The story of that article begins like many other stories, at a sidewalk table outside the Café du Dôme. There one summer afternoon I found Ivan Opffer, a feckless Dane I had known in the Village. Ivan told me that *The Bookman* had commissioned him to draw portraits of the best-known French authors. "Why don't you come along and do an article to go with the next picture?" he said. His next scheduled visit was to Henri Barbusse, author of a famous antiwar novel, *Le Feu*. We found that the roads around his little country house were patrolled by gendarmes in pairs, on bicycles; one pair stopped us and asked to see our passports. "That's how things go in France," Barbusse said as he offered each of us a long, emaciated hand; he had the visionary look of a John the Baptist. I asked him questions and took notes in two languages while Ivan made hasty sketches on big sheets of drawing paper. Ivan was wonderful at catching facial expressions, but he had never learned to draw hands. My little profile in words was of course written on spec, but it resulted in a commission to do six others, all with Ivan's handless figures as illustrations. Lectured at by one author after another, I learned something about French literary politics and was modestly paid for writing what amounted to classroom reports on my studies.

I also contributed to magazines published in Europe, sometimes rather obscure ones, as Mrs. Eisenberg's checklist shows. One item recalls a story:

> M73 "Madrigals." *Mécano* (Leiden), numbers 4 and 5 (1923), n.p.
>
> Three short, rather scabrous poems printed in a Dutch Dadaist magazine edited by Theo van Doesburg. Never reprinted.

Again the story starts at the Dôme, where, one spring afternoon, I found my good friend Tristan Tzara, the founder of Dada. A Rumanian living in Switzerland, he had been brought to Paris in 1919 by Louis Aragon, also my friend, and André Breton. Now he was having quarrels with the French Dadaists, originally his disciples, but he was still held in reverence by Dadaist groups sprung up in Germany, Belgium, and Holland. That afternoon Tzara was sitting with an eager, rather innocent—so it seemed to me—Dutch Dadaist named Theo van Doesburg; later he was to become internationally known for I forget what. Tzara introduced me as a *poète Dada américain.* Van Doesburg asked whether I wouldn't contribute to a little magazine he was publishing in Leiden. Why, yes, *volontiers,* I said, thinking of some scabrous songs I had written for my own entertainment. It would be amusing to print them in a Dutch Dadaist paper when they couldn't appear, at the time, anywhere in the English-speaking world:

> *masochistic Mazie*
> *very nearly crazy*
> *almost*
> > *very nearly*
> > > *quite*
> *insane*
> *scratched her pretty asshole*
> *over broken glass*
> > > *coal*
> *cinders*
> > *Joy*
> > > *Sex*
> > > > *Pain*
> *WASn't she insane?*

That was the first of the "Madrigals." There was another about Sadic Sam from Alabam, there were two lines about fetishistic Fanny, who married Jack the Ripper, and they were duly printed in Joint Nos. 4 & 5 of *Mécano.* A year later Hemingway published other scabrous lyrics in a German semi-Dadaist magazine called *Der Querschnitt,* one which had the greater distinction of paying its contributors.

In the late spring of 1923 my fellowship expired, money ran short, and we started to think about going back to New York. We were then living in three rooms above the former blacksmith shop in Giverny, a Norman village fifty miles down the Seine from Paris. Bob Coates, our big red-headed friend, agreed to take over the rooms and we began to pack our few possessions into a wicker trunk. I felt that there ought to be something more ponderable as a memento of those two years in Europe. An essay on

Racine, just finished, was a brief work in which I took pride. I carried the essay to a printer in Paris and received his estimate: for two hundred copies of a stapled pamphlet he would charge me less than thirty-five dollars at the current rate of exchange. That brings me to the very first item in the Malcolm Cowley checklist:

> A1  *Racine.* Paris: Privately printed, 1923.
>
> Of the 200 original copies only 15 are known to survive.
> . . . Later appeared in the *Freeman* (see G15, G16).

Let me explain why the pamphlet is so rare. The two hundred copies, dedicated to Copey, "In default of a better gift," I said, went back with us to New York, and there I started mailing them out to friends. There too I made the humiliating discovery that I hadn't two hundred friends or bowing acquaintances who might be interested in Racine; at most I could stretch the list to forty or fifty names. The remaining copies of the pamphlet lay piled in various closets for several years, until I got tired of carrying them from one habitation to another; then I dropped them into a wastebasket except for a dozen or more copies that I saved. In 1960 or thereabouts I looked at the catalogue of a rare-book dealer and found that one copy of the pamphlet, "slightly foxed," was being offered for thirty-five dollars, or a little more than I had paid for the whole edition. The price ten years later had risen to seventy-five dollars. By that time, however, I had only two copies left and couldn't be tempted to sell them.

When we got back to New York in August 1923 I had only five dollars in my wallet, but this time my prospects were somewhat brighter than they had been in 1920. I paid a visit to my former boss at *Sweet's Architectural Catalogue* and was promptly hired back at a better salary. For a long time I was kept too busy to write anything for publication except a few reviews for *The Dial* and for Dr. Canby. But I dreamed of going deep into the country and living once again as a free-lance writer, and already I was moving in that direction, one step at a time. First I began to look for other periodical outlets, then I rented a little house on Staten Island that had a vegetable garden to practice in, then I bought a very old Model T Ford, and then, as a decisive step, I resigned from *Sweet's* to see whether I could live for a year by writing. After living out the year, which ended in the spring of 1926, I helped to load our three sticks of furniture and our four boxes of books on a wheezing Model T truck, and we set out for Sherman, Connecticut. Friends of mine—Hart Crane, Allen Tate, William Slater Brown, Matthew Josephson—lived in the neighborhood, and they had found us an old farmhouse with exterior nonplumbing that rented for ten dollars a month. The wheezing truck broke down at the top of Briggs Hill, half a mile from its destination, and our belongings arrived on a farm wagon.

I note some further entries that explain how we had kept ourselves going.

> G19 "Parnassus-on-the-Seine." *Charm* I (July 1924): 19, 80, 83.
>
> "Montparnasse, the art student quarter of Paris, is the rendezvous of the world."

*Charm* was a rather elaborate magazine that had just been started by Bamberger's department store in Newark, New Jersey, for distribution to its charge customers. Its first editor was Bessie Breuer, a friend of Peggy's; later she became a novelist, sound and perceptive but not widely perceived. Bessie tried to help us by dreaming up articles for me to write—outlandish articles, so it seemed to this serious literary person, but still I accepted the challenge, much as if I had been an engineer asked to design an outlandish bridge. When Bessie was succeeded by another able editor, Lucie Taussig, I began suggesting my own subjects, often drawn from New Jersey history. I also wrote a monthly book page for *Charm* and presented the literary scene in terms that I hoped would interest New Jersey housewives.

> F51 "Mr. Moore's Golden Treasury." *New York Herald Tribune Books,* August 2, 1925, p. 5.
>
> *An Anthology of Pure Poetry,* edited with an introduction by George Moore.

That must have been the first review I wrote for Irita Van Doren. I don't remember whether I asked her for the book or whether she suggested my reviewing it after her friend Harrison Smith had written a front-page article about my first translation from the French, *On Board the Morning Star,* a cycle of pirate stories by Pierre MacOrlan. In either case I was soon contributing regularly to Mrs. Van Doren's book section. Among the kindhearted editors I have known, she was by far the kindest. She had taken over *Herald Tribune Books* after the sudden death of Stuart Pratt Sherman, its first editor, and had directed it successfully from the beginning. Young ambitious people wanted to write for her. On Wednesday afternoons, I think it was, when she held a sort of open house for reviewers and would-be reviewers, they used to gather in her waiting room from their garrets and cellars. That year it always rained on Wednesday afternoon, or so it seems to me now. The picture that stays in my mind is of one young woman—I never learned her name—sitting with wet shoes and a dripping skirt, her lank hair framing a long-jawed, pale, moist, eager face, as she waited for a word or still better a book from Mrs. Van Doren.

Irita was an Alabama woman with a soft voice and an enchanting smile, but she could be firm at moments; she could even be ruthless when that was the kindest thing to be. Once she had accepted a reviewer, she kept him on her staff year after year— sometimes too long—and looked for interesting books for him to write about. It was partly owing to her loyal friendship that I was able to carry out my project of living deep in the country with nothing to sell but words.

We didn't live very well. There was always something to eat in the house, but sometimes there wasn't very much, and on those days I would wait for the mailman in hope of his bringing me a nick-of-time check. If the check arrived, I would drive over back roads to New Milford, Connecticut, and deposit it in what passed for my bank account. I didn't dare to cash the check in New Milford, since the account was seldom large enough to cover it. Instead I would drive sixteen miles to Pawling, New York, buy groceries, and pay for them with a check drawn on New Milford.

It would have to pass through the New York clearinghouse and the Boston clearinghouse before it reached the bank, a process that would take three or four days. By that time my deposit would have been collected and credited to my account, and the check written in Pawling would be honored. It sounds complicated, but it was all part of the writer's trade, just as much as the proper use of semicolons.

3 ⬧ There is one more of Mrs. Eisenberg's entries to mention, the one that records publication of my first book and hence the end of a literary apprenticeship. Once again it recalls a story.

> L2 *Blue Juniata.* New York: Jonathan Cape and Harrison Smith, 1929. 115 pp.
>
> 56 poems in five parts: 1. Blue Juniata; 2. The Adolescent; 3. Valuta; 4. The City of Anger; 5. Old Melodies: Love and Death.

Hart Crane is the hero of the story. It begins in the summer of 1928, when Hart came back to the rooms he rented in Addie Turner's bleak house, five miles from Patterson, New York, after a disastrous winter in California. I had moved across the state line that spring after contracting to buy, if I could make the payments, sixty acres of abandoned farmland and a hungry-looking house half a mile from Mrs. Turner's. We saw Hart almost daily that summer. Like everyone else we noted that his bristly hair was turning gray and that his face was redder and puffier. Those were signs of a physiological change, from being a "heavy social drinker," as we had always known him, to being a "problem drinker," the first stage of true alcoholism. He was paying more and more visits to Wiley Varian, the cashiered army officer who ran a speakeasy on Birch Hill. "Sometimes Hart gave a party," and then, says Nathan Asch,[2] who was living in the same big

---

2. Nathan Asch, a tragic figure in retrospect, hated to be known as a son of the famous Yiddish novelist Sholem Asch. Still in his twenties

house that summer, "we, the writers rejected by New York booming with the market of the twenties, consoled ourselves with the gaiety we could engender ourselves. We drank the liquor from either Varian's or one of the other bootleggers, and then we shouted and then we danced. . . . We did not speak to each other, but rather each of us howled out, and we did not dance with our wives or even with each other, but whirled around Hart's room, faster and faster, as if we were truly possessed." Yes, we did all that and more, with the phonograph blaring and Hart leading the revels, but we did it on only one occasion; I think it was on his birthday, July 21. Hart wasn't much of a party giver.

Instead he was a party goer. He distinguished himself, though I don't remember how, at the Fourth of July party given by Slater and Sue Brown, and he came back from New York for the party on Labor Day. Everybody speaks of that summer in terms of parties. What I remember with more pleasure are the long, intensely quiet mornings, the games of croquet at the Browns', where we gathered on Sunday afternoons, the weekday afternoons spent fishing by myself or walking in the woods with Hart, and the talks about poets and poetry. Hart had a purely unselfish project that summer; he was going to prod me into collecting a book of poems. "I have it at least in mind," he wrote to Isidor and Helen Schneider in July, "to try my best to get his poems accepted by some publisher or other before a twelvemonth. He'll never do much about it himself, as you know, and his collection is really needed on the shelves these days."

Hart was right in thinking that I would have been slow to do anything about it myself. I had sixty-odd poems, all printed in magazines during the preceding ten years—there was an im-

---

when he lived in Addie Turner's house, Nathan had already published two novels and was working on a third (*Pay Day*, 1930). He thought he was a better writer than his father, and indeed he wrote more lyrically, sometimes with deeper feeling, but he lacked the father's simple vigor and breadth of conception. After World War II, in which he served with courage, he couldn't get his books published any longer, at a time when his father's books were selling more widely than ever. Nathan's death in 1964 went almost unnoticed.

mediacy that I enjoyed in magazine publication—but I felt no urgent desire to make a book of them. Although the book would come in time, I rather preferred to be unknown for the moment, except to magazine readers, and therefore unclassified, free to move in any direction. But Hart kept prodding me. Early in July he had made me assemble a sheaf of poems; then we went over them together, rejecting some by mutual consent and discussing which of the others belonged together, in exactly what order. Hart believed that emotions, and the poems that expressed them, should follow one another in the right sequence. He thought naturally in terms of structure and of "the book," which, he insisted, should be more than a random selection of poems by one author. In the poems themselves he did not change a word—not even later, when he retyped the whole manuscript—since both of us felt that a poet should speak in his own voice.

When he left for New York early in August there was a book of sorts and one that might have been printed, but I still had only a vague notion of showing it to a publisher. Hart's notion was more definite. On October 24 he asked me—it wasn't the first time, since some of his letters have been lost—"to bring in all the mss material of your poems which I was in the process of editing last summer. I'll soon have plenty of time to give the matter, and I have a suspicion that something will come of it now." On November 20 he announced in a drunken early-morning letter that the poems had arrived the day before. "I'll be careful with the mss," he said, "and your book'll be out within 7 months," that is, within the "twelvemonth" he had mentioned in his letter to the Schneiders. On December 1, a week before sailing for Europe, he wrote, "It has been a pleasure for me to spend part of the last two days in typing the mss of your book. . . . I now have two copies, one to turn over to the 'secret' arbiter here and one to take with me to England." He had omitted one poem that both of us had questions about and had changed the position in the manuscript of three others. "Really the book as we now have it," he said, "has astonishing structural sequence," thus ending the sentence with two of his favorite words. The original manuscript was being returned to me by registered mail.

A few weeks later, when Hart was in London or Paris, I heard from the "secret arbiter." He turned out to be Gorham Munson, then an editor of the George H. Doran Company (which later merged with Doubleday). Munson and I had been on opposite sides of the quarrels in 1923 that hastened the deaths of two little magazines, *Broom* and *Secession;* that was why Hart hadn't mentioned his name. Now Munson laid the quarrels aside. In the name of his company he offered me a contract for the book—it had by then acquired a title, *Blue Juniata*—together with a modest advance against royalties. Hart's project was bearing fruit, and in less than the twelvemonth he had specified.

At this point, however, the project was interrupted by the stiff-necked character of the author. Grateful as I was to Hart, I had a Pennsylvania Dutch side that hated to be—as my forebears would have said—"beholden" to anyone for the structure and publication of my first book. I thanked Munson for the offer and said I would think about it. Then I showed the original manuscript to Harrison Smith, a friend of mine (of Hart's too, and of the Van Dorens'), who had started a publishing house in partnership with Jonathan Cape of London. Hal, as everyone called him, promptly accepted it and gave me a slightly larger advance than Doran had offered.

I took the manuscript home—we were spending the winter in a cramped apartment on Avenue B, south of the present East Village—and set to work on it. First I gave the poems a completely different sequence, not emotional or dialectical, as Hart had suggested (and as he himself had followed in *White Buildings*), but autobiographical. The new framework made it possible to use a few of the poems that Hart and I had earlier decided to omit; they were callow, as we agreed, but callowness was part of the story I was telling. Then I divided the book into five sections and furnished notes, in prose, to introduce three of these. I revised most of the poems once again, a task that continued through the winter (though it was interrupted when I had to do translations to pay the rent). Meanwhile Hart had carried his copy of the earlier manuscript to Paris and was trying to persuade his rich friend Harry Crosby to publish it at the

Black Sun Press. I learn from John Unterecker's biography of Hart that he was on the point of succeeding when I wrote him late in January that the book was coming out in New York.

By the middle of June *Blue Juniata* was in type and I sent an extra set of galleys to Hart. I was a little afraid that his vanity would be wounded by my failure to accept his suggestions, but I need not have been, for Hart had almost no vanity of the sort. He was not interested in whether the book embodied his ideas, but only in whether it was put together effectively. "Since reading the proofs," he wrote me on July 3, 1929, "I'm certain that the book is even better...a much more solidified unit than it was before. I haven't had the original mss with me for comparison, but wherever I have noted changes they seem to be for the better. Really, Malcolm—if you will excuse me for the egoism —I'm just a little proud of the outcome of my agitations last summer." It had been exactly a twelvemonth since he started them.

So I end with this message of gratitude to a dead friend. As I piece together the story, I think again how different Hart was, on that wise and amiable side of him, from the drunken rioter he is often pictured as being. All this took place in the time of his noisiest riots, and yet he devoted sober weeks to editing and typing and peddling someone else's manuscript. He was absolutely lacking in professional jealousy—except toward T. S. Eliot, and that was a compliment to Eliot; otherwise Hart was jealous only of the great dead. The little victories gained by his friends delighted him more than his own victories. "You're a lucky boy!" he wrote me after reading some favorable reviews of *Blue Juniata*. "I'm very glad about it all"—and he truly was. He was the first person to whom I sent an inscribed copy of the book. "If it's bad," I wrote on the flyleaf, "the sin be on your head." He carried the book with him when he went to Mexico in 1931. My first wife was there too, getting a friendly divorce, and finally they sailed for New York together. Peggy retrieved the book from his stateroom on the *Orizaba* the day he jumped overboard.

# V LAFORGUE
# IN AMERICA
# A Testimony

1 ✍ *Deponent states:* My name is Malcolm Cowley and I am
by profession a literary historian. In 1929 I published a first book
of poems, *Blue Juniata,* which was divided into five sections arranged in roughly chronological order. Three of the sections were
each preceded by an explanatory note intended to set the tone of
what followed. The note preceding a section called "The Adolescent" began as follows:

> After the war we drifted to New York, to the district
> south of Fourteenth Street, where we could occupy a hall
> bedroom for two or three dollars weekly and rent the un-
> furnished top floor of a rickety dwelling for thirty dollars a
> month. There were two schools among us: those who painted
> the floors black (they were the last of the aesthetes) and
> those who did not paint the floors. Our college textbooks and

the complete works of Jules Laforgue gathered dust on the mantelpiece among a litter of unemptied ashtrays.

Two questions that might strike a reader are, first, why and how the works of Jules Laforgue, an early Symbolist poet (1860–87)—said works then consisting of three yellow-backed volumes published by the Mecure de France—found their way to a mantelpiece in an old brick rat-infested house on I remember it was Bedford Street, in the territory of a West Side gang, the Hudson Dusters; and second, what influence they had on the poems that some of us were writing in those days. By "us" I mean the apprentice writers of 1919–20, those who had interrupted their college years by enlisting in one of the armed services or, more likely, in the unarmed American Field Service attached to the French armies. Now we were back in the States, and Laforgue must have stood for something in the civilian lives we hoped to lead.

What that something was and how it got into our lives is a story that goes back to a time shortly before we were born. At Harvard in the early 1890s there were several gifted poets, all of whom died young; collectively they deserved the name that Yeats applied to his friends of the same age in London: the Tragic Generation. William Vaughn Moody and George Cabot Lodge were members of the group, but the best of them was Trumbull Stickney, who was born in 1874 and died of a brain tumor at the age of thirty. Most of those Harvard poets had a particular sense of life and literature that was based partly on Greek classicism and partly on French Symbolism. It was strictly in character that Stickney not only was the first American to be granted a *Doctorat ès Lettres* by the Sorbonne but also chose as the subject for his French dissertation "Axioms in Greek Poetry from Homer to Euripides." His poems showed a similar combination of Greek learning with a number of qualities cultivated by French poets of his time, among others, the use of daring metaphors controlled by irony. Greek and French: the combination reappears, if not so strikingly, in other poets of the group.

After the undergraduate years of the Tragic Generation,

there was always an undercurrent of interest at Harvard in French Symbolist poetry. The interest was kept alive partly through efforts of an instructor long remembered by his students and his friends at the Signet Society, though almost lost to academic history; his name was Pierre de Chaignon La Rose. T. S. Eliot, also a Signet member, must have known him when Eliot was an undergraduate in the class of 1910, but at any rate he knew others familiar with the Symbolist poets. Eliot carried on the tradition of the 1890s, and by his junior year he was contributing poems to *The Harvard Advocate* that were written in an undeniably Laforguean manner. The story continues with Eliot's early years in London, when he was unhappily teaching school and, in his leisure time, writing the poems that followed his "Prufrock" period. In 1914 he met Ezra Pound, who introduced him to many French poets he had not read, or had not read attentively, but in one case the introduction was reversed: it was Eliot who taught Pound to admire Laforgue.

Pound's new admiration was expressed at some length in an article he wrote for the February 1918 issue of *The Little Review*; he used most of the issue to present a number of French Symbolists, including Laforgue, with sweeping comments and with samples of their work in the original. In those days Pound was a marvelous impresario, even if he did not always grasp the best elements of the poets he was presenting to a new audience. With Laforgue, for example, if Pound came to a passage he did not understand—either in the poems or in the *Moralités Légendaires*, some of which he translated in another article—he simply omitted the difficult sentence or stanza or paragraph. But he had an assured manner that overwhelmed his readers, so that everything he wrote about French poetry—and especially the *Little Review* article in 1918—had a lasting influence on younger American poets.

Such poets were then appearing in somewhat larger numbers than before the Great War. Many of them had become familiar with Laforgue, in some cases through the Harvard tradition, in some cases through Pound's article, and there were other sources as well. I suspect that several of the young poets owned (as did I) a two-volume collection by Van Bever and Léautaud, *Poètes d'Aujourd'hui*, from which they could have learned rather more than they were eager to know about the French and Belgian Symbolists. For a long time I couldn't remember who precisely had introduced me to Laforgue. Then—as related in an earlier chapter—I asked Foster Damon and he answered the question. "Yes," he told me, "I remember showing you the poems of Jules Laforgue. We went over them together." Foster also passed along his discoveries in French poetry to Cummings and I think to John Brooks Wheelwright. Kenneth Burke, to mention another name, had been making his own explorations of modern French poetry at the New York Public Library. After dropping out of Columbia in the winter of 1917, he had taken to writing Laforguean complaints and moonstruck rhapsodies in free verse. Others who read Laforgue with professional interest in the years around 1920 were Hart Crane, Allen Tate, Louise Bogan, Rolfe Humphries, and Yvor Winters (but not Léonie Adams, who read him later). Perhaps I was more enthusiastic than the others. That explains, at any rate, why those three yellow-backed volumes of Laforgue (with not all the pages cut in the third volume)[1] stood gathering dust on my mantelpiece among the litter of unemptied ashtrays.

2 ᵏ But what was it that we saw in Laforgue and that some of us tried to reproduce in our own work? I have to admit that most of us read French poems with the help of a dictionary (which we were sometimes too lazy to use), that we were not at the time well versed in the rules of French prosody, and that we often misunderstood what we were reading. Not long ago I was shown a document that revealed what might be called our typical

---

1. There was to be a fourth volume, *Mélanges Posthumes*, not published until 1923, when my enthusiasm was waning. I have it still, but with few of the pages cut.

ignorance. It was the volume of Laforgue that Hart Crane had owned, with two stanzas of the *Complainte des Nostalgies Préhistoriques* annotated in Hart's handwriting. Here are the stanzas and the annotations:

          darkens
*La nuit bruine sur les villes.*
*Mal repu des gains machinals,*         mechanical gains
*On dîne; et, gonflé d'idéal,*         swelled with ideals
*Chacun sirote son idylle,*       each one sighs his idyll
    *Ou furtive, ou facile.*

*Echos des grands soirs primitifs!*
*Couchants aux flambantes usines,*      factories

       earth    childbirth
*Rude paix des sols en gésine,*
*Cri jailli là-bas d'un massif,*
    *Voluptés à vif!*

The least one can say after reading the notations is that Hart's French vocabulary was not extensive. I wonder if he guessed at the combination of two words in *voluptés?* Possibly he did, for he enjoyed making the same sort of combinations in English. But his translations of the first three *Locutions des Pierrots* were so far from the original that he had to apologize in a footnote. "A strictly literal translation of Laforgue," he said, "is meaningless. The native implications of his idiosyncratic style have to be recast in English garments." My own knowledge of French at the time was a little greater than Hart's; after all I had spent those six months with the French Army and had even acquired a wartime godmother, a *marraine*. Still, there were broad gaps in my learning, as in that of every other young American poet. What puzzles me is how it came about that Laforgue had a deep influence on many of us, considering that we had to approach him through a screen of ignorance.

It was probably because there were a few of his characteristics that penetrated the screen. First of all, we were impressed by his subject matter. Most of our reading had been among country poets, and Laforgue seemed new to us partly because he was urban. Moreover, we were young and yearning, and we found it exciting to read a poet who regarded adolescence as a time of life that deserved as much serious attention as any other time. He perfectly expressed our feelings about women (excepting mothers and aunts) when he singularized and rarefied the petticoated multitude into the Eternal Feminine:

> *Vous n'êtes que de naïfs mâles,*
> *Je suis l'Eternel Féminin!*

She, that is, womankind, was at the same time our hope and yearning, our necessity, and the ogress who would lock us in her dungeon. Weak and irresistible, compassionate, pitiless, and perhaps essentially stupid, She would snatch us from our lonely divagations under the moon and make us the daytime prisoners of convention. All this we found in Laforgue, and we also found confirmation of our instinctive notion about the best means of defending ourselves. The best means was a style, a literary attitude applied to life; it was irony, paradox, and a parade of learning. If we laughed at ourselves and Her in the same breath, we should be safe even against tears, even against the heartbroken "Ah! you don't love me!" We could always dream of answering coldly with Lord Pierrot, "The sum of the angles of a triangle, dear heart, is equal to two right angles."

Besides a subject and a strategy that seemed close to us in that forgotten, that almost incredible time, we also found a language in Laforgue. I don't mean that we mastered French, but rather that we sensed another language in his poems for which French was chiefly a mode and a mask. The other language was a new, at the time, amalgam of learned words from philosophy, medicine, and the natural sciences with familiar expressions, street slang, and newspaper phrases beautifully misapplied. Ezra Pound spoke of Laforgue as being the poet who had most highly developed the art of what he called "logopoeia," that is, a playing about with the ordinary meanings of words, and certainly, in those days, a little band of young American poets would have liked to become logopoeists.

Then comes one other characteristic of Laforgue that was striking enough to be perceived through the screen of ignorance. It was the free but singing rhythm of his verse, especially in the *Complaintes*. This might seem a curious thing to say, considering that there have always been learned arguments about the rhythm of French verse and considering that French prosody is based on a syllabic count of the lines and not on accents recurring at more or less regular intervals. But the *Complaintes* are built around popular songs, of which the pounding rhythm is suggested by Laforgue's refrains. A transatlantic reader could sense the rhythm, whether or not he was familiar with the song—

> —*Pré*aux des *soirs,*
> *Christs* des dor*toirs!*
>
> *Tu* t'en *vas* et *tu* nous *laiss*es,
> *Tu* nous *laiss's* et *tu* t'en *vas,*

—Hearing the words that echo through my mind after so many years, I realize that I was misplacing the accents in the next two lines of Laforgue's "Complaint of the Pianos That One Hears in Residential Streets." But if I had then known the children's burlesque dirge around which he was writing variations, I might have found an excuse for my reading the lines, not as French octosyllables, but as English tetrameters:

> Dé*faire et refaire* ses *tresses,*
> Broder d'éternels *canevas.*

The chant that we heard, or fancied we heard, in lines like these was something we tried to reproduce in our own verses, where we also used, on occasion, the Laforguean device of a couplet, usually in a different meter, that summarizes or comments upon the preceding stanza:

> —*Coeurs en prison,*
> *Lentes saisons!*

—an effect brilliantly reproduced in J. Alfred Prufrock's

*I grow old . . . I grow old . . .*
*I shall wear the bottoms of my trousers rolled.*

Merely as confirmation of these statements, the deponent wishes to place in evidence some of the poems he wrote in the 1920s that reveal the influence of Laforgue or attempt to reproduce some of his qualities in English. Exhibit A might be the first stanza of a poem printed in *The Little Review,* called "After Jules Laforgue." It comes pretty far after him, but the poet might have offered Hart Crane's excuse, that the "native implications of his idiosyncratic style have to be recast in English garments":

> *Sundays in my bedroom staring*
> *Through the broken window pane*
> *I watch the slanting lines of rain*
> *And since I have an empty purse*
> *Turn to philosophy again—*
> > *The world is a potato paring,*
> > *Refuse of the universe,*
> > *And man excrescent,*
> > *Adolescent.*

Although the English garments might be better cut, still we have the short couplet rhyming on Latinate words and offered as comment upon the preceding stanza, we have the philosophy that is less cosmic than it sounds, and we have the word "adolescent," a key to much that we found in Laforgue. Exhibit B is part of a poem called "Nocturne," first printed in the *Hound & Horn.* Obviously to us, though not to the young author who wrote it, the poem was inspired by Laforgue's "Complaint of the Pianos":

> *Mother has washed the dishes, limped upstairs;*
> *Mother has disappeared into the light;*
> *porches are filled where wicker rocking chairs*
> *creak . . . through the emptiness of night*
> *. . . creak . . . scrape, as if they would repeat*

*the litany of the daughters of the street:*
> "Hamburg steak for dinner, runs in our hose,
> nobody speaks of them, everybody knows;
> meeting me at twilight he handed me a rose:
> will he come?"

"Nocturne" is close to the form and spirit of its French model, especially when Laforgue's young man appears at the end of the poem (though not in his disguise of Pierrot) and explains himself to the quasi-eternal young woman:

> *"Your folk are stronger than mine,*
> *being less bold;*
> *your arms are stronger than mine,*
> *willing to hold;*
> *your faith is stronger than mine,*
> *founded on lies;*
> *my faith is no longer mine,*
> *but melts away in your eyes,*
> *in the syrup of your eyes.*
> *I can never belong to you."*

> *And she: "It is not true."*
> *My words have tapped like pebbles*
> *in the dry well of her mind.*
> *She only smiles and echoes,*
> *"It is not true. You are unkind."*
> *Or else she answers nothing of the kind.*

Exhibit C is submitted to show how Laforgue's practice encouraged us to experiment with a Latinate vocabulary. The poem here quoted in part was called, quite briefly, "Time":

> *Twilight. And still the clock*
> *ticks viciously at every second;*
> *the minutes stalk*
> *slowly across the field of consciousness;*
> *an hour is a time unreckoned;*
> *precise and categorical*
> *the seconds hammer on the wall.*

*At their touch the flesh disintegrates:*
*the mind is a cerebrum, a cerebellum,*
*in tangles like a ball of cotton waste,*
*like bundles of soiled linen or bales of shoddy.*
*The seconds drip from a great height,*
*exploding one by one against the nerves,*
*against the broken carapace of body;*
*each second is eroding like the rain*
*its bit of flesh or deliquescent brain.*

The final piece of evidence, exhibit D, is one that I present with some embarrassment. It is the first and last stanzas of a poem that I felt was too juvenile for publication when I wrote it at twenty-one, in that room on Bedford Street where the dust-covered volumes of Laforgue looked down at me from the mantelpiece. Perhaps I dusted them off before writing the poem. Once again it sounds the note of adolescent yearning, and it also depends on one of Laforgue's favorite devices, that of using out-of-context refrains from popular songs (in his case the songs were *complaintes,* that is, laments corresponding in mood, though not in music, to Negro blues). Even the title of the poem is Laforguean: "Variations on a Cosmical Air."

*Love is the flower of a day,*
*Love is a rosebud—anyway,*
*When we dissect its every feature*
*We find it something of that nature,*
*And even in our puberty*
*We drown love in philosophy.*

But I'm coming around in a taxi, honey,
Tomorrow night with a roll of money;
You wanta be ready about ha-past eight.

.   .   .

*Before I start let planets break*
*And suns turn black before I wake*
*Alone tomorrow in this room;*
*I want a cosmic sort of broom*

> To reach the Bear and Sirius even,
> Annihilate our ancient heaven,
> Or rearrange in other pairs
> Those interstellar love affairs,
> Finding a mate for everyone
> And me, and me, before I'm done.

> Ashes to ashes and dust to dust,
> Stars for love and love for money:
> If the whiskey don't get you the cocaine must,
> And I'm coming around in a taxi, honey.

3 ⚑ Having submitted these exhibits, I attest and depose that they constitute, with the preceding statements, a true record of one poet and his early debt to Laforgue. It is possible that the debt may have been somewhat smaller than the exhibits would seem to indicate. In talking about literary sources, we always run the danger of assuming that because something is *post hoc*—in this case, post Laforgue—it is also *propter hoc*. Some of the resemblances are due to the air of the times, in 1919–20, and the common perplexities of adolescence. But there *was* an influence, and a great one, and I suspect that several other poets who started writing at about the same time might be willing to offer depositions of much the same nature. Of course the great example of a Laforguean poem in English is "The Love Song of J. Alfred Prufrock," which combines such characteristics as the urban background, the timidly yearning hero (in this case older than Laforgue's beardless Pierrots), the self-protective irony, the bold figures of speech, the mixture of colloquial and academic language, the rhythms that might be those of popular songs, and the rhyming couplets serving as refrains. Besides presenting all those Laforguean elements, "Prufrock" ends with perhaps the most effective use in English or French of a device to which Kenneth Burke gave the name "tangent ending." Laforgue was fond of

the device and apparently discovered it for himself, even if he was not the first to adopt it. Essentially it consists in rounding out a story or a situation, then moving away from it at a tangent, as if, after making a tour of the house, one had found a door that opened on a new landscape. Such a door is what Alfred Prufrock finds after making his tea-time visit and deciding that he will never have courage to confess his yearnings. The episode and the poem seem to be ending together, when suddenly Prufrock dreams of walking on the beach and listening to the mermaids' songs:

> *I have seen them riding seaward on the waves*
> *Combing the white hair of the waves blown back*
> *When the wind blows the water white and black.*

> *We have lingered in the chambers of the sea*
> *By sea-girls wreathed with seaweed red and brown*
> *Till human voices wake us, and we drown.*

That is, for me, one of the great moments in twentieth-century English poetry, and I do not think it is equaled by any moment in *The Waste Land,* which has dozens of tangents running off in all directions from a circle that is never clearly drawn. Even before *The Waste Land,* but after the period of his Laforguean poems, Eliot had entered a different stage in which, cheered on by Pound, he was trying to reproduce the qualities of other French poets, and notably of Tristan Corbière. Almost all that remains of Laforgue in this so-called "Sweeney" period of Eliot's is the popular songs in "Fragment of an Agon" and the poly-syllabic language of "The Hippopotamus."

Pound himself was never deeply influenced by Laforgue, and what he got out of him was hardly the best that the poet had to offer. He seems to have been impressed chiefly by the dexterity in playing with words and by the tone of sophisticated detachment, so that Pound's Laforgue is a *boulevardier* rather than a sensitive adolescent. What Pound then enjoyed was savage wit, and he found more of it in Corbière, as in Laurent Tailhade, whom he regarded as one of the great. The younger poets who had been influenced by Laforgue also looked for other masters before they were ready to stand alone. He is not particularly admired by the present generation. It remains true, however, that his work helped to change the course of American poetry and that its influence here was based on an instinctive sympathy amounting almost, at the time, to an identity of spirit. That explains why Laforgue was a liberating force, in style and form and subject matter. I attest and depose that he encouraged a number of American poets to speak with greater freedom, in voices that later proved to be their own.

# VI FIGURE
# IN A CROWD

1 ⚚ When we packed our wicker trunk to come home from Europe, it was Bob Coates, as I said, who moved into the rooms over the blacksmith shop where we had lived in Giverny. Robert M. (for Myron) Coates: he was a writer of talent whose reputation has lagged well behind his merits, and I have always wondered why. I had first met him in Paris, 1922, and later I was his friend, sometimes his neighbor, for more than fifty years. But did I really know him? Open to friendship as he seemed to be, always ready to explain himself, there was in him something inaccessible. It was as if, in his travels through the world, he carried with him a portable, unwindowed room into which he sometimes retired, and locked the door.

Oh, I know the exterior facts about him. Born April 6, 1897, in New Haven, Connecticut. Only child of Frederick and Harriet Davidson Coates. The father, descended from a line of

Yankee mechanics, was a tool designer who wandered from New England to the Pacific Northwest and back again, usually as head of his own small enterprise; once he leased a gold mine near Cripple Creek. The boy grew up in more cities than laid claim to Homer; some of them were Springfield (Massachusetts), Portland (Oregon), Seattle, Denver, Cincinnati, Buffalo, and New York. As a rule he was the lonely new boy in each school he attended, with the result that he was thrown back on his own resources; he read and dreamed. But the family perched longer than usual in Rochester, New York, and there he finished high school after making friends.

Yale, class of '19. Served for some months as a cadet in Naval Aviation, but the war ended in time for him to go back to college and graduate with his class. Did publicity work in New York and dropped it to write poetry while living chiefly on lentils. Went to France in 1921 (his father helped) and stayed there for five years. After 1923 he lived mostly in that Norman village fifty miles from Paris, but he also became a familiar figure in Montparnasse, almost a perambulatory landmark. Very tall, square-shouldered, close to being gaunt in those days when money for meals was a problem, he had a big head (7¾) and a solemn oblong face surmounted by a jungle of crinkly red hair through which he couldn't push a comb. His eyes were sky-blue, his cheeks were pink, and, as he slowly bicycled through the Paris streets, people stared at him from sidewalk tables. "He looked like a flag," Janet Flanner said.

He came back to New York in 1926 with two novels, the first of which remained in manuscript. The second was *The Eater of Darkness*, already published in Paris, but in a very limited edition; it combined a scrupulous accuracy of detail with a headlong impossibility of plot. Republished here in 1929, it has enjoyed an underground reputation as the first, and for some time the only, Dadaist novel in English. Before it appeared, Coates had joined the staff of a very young magazine, *The New Yorker*. There he collaborated on "Talk of the Town," then wrote a weekly book page, then finally—for thirty years—served as art critic. He did his journalistic work in the city, but during most of those years he also had a country house—two houses in succession, both among fields and woods—where he wrote his novels and stories. His avocations were chess, gardening, skiing, and wandering alone in the Manhattan streets.

He published a dozen books, most of them fiction, all of them truly *written*, with an appearance of ease that is among the hardest qualities to master; the question is why he never became so famous as some of his friends and coevals. Twice he stood on the front doorstep of fame while we waited to see the door open and hear the band strike up. The first time was in 1930, when he published *The Outlaw Years*, about the land pirates of the Natchez Trace, a history that has been many times reissued. It was chosen by the Literary Guild, but the royalties went into the first of his country houses (that one in Sherman, Connecticut, on a back road to which I moved a few years later). Coates finished the house with his own hands. He says of it in *Yesterday's Burdens*, "I test the floor I laid to see that it does not creak; I inspect the joinings of the door-casings I put in place, the smooth surface of the table I built. These are joys stolen from past centuries. Who nowadays can point to a tree he planted or hang his immortality on a nail of his own driving?" But houses change hands, as this one did later, and Coates's friends concluded that building it had cost him the writing of at least two books for which a public was waiting. His other approach to fame was in 1948, when *Wisteria Cottage*, a novel about a homicidal maniac, almost became a best seller and was almost bought by the movies. But he waited seven years to publish his next novel, *The Farther Shore*, which almost failed to have an audience. It proved to be the last of Coates's longer fictions. He continued, though, to write short stories that should be reread and reissued; perhaps their time will come.

During the last three years of his life he was trying to finish one story—only one—to round out a book that he hoped would be his best collection. But he was wasting away with cancer, and he died February 8, 1973, with the story and the book unfinished.

Those are the facts of his career, and they don't tell us

much about the inner man. After fifty years of companionship, and affection too, I still feel that he eludes me. Why, for example, did he reject the notion of trying to become a famous writer? He must have played with the notion more than once, and he must have felt that fame would be gratifying if it came as the un-planned-for result of something he had worked on for years, but he didn't promote his work or trumpet himself. He was more admired by fellow writers and by magazine editors, who printed almost everything he offered them, than he was read by the public at large. He never taught, never went on lecture tours, and never addressed a public meeting, although, in the contentious 1930s, he attended some of these. If he spoke from the floor, it was only to offer a suggestion in a low, stammering voice, as if to apologize for his conspicuous appearance. Why did he prefer to stay in the background? I am sure it was not because of uncertainty about the rightness of his opinions or the value of his work. Perhaps he felt that too much fame would involve him in temptations like those to which some of his early friends had yielded.

A letter of August 8, 1966, was one of the very few in which he allowed himself to complain. There he said in part:

> Hemingway—well, he is one of the problems that have al-ways defeated me—like Jim Thurber; the man who gets worse, both as an artist and as a person, when he should be getting better. Jim when I first knew him, and he was then my closest friend (and, as on the New Yorker, my helper and benefactor) was, without listing attributes, just about the all-round nicest guy I've ever known. And then—what was it: blindness? drinking? something physical?—he got to the stage where Joe Sayre, in a piece for TIME could say, quot-ing someone maybe invented, "he's the nicest guy in the world—till around nine o'clock in the evening."
>
> And then, finally, well, outrage. And why?
>
> With Ernest it seems to me it was a similar sort of thing, although, being a greater man and uncluttered with side issues, the thing seems simpler. As you know, he and I were fairly close friends back in the Paris days. I was one of those

who "boxed with Hemingway." But we also walked about a good deal, visited back and forth (in Paris) and so on. But there was always something a little wary about him. As I see it now, and I believe I'm right, Ernest was one of those not-so-terribly-rare people who can't stand feeling obligated to anyone. If you did him a favor, you were dead, and it was on that note—when he turned so atrociously on Gertrude Stein (who had done so much for him) and on poor old Ford (same help and even worse treatment) that our friendship (as if that mattered) ended. He had also, with the first two novels, met success and had gotten out of the Quarter.

For some reason Coates did not save the letters he received from famous friends. He preferred not to trade on other people's names, and he may have felt—though here I have to guess—that the mere thought of preserving a correspondence for future readers would deprive it of frankness and spontaneity. Once a scholar asked to see his letters from Gertrude Stein. "Sorry, but I didn't keep them," Coates answered. "That's funny," the scholar said. "Miss Stein kept *your* letters." It was a merited rebuke, but a mild one, since the scholar realized that Coates had acted in accordance with his own strict notion of literary and personal ethics. Having resisted success, he continued to be the all-round nicest guy in the world, even after nine o'clock in the evening. He was deferent, unassuming, fond of playing immense but innocent jokes, and punctilious about returning favors. At other times, not often, he had lapses in kindness that troubled his friends; they were due, I think, to a compulsive need for going his own way. People often spoke of his sunny disposition, but his face in repose had a melancholy look and there must have been the streak of morbidity that was revealed in some of his best fiction, for instance, in *Wisteria Cottage* and in that often-anthologized tale, "The Fury."

I am still puzzled by these and other contradictions in his character and in his writing. *Item,* to start a list of these, he was both solitary and gregarious. He loved boisterous parties and raffish companions, but I suspect that he was happiest when alone. *Item,* he was romantic by disposition, almost nympholeptic, dreaming for years of an impossibly beautiful woman in gray for whom he would eagerly sacrifice his future; but he was also a realist who worked, paid his debts, and had a hard observing eye for objects. *Item,* he was a city man who fled to the country, where he lived in tune with the earth and in time with the seasons, as one learns from the lovely first section of *Yesterday's Burdens;* but from time to time he fled back to the city and roamed the streets from Harlem to the Battery. And a final item chosen among others: in spite of his boyhood travels over the United States and all those apprentice years in Paris, he remained in some ways a Connecticut Yankee like his father. I think of him as a craftsman, an inspired mechanic working with words as his father had worked with bits of metal, choosing and calibrating, fitting together, then grinding and polishing in the hope of achieving some ultimate invention.

In his writing it is hard to distinguish the influence of any single author (unless it might be James Thurber in some matters of style). He acknowledged a debt to Gertrude Stein, but I cannot find in his work a single phrase that he owed to her; perhaps what he had in mind was her freedom of judgment. He owed another debt to the Dadaists, among them Louis Aragon and his *Paysan de Paris:* in Aragon's fashion he tried to be a wandering peasant in Manhattan. Some of his writing resembles the early fiction of Kenneth Burke, but I think he arrived independently at the same sort of devices. His impulse was to invent, to do surprising things, to be accuratistic and conversational while abandoning the pretense that he was writing anything but fiction; then to give everything a consistent finish as if he were polishing steel. Each work he produced was die-stamped with his own trademark.

$2$ゑ Among Coates's twelve books, *Yesterday's Burdens*—reissued in 1975 by the Southern Illinois University Press—has always been my favorite. It contains more of himself than the others: more of his contradictions, more of his inventiveness, more of his nympholepsy, more of his double feeling for city streets and the deep country. It is also a completed act rather than a mere novel. In the end it impresses me as a sort of leavetaking, almost a symbolic suicide.

There is a passage beginning on page forty-one in which the author sets forth his program. "But let me tell you about this book I'm trying to write," he says, "in between bouts of book-reviewing":

> It's a novel, or rather a novel about a novel, or perhaps one might better describe it as a long essay discussing a novel that I might possibly write, with fragments of the narrative inserted here and there, by way of illustration or example.
>
> Or—again one might say—the attempt is to make it as nearly as possible a true example of the roman vécu. Nothing in it that I myself have not seen, heard, felt—or seen or felt in some other so vividly as almost to make the experience my own.
>
> The plot, of course, is the difficulty. You know my idea about plots—pick a good lively one and then forget about it. In this case, though, I don't think that formula would work. I have this young man, Henderson, and the process would seem to be to take him to the city and there lose him, as thoroughly as possible. Or at least to reverse the usual method, and instead of trying to individualize him and pin him down to a story, to generalize more and more about him —to let him become like the figures in a crowd, and the crowd dispersing.
>
> But isn't that, after all, the authentic thing—the thing that happens to all of us nowadays, and to all our friends?

"This book I'm trying to write" is *Yesterday's Burdens*—of course, of course—and its author is like a conjurer laying his cards face up on the table. He has every right to be confident that there are enough tricks up his sleeve to keep the audience amazed. One trick among others is this: Henderson is so thoroughly lost in the city that his story can be given three possible endings. He will be (1) reconciled with his wife, who has come back from Paris unseduced and without a divorce—or (2) shot and killed by his lover's husband—or (3) left alone despondent—jobless, probably—and will jump to his death from a high window. Coates inclines toward the third ending, but without quite making up his mind. "I never saw him again," he repeats on the last page, as if throwing up his hands.

Meanwhile the conjurer is palming another card, or item of information. He does not tell the reader, but does allow him to guess, that "this young man, Henderson"—at least in one of his aspects—is the author himself. In another aspect, the social one, Henderson is vaguely connected with James Thurber (or so Coates told his second wife many years later). The book is dedicated to Thurber, but the connection between its hero and Coates himself is better documented in the story. Henderson is given Coates's birthday, April 6, his red hair, some of what we recognize from other books as his boyhood memories, and also, clearly, the group of his Village friends. He impresses us as being one side of Coates's past, and also what Coates might have become if he had chosen to hold a job in New York and make a big income instead of escaping to a country house without running water. That is why one thinks of the book as a symbolic or vicarious suicide. In making Henderson a scapegoat burdened with the author's sins (or what he had come to regard as sins)—in letting him vanish into the crowd (and the crowd dispersing)—Coates is abolishing part of himself while hoping, one strongly feels, to be reborn into a different future.

(One notes that death-and-rebirth was the underlying theme of many books published during the early Depression years. Two of these were written by Coates's friends: *Towards a Better*

*Life,* an extraordinary "novel in the form of declamations," by Kenneth Burke, 1932; and my own *Exile's Return,* 1934. Also to be mentioned is Waldo Frank's big turgid novel *The Death and Birth of David Markand,* 1934.)

Coates thought that *Yesterday's Burdens* was an ideal title for such a work, though his publisher didn't agree. His publisher was the Macaulay Company, a small house that specialized in mildly salacious novels and ghosted autobiographies. Lee Furman, the head of the house—we called him "Mr. Macaulay"—had been persuaded by Coates's friend Matthew Josephson to add a few avant-garde authors to his list. He thought they would lend it distinction, and also he had a wistful idea that he could sell their books if they were attractively priced and labeled. Mr. Macaulay believed in the magic of titles. "Let's have a big novel written to order," he told an editorial meeting, "and let's give it a tremendous title—you know, something that will make people think of *The Good Earth* and *All Quiet on the Western Front.* Any bright ideas?" Of course someone suggested "The Bad Earth." "Or," Isidor Schneider said—he was the poet who served as advertising manager—"what about 'All Noisy on the Eastern Behind'?"

Mr. Macaulay was distressed by Coates's title. "This year," he told the author—it was in 1933—"nobody wants to hear about yesterday's burdens or any other burdens. Can't you think of something upbeat and catchy?" Coates stammered a little, as always, but insisted on his downbeat title, and Mr. Macaulay accepted it, though with misgivings that he must have passed on to his salesmen. He was an amiable businessman on the edge of failure, and he hated arguments. Perhaps he was right about the mood of the time, or perhaps he made himself right by giving the book no advance promotion. It did receive some appreciative reviews, including one I wrote for *The New Republic,* but, on the whole, it attracted little notice in a year when critics were arguing about proletarian literature. Like *Miss Lonelyhearts,* by his friend Nathanael West, also published in 1933—and also dismissed as being "of the 1920s," a period then held in low esteem—it became an example of the good book that some people talked about, but almost nobody bought. It is my impression that most of the first and only printing was sold cheaply as overstock. Two years later the Macaulay Company went out of business— not because of *Yesterday's Burdens*—and the book was quietly interred. My tardily written review might have been the tribute spoken over a grave.

3 ✍ The review had indeed praised the book, but not nearly enough—or so it seems to me now—and chiefly for the feeling it conveyed of a given social caste in a given year. The caste was the new one to which Henderson belonged, composed of young people on the fringes of the arts who had flocked to Manhattan chiefly from Midwestern cities: Columbus, Minneapolis, Davenport. As contrasted with their English contemporaries, the Bright Young People of Evelyn Waugh's early novels, they had no social standing or family connections. They had prospered, though, by serving the business community. "As American business entered the boom era," I said in the review, "it needed more and more propagandists to help in the increasingly difficult task of selling more commodities each year to families that were given no higher wages to buy them with, and therefore had to be tempted with all the devices of art, literature, and science into bartering their future earnings for an automobile or a bedroom suite. Business needed public-relations counselors, it needed advertising artists and copywriters, it needed romancers to fill the pages of magazines in which its products were advertised, and illustrators to make the romance visible (and pyschologists to explain how the whole process could be intensified); it needed stylists, designers, editors"; and I went on to say that in the boom years it conferred high rewards on not a few of these. There was a time when those young people, as a caste, regarded New York as a grand yearlong party given strictly for themselves. But their mood, as I observed and partly shared it, was changing even before the Crash, and many of them had come to be painfully dissatisfied with their lives.

The Crash is not mentioned in Coates's novel, though perhaps it can be sensed there as an undertone. As for the "given year" depicted, it is obviously not 1932, the year before the novel was published, considering that the narrator goes rambling through Manhattan without seeing breadlines or boarded-up stores or demonstrations of the unemployed led by Communists and broken up by the police. Coates was to play a distantly sympathetic part in the political revolts of the 1930s, but there is not a hint of them in his novel. He was a slow writer who liked to mull over his impressions before setting them down. The time of his story could only be 1930, the strange year that followed the Crash and served as an epilogue to the Boom. Hardly anything had changed that year on the surface of Henderson's world. Jobs could still be found in New York (or at least held on to); there were as many parties as ever (though more often with glum or violent sequels in the early-morning hours); and meanwhile everything was imperceptibly going to pieces, including long-established marriages and friendships.

"Often it seems I have no friends" is one of the "topic sentences" that Coates repeats with variations as if they were musical themes. At one point he continues:

> —or rather, I have friends, but all of them have Watkins, Algonquin or Stuyvesant telephone numbers and live in the Village. Tonight, I will have none of them; I know so well what they are doing. I know so well those green-tinted apartments, the furniture that has so much the air of being fresh from the furniture stores, the standing lamps arranged to illuminate the pages of the books no one ever has time to read in the easy chairs.
>
> There will be greetings and ringings of the telephone; cocktails will be poured and drunk, cigarettes held in nervous fingers. Towards eight o'clock or later, women will be crowding before the mirror in the bathroom, men will be hunting out overcoats from the tangle of clothes on the bed in the alcove and shoving their arms into the sleeves; people will be going trailing laughter down the stairs. We shall all gather

on the sidewalk in a little noisy cluster, deep down among the silent unfriendly houses.

It is a pleasure to transcribe those lines that suggest a vanished way of life. Each word is in the right place—as always in Coates's prose—and each phrase is an incantation against the danger of remaining in Henderson's world. It was in 1930 that Coates took flight into the Connecticut countryside, into a farming community already invaded by others whom Henderson might have known. Few of the others made the same effort to put down new roots. Coates says of the invasion in another passage that conveys the feeling of the year, this time in country terms:

> On all sides one sees writers, painters, fashion designers buying acres of tillable land or pasture and dedicating them to the cultivation of sumac, goldenrod and blackberry brambles. Is it for revenge? The artist's tendencies, it would seem, are always atavistic; he would raze cities, he would remake New England into a wilderness. But what of the land itself?
>
> I sometimes feel a strange uneasiness: the trees look hostile, the very grass seems to regard me with a venomous air. I have bought these fields and doomed them to sterility. Can you tell me if there is anything in common law concerning the rights of the soil to expect careful husbandry on the part of its owner?

Those lines were written at an early stage of the invasion, before artists and fashion designers were followed by real-estate men. There were still working farms in Coates's neighborhood (which would soon be mine). Many fields had been recently abandoned, but they were still open to the sky. Later the horizon closed in, field by field, as sumac and goldenrod and broom sedge were shaded over by scruffy forest. The New England countryside has changed as definitely as New York City, and much of it—between the new housing developments—has indeed become a wilderness crisscrossed by stone fences. Not a few books of the 1970s deal with efforts to reclaim portions of that wilderness for grazing or tillage, and they are echoes, as it were, of Coates's feeling about the soil.

In that respect and others—notably in the cards-on-the-table attitude revealed toward the art of fiction—*Yesterday's Burdens* has a prophetic quality, and this is one reason for my admiring it more today than when it first appeared. Of course there is another reason too. I had praised the book long ago as a sort of contemporary history, as a subjective but accurate picture of a social order just on the point of being destroyed, or self-destroyed. Now it seems to me that a special moment of time has been so well depicted, in a novel so full of inventions and yet so solidly put together, that the moment ceases to be something merely recovered from the past. It lives for us again, both in itself and for what it portends; both in the way people acted at the time and in the feeling they had that their world was going to pieces while they yearned for a different life in a new age.

# VII THE 1930s
## Faith and Works

1 ✍ In literature as in other arts, the representative works of
the 1930s were strikingly different from those of the period that
followed. The sequence was not an orderly development, but
rather an abrupt reaction. If we skip over the war years as a time
when not much was happening in the world of letters because
too much was happening in the world outside, we might say that
later the 1950s went to one extreme largely—though of course not
entirely—because the 1930s had gone to another.

The phenomenon is not at all unique in literary annals.
Writers of any new age group try to avoid the mistakes and enthusiasms of the group that preceded them. As the groups follow
each other at intervals of ten or fifteen years, there seems to be
an alternation of expansive and contractive moods, of interests
turned outward to social problems and of those turned inward to
dilemmas of the author; it suggests an immensely slow heartbeat

rhythm of diastole and systole. The cycle may take thirty years or more to complete, something close to the span of a biological generation, with the result that periods separated by thirty years often bear some resemblance to each other. Thus, the 1950s were like the 1920s in being a contractive or systolic period devoted to the quest for personal fulfillment; "identity" was a watchword of the time, as "experience" had been a watchword of the 1920s. The 1930s, on the other hand, were like the early 1900s in being a diastolic period that admired breadth, observation, and social purpose.[1]

Indeed, such outward-turning qualities were only too much admired, to the frequent detriment of fiction. Books of the period were sometimes all surface, merely a system of values applied or appliquéd to a colorful situation. Many of the books were schematized, absurdly confident, lacking in irony—and that helps to explain why writers of the next age group reacted against them —but they did have a system of values, even if it was too simple to be true, and they had the further advantage, among others, of dealing with fresh material. The writers of the 1930s inspected the whole country, they re-examined the American past, they looked abroad in search of dramatic conflicts, and they found a new subject at home in the sorrows of the working class.

"Men of literary tastes," Frederick Law Olmsted wrote long ago in his *Journey in the Seaboard Slave States,* "are always apt to overlook the working-classes, and to confine the record they make of their times, in a great degree, to the habits and fortunes of their own associates, or to those people of superior rank to themselves, of whose sayings and doings their vanity, as well as their curiosity, leads them most carefully to inform themselves. The dumb masses have often been so lost in the shadow of egotism, that, in later days, it has been impossible to discern the very real influence their character has had on the fortune and fate

---

1. This paragraph had been quoted in the chapter on literary generations, "And Jesse Begat..." Here I let it stand in its original context—and without adding that the 1960s were to be another diastolic period recurring after thirty years.

of nations." Those dumb masses found a voice, or were lent a voice, in many novels and plays of the 1930s. I thought at the time that their appearance on such a broad scale in American literature was a permanent addition to its subject matter, a means of achieving more richness and variety, but I was rejoicing too soon. The new writers of the fifties went back "in a great measure," to use Olmsted's words, "to the habits and fortunes of their own associates" as the record they made of their times, and they also kept asking the question, "Who am I as a person?" It was a contraction of interests and a loss of social commitment that made their work—though better in many respects, more carefully written and more conscious of human limitations—seem narrower in scope and less dramatic than the best work of the years before World War II.

2 ∡ I think of the 1930s as an age that was announced by the Wall Street Crash of October 1929, but that really began several months or more than a year later, perhaps with the second quieter and more disheartening crash of the following spring, which has been neglected by historians. In literary circles the old era took a long time to die, as I suggested in my rereading of *Yesterday's Burdens*. Not many young writers of my acquaintance had money enough to gamble in the stock market, but most of them had their little checking accounts, often at the Bank of United States, which was obliging in the matter of minimum balances. When the bank with its many branches failed resoundingly in December 1930, they began to look around them and to find that others were vastly more unfortunate; or else their eyes were opened by simply losing a job. Their picture of capitalism changed rapidly, and by 1932 young writers had gone far beyond the rest of the nation in their feeling that everything had to be changed.

The age did not really end with the Russo-German Pact of 1939 or even with the fall of France in 1940. For most writers, as for the country at large, it continued till the attack on Pearl

Harbor in December 1941. We must also remember, in this matter of dates, that books take a long time to be conceived and to write and to be published. Not a few of the works that best represent the period did not appear until the early forties, as, for example, James Agee's *Let Us Now Praise Famous Men* (1941) and Nelson Algren's *Never Come Morning* (1942).

In literature the distinguishing mark of the age was its pervasive interest in social ideals. This continued to the end, but with different manifestations, so that the age might be divided into three shorter periods. During the first years of economic collapse, there were feelings of bewilderment, despair, and anger, but all these were mingled—especially among younger writers—with wild hopes for an order that would supervene after the defeat of American capitalism. Some of those hopes persisted into the middle years, from 1934 to 1938. For a time they even grew stronger, but gradually they were poisoned by doubts about Russia under Stalin, which were generally repressed by livelier fears of international fascism. Then, after the Russo-German Pact, there was a new mood of disillusionment and self-appraisal, a moral crisis. Although this helped to produce what was to become the literary climate of the 1950s, it was essentially of a different nature. Disillusionment with a particular set of social aims is far from being the same as indifference or what the social psychologists of the 1950s were to call privatism.

I have read often, and in the past have even repeated, that the 1930s were a period of literary naturalism. The judgment now seems to me shallow. A truly naturalistic writer thinks of his works as presenting a verifiable picture of society. As a scientist of sorts he does not preach, but merely records and holds up for inspection. It is true that the American novelists of the 1930s often wrote in a naturalistic or "documentary" manner—hence the confusion—but many of them had a different purpose in mind. Instead of making scientific reports, they were offering parables of virtue oppressed by wickedness while waiting for its day of vindication.

Some of their novels have biblical titles: *The Land of*

*Plenty, The Judas Time, Judgment Day, Christ in Concrete.*
Often the story they tell is like that of the Gospels, with another
Jesus taking up his cross and dying for mankind. John the
Baptist, Mary, Mary Magdalene, Judas (most frequently), Paul,
and other New Testament figures reappear in more or less pene-
trable disguises. Once again Peter draws his sword on the Mount
of Olives and Pilate washes his hands. It is hard to say in specific
instances whether such biblical effects were calculated by the
author. At times they must have risen spontaneously from those
depths of the mind in which the Passion survives for most of us,
religious or irreligious, Jew or gentile, as the archetypical story.
But when the Christ figure is surrounded by exactly twelve companions—as in *The Grapes of Wrath,* where Preacher Jim Casy
(J.C.) is surrounded by exactly twelve Joads when he makes
his trip to California, and in *For Whom the Bell Tolls,* where
Robert Jordan has twelve Spanish guerrillas with him when he
rides out to die at the bridge—then it seems likely that the author
has counted disciples on his fingers, and two besides.

The 1930s were an age of faith, although the essence
of the faith is hard to define. In spite of the biblical echoes, it
was not Christian except in the case of a few writers, Thornton
Wilder, for instance, and James Agee and, with many reservations,
Faulkner. It was not the religion of art that flourished in the
1920s, and definitely not the psychoanalytic faith of many writers
in the 1950s. The saints revered at the time were not Sigmund of
Vienna or Carl of Bollingen, but rather the older Karl of the
British Museum, with Vladimir Ilyich of the Finland Station and,
for some, St. Leon Trotsky the Exile. Stalin was not a saint even
for his loyal admirers, who included very few American writers;
he was a pope or antipope throned in the midst of his Politburo,
or college of cardinals.

One might say that the age was Marxian in a broad sense,
but here again there are qualifications to be made. Even the
devout left-wing writers of the time were not much interested in
Marx as a philosopher, or Marx as an economist, or Marx in his
favorite role as a scientist of revolution. Instead they revered him

as a prophet calling for a day of judgment and a new heaven on earth. Sometimes they mentioned dialectical materialism, but without trying to understand the Marxian or Hegelian trinity of thesis, antithesis, and synthesis. They were not trinitarians, but dualists and Manichaeans. They bisected and bifurcated, they dichotomized, they either-ored: either light or darkness, but nothing between; either socialism or fascism, our side or their side, Russia or Germany, the glorious future or a reversion to the Middle Ages.

Their faith was apocalyptic and millennial. That is, they looked forward to something like the destruction by fire of the old Babylonian order and the establishment of a universal commonwealth that would correspond in secular terms—one cannot help thinking—to the Holy City announced in the Book of Revelations: "that great city, the holy Jerusalem, descending out of heaven from God, having the glory of God: and her light was like unto a stone most precious, even like a jasper stone, clear as crystal." The vision had been most crystalline in the years when the old order seemed to be falling to pieces. After the middle of the decade, it was to exist side by side with the apocalyptic fear that the world would be ruled by Antichrist—perhaps for a thousand years, as Hitler had promised that his empire would endure.

But this chiliastic dream and this nightmare of the future were only two manifestations of the faith I am trying to describe. Perhaps more fundamental was a longing for communion with others in some great endeavor. The writers of the time were trying to escape from a feeling of isolation and ineffectuality. They wanted to merge themselves in some great aggregation of suffering men and women, "the workers," "the dispossessed," not to lead or even advise them (though there were exceptions here in the shape of bad writers who became worse politicians), but simply to link arms with them and march forward together into a new life. "No matter how a man alone ain't got no bloody fucking chance," says Hemingway's working-class hero, Harry Morgan, near the end of *To Have and Have Not* (1937). It was a curious moral to draw from that blustering, blood-spattered, rum-drenched tale, but still it was to be repeated with variations by other novelists. Already a more grammatical motto of the same type had become a central precept of the 1930s: "Not I but we; not mine or theirs but *ours*."

The age had other precepts that were each embodied in a mass of fiction. One was the old revolutionary slogan of liberty, equality, fraternity, but with a fourth term added: dignity. What the age meant by it is best expressed in André Malraux's *Man's Fate*, a novel that was closely read by American writers. Dignity is the favorite word of Kyo, its Communist hero. Taken prisoner by the Kuomintang, he is condemned to be burned alive in the firebox of an old locomotive, but first he is given a chance to survive if he will take service as a spy. Kyo's sense of dignity keeps him from even being tempted by the offer.

"What do you mean by dignity?" the chief of police asks him. "It doesn't mean anything."

Kyo thinks to himself, "My life," but aloud he answers, "The opposite of humiliation."

His remark echoes in dozens of books published during the 1930s, as does the feeling on which it is based. Dignity is what Steinbeck finds among the Okies, Faulkner among the Mississippi Negroes, Hemingway among the Spanish guerrillas, and Agee among the white Alabama sharecroppers, where he also finds a deep fear of being humiliated. He watches the "fear from behind the glittering of laughter" in the eyes of old Fred Ricketts and interprets it as saying, "o lord god please for once, just for once, don't let this man laugh at me up his sleeve, or do me any meanness or harm"—or in brief, "Preserve my dignity as a man."


3 ⟨ An age of faith is almost certain to become an age of quarrels among the faithful. They divide into bitterly hostile sects, each with its own leader and each hoping for support from one group or another among the infidels. Especially toward the end, such quarrels disfigured the pattern of the 1930s—or should one say that the quarrels were an essential part of it? Different

conclusions were being drawn from not very different premises. Looking back from another age, one is surprised to find how much the writers in different factions, as well as those standing apart from any faction, radical or conservative, were affected by the same fears and aspirations for human society. "There is a great destiny," Emerson says in his journal for 1841, "which comes in with this as with every age, which is colossal in its traits, terrible in its strength, which cannot be tamed, or criticized, or subdued. It is shared by every man and woman of the time, for it is by it they live."

The spirit of the 1930s exerted that same terrible strength, at least in the literary world. Different age groups among them were affected in different fashions—for example, it was mostly those of the youngest group who tried to write proletarian novels and poems—but those of the middle group also responded to the new spirit. I keep reading about authors who "did not share the social interests of the time"—here Faulkner is always mentioned —or who "belonged to the twenties and never adapted themselves to the new era," as notably Fitzgerald and Thomas Wolfe. But hasn't it been noted that there is a change between the patronizing attitude toward Negroes expressed in Faulkner's early work and the respect and sympathy for them, mingled with a feeling of social guilt, that one finds in *Go Down, Moses*, published in 1942? The spirit of the age was speaking through Faulkner, as it also spoke through Fitzgerald, though in a different fashion. Has it been forgotten that *Tender Is the Night*, though the book changed in the writing, was replanned in 1932 as almost a tract against the upper bourgeoisie? "The novel should do this," Fitzgerald said in a misspelled memorandum to himself. "Show a man who is a natural idealist, a spoiled priest, giving in for various causes to the ideas of the haute Burgeoise, and in his rise to the top of the social world losing his idealism, his talent and turning to drink and dissipation. Background one in which the liesure class is at their truly most brilliant & glamorous such as Murphys." As for *The Last Tycoon*, unfinished when Fitzgerald died, it is concerned with the defeat of a genius by social forces, including finance capital and union labor. The novel he planned would have been almost as much "of the thirties" as *Gatsby* is of the twenties.

Thomas Wolfe's connection to the spirit of the age is a somewhat more complicated question. As late as 1933, when he published *Of Time and the River,* he was writing in the mood of the preceding decade. But *You Can't Go Home Again,* the book on which he was working before his death in 1938, contains one section—"The Party at Mrs. Jack's"—that is a short antibourgeois novel in itself, and another that is the compulsory, at the time, anti-Fascist pamphlet (a good one, too, called "I Have a Thing to Tell You"), while the book ends with his apocalyptic dream of a new America.

> I believe that we are lost here in America [he says], but I believe we shall be found. And this belief . . . is for me—and I think for all of us—not only our own hope, but America's everlasting dream. I think the life which we have fashioned in America, and which has fashioned us—the forms we made, the cells that grew, the honeycomb that was created—was self-destructive in its nature, and must be destroyed. I think these forms are dying, and must die, just as I know America and the people in it are deathless, undiscovered, and immortal, and must live.
>
> I think the true discovery of America is before us. I think the true fulfillment of our spirit, of our people, of our mighty and immortal land, is yet to come. . . . And I think that all these things are as certain as the morning, as inevitable as noon.

That same apocalyptic dream, in one or another of its aspects, affected almost everyone in the literary world except the professional entertainers. Some of these were affected too. For example, not a few of the historical romancers who flourished in those years revealed a social purpose in their writing: at a time of crisis they were turning to the past, not simply because it was picturesque, but also to find American heroes whose example would hearten the nation to confront the future. Even the novelists who studied the American upper-middle classes in a more or less conservative temper—more in the case of Cozzens and Marquand, rather less, at the time, in that of John O'Hara—felt that they should and must take account of economic forces and the laws that govern the rise and fall of social groups.

Of course there was Ezra Pound, apparently moving against the current of the times; and yet, when he supported Italian fascism, it was largely because he dreamed of saving the world by abolishing usury. The Nashville Agrarians—Ransom, Tate, Warren, and others—had no sympathy for Pound's notions, although they were as deeply opposed to socialism. Their dream for America was to preserve and extend the old Southern values of the yeoman farmer. Almost the only writers of standing who completely resisted the social impulse of the 1930s were a few professional cynics such as H. L. Mencken and a few gifted poets. Among the latter, Robert Frost proclaimed his Yankee independence. Robinson Jeffers and, in a different fashion, E. E. Cummings reacted by defending the separate person as against any sort of association for the common good. But one notes with Jeffers and Cummings that this truculent defense of separateness was a reaction to the dream; at another time they might not have been driven into that sort of antisocial rebellion. They were trying to escape the destiny of the age "which ponders in the philosophers," as Emerson said, "which drudges in the laborers, which basks in the poets," but it left its mark on their work.

4 ✒ Looking back on the 1930s, I once asked myself a question. "Out of all that activity," I said, "all those dreams of universal change, and brotherhood with the workers, and those quarrels among the dreamers, what books remain that can still be admired?" Long ago I tried to draw up a reader's list of them, but the list had to be revised several times and then abandoned. I was uneasy about the good books that must have been overlooked, and besides, the whole project smacked of the critical canonmaking to

which I had always objected. Still, working over the list had helped me to reach a few conclusions.

I found, not to my surprise, that all but a very few of the lasting books were not the ones praised in the beginning for their revolutionary sentiments. Those proletarian novels that aroused so much discussion, especially during the first half of the decade, have mostly become unreadable. In an appendix to *The Radical Novel in the United States* (1956), that level-headed scholar Walter B. Rideout gives the names of fifty such novels for the years from 1930 to 1939, and there are others he might have mentioned. Almost all of his fifty are now historical curiosities; the likeliest exceptions are James T. Farrell's *Studs Lonigan* trilogy (1932–35), which still conveys its feeling of raw outrage, and Robert Cantwell's *The Land of Plenty* (1934). Later decades have been more impressed by novels that were neglected for years because they seemed to be outside the current of the age; one thinks of *Miss Lonelyhearts* and *Call It Sleep*. It would be easy, though, to demonstrate that each of these was affected by the current and could have been written at no other time.[2]

As might have been expected, the 1930s showed a strong interest in documentary writing, then known as "reportage." Shaken by the national crisis, or persuaded by the Communists to report a strike, young men of letters traveled west of the Hudson or south of the Potomac into regions they had never explored. They sat in dingy hotel rooms typing out their furious impressions of hired gunmen in Harlan County or of the Ford plant in River Rouge. Among those literary pilgrims, or tourists, the most brilliant was Edmund Wilson, who wandered over the country by train and sent back articles to *The New Republic*: later these were collected in *The American Jitters* (1932). Wilson was read with attention by his fellow writers, some of whom followed his example with variations. Nathan Asch, for instance, went everywhere by bus and wrote *The Road* (1937), a book that has been unjustly forgotten together with its talented author. But the best

---

2. It mightn't be so easy, though, with another admired novel, Djuna Barnes's *Nightwood* (1936).

of the documentaries is one I have mentioned already, *Let Us Now Praise Famous Men,* James Agee's book about Alabama cotton tenants that was five years in the writing. It finally appeared in 1941, with photographs by Walker Evans that are as detailed and eloquent as Agee's prose.

The age took a similar interest in autobiographical writing, especially of the sort that described the author's progress toward faith in a new society. Thus, Vincent Sheean's *Personal History* (1935) was widely praised. It proposed what Sheean called "the long view" of wars and revolutions he had witnessed as a foreign correspondent; that view was essentially Marxist. *An American Testament* (1936) is Joseph Freeman's account of his political conversion and of a life spent mostly among Communists, American and international. The account is as honest as he could make it while following the party line. All the political autobiographies are lacking in the extreme candor about personal relations that is now demanded of authors. The candor, though, was abundantly supplied by Henry Miller in *Tropic of Cancer* (1934), a book that was to be widely imitated thirty years later. Miller, incidentally, was among the very few writers unaffected by the political dreams of the age. There had to be exceptions even in the 1930s.

From an age so much concerned with class struggles, one might have expected some permanent works on political or economic theory or international affairs. The age was disappointing in this respect. Most of its social essays were shallow, contentious, polluted with jargon, and devoted to questions of the day presented in terms of liberal or Marxian or Freudian orthodoxies. Among the few exceptions were two books by Lewis Mumford, *Technics and Civilization* (1934) and *The Culture of Cities* (1938), in which he was preparing to offer his own prescription for social survival. Kenneth Burke, from a basis in literary criticism, was slowly evolving a philosophy of human motives to which he would later give the name of Dramatism. His longest work of the period, one which went almost unread like the others, was *Attitudes toward History* (1938).

In poetry the 1930s were a period when Frost, Stevens,

Williams, Moore, Jeffers, and Aiken were doing some of their best work. These were older poets, all in their fifties or sixties by the end of the decade, and their talents reflected an earlier time. All except Williams tried to stand apart from the new social currents, but these affected their work, if only by opposition. Another form of opposition was displayed by the talented poets who appeared at the end of the decade. They were Robert Lowell, Theodore Roethke, Delmore Schwartz, Randall Jarrell, and John Berryman, none of whom except Schwartz published their first books before the early 1940s. Schwartz described himself in a phrase that might be applied to the others, "as having a post-Munich sensibility," in other words, a feeling of skepticism toward the social movement. As for the earlier poets of the 1930s who plunged headlong into the movement, their work was less assured and impressive than that of their English contemporaries; perhaps that was because they had no spokesman like Auden to teach them a new language. As Auden was to say in his great elegy for W. B. Yeats (and later was to regret having said),

> *Time that is intolerant*
> *Of the brave and innocent,*
> *And indifferent in a week*
> *To a beautiful physique,*
>
> *Worships language and forgives*
> *Everyone by whom it lives.*

The young American poets of the early 1930s were embarrassed by a contradiction between language and subject matter; they were trying to convey a public message in a style they had adapted from Symbolist or Imagist poets, that is, a style best suited to private visions and nightmares. "Social symbolism" was what they called the result, but the term itself is a two-headed beast. Archibald MacLeish, a poet then in his forties, had found a style of his own that had been a grand vehicle for his lyrics and personal statements. More temperate in his opinions, but no less disturbed by threats to the American future than were his younger colleagues, he now wrote social poems that were more effective than theirs. Still, his work during the 1930s proved once again that *Public Speech*—his title for a book of poems published in 1936—is always in danger of becoming forensic.

So, much against my intention, I have after all compiled a list of titles and authors. The list is obviously incomplete; for example, it does not even glance at such broad fields as drama, criticism, and history. In the fields it does cover briefly, it fails to mention some lasting books while naming others that have a chiefly symptomatic interest. It omits whole categories of writers, such as the hard-boiled novelists of the 1930s. It does suggest, however, that the productions of the age were more varied and substantial than they are remembered as being. Fiction was of course the central field for writers. Faulkner seems more and more to have been the major novelist, and his best books were all published in the years from 1929 to 1942—eleven books in thirteen years, each different from any of the others. I said that Faulkner too was affected by the spirit of the age, but obviously he reacted in his own fashion. For the clearest expression of the age in its successive moods of anger, millennialism, and discouragement, one must turn to three big novels by others.

5 ✐ The three novels are *U. S. A., The Grapes of Wrath,* and *For Whom the Bell Tolls.* Let us see what each of them reveals about the mood of the years in which it was being written.

*U. S. A.,* the trilogy by John Dos Passos of which the first volume was published in 1930 and the last in 1936, comes first in time and is broadest of the three works in subject matter. By presenting many lives in brief—and, I might add, in varieties of harsh and rather dull prose that he regards as appropriate to their narrow fields of consciousness—Dos Passos tries to suggest what happened to the whole nation during the first thirty years of this century. The story ends just before the Wall Street Crash, but its somber mood is that of the early Depression years when everything was going to pieces as if by the operation of inexorable processes beyond human control. The author is bent on showing that more and more financial power was being concentrated in fewer hands, that the middle class was losing its independence, and that the poor were being driven from their homes. "All right we are two nations," he says in one of the Camera Eye passages that reflect his own feelings. One nation is represented at the end of the trilogy by a starving vagrant who stands beside the road trying to thumb a ride, and the other by a businessman who eats too well and vomits as he soars overhead in a silvery plane.

Dos Passos finds no hope of salvation for individuals in either the nation of the rich or the nation of the poor. The businessmen of his trilogy go bankrupt or suffer from heart attacks, the star of silent movies finds that she has no voice for talking pictures, the rising young executive becomes an alcoholic black-mailed by Negro homosexuals, the pure-hearted radicals are either corrupted or else expelled from the Communist party and cast into darkness by their friends; everybody good and bad is involved in a common disaster. There is no hint of the wild hopefulness felt by many young persons who believed that everything must soon be changed. When one rereads *U. S. A.* in the light of later events, it seems to be an absurdly pessimistic novel, but even the bleak prose of the narrative section has the power of deeply held convictions. The book holds together like a great ship freighted with the dead and dying, and it expresses what many people besides the author felt in those years when the nation seemed to be careening into the depths.

*The Grapes of Wrath,* on the other hand, is an optimistic tragedy. We know from the beginning that the Joad family, starving like the Jews in the land of Egypt, is making a hopeless pilgrimage. We know that the Joads will starve in the land of Canaan too. We are not surprised when some of them die on the journey through the wilderness or when others become disheartened and wander away. Memories of the New Testament are mingled with those of the Old. After Preacher Jim Casy, the Christ figure, is cornered and killed by vigilantes ("That's him. That shiny bastard"), Tom Joad takes up the Preacher's mission like another Saint Paul. We know that he will not surrender, but that he is certain to be tracked down and martyred. Tom, though, is willing to face death for the great aim of bringing the people together. After death, "I'll be ever'where—" he says to Ma Joad, "wherever you look. Wherever they's a fight so hungry people can eat, I'll be there. Wherever they's a cop beatin' up a guy, I'll be there."

Tom has completely merged his life in that of the people. When many others have done the same—when the people have finally come together for defense, with every "I" merged in a great "we"—then they will triumph over the oppressors and Tom, though dead, will be with them. That was his faith, or Steinbeck's faith at the time. Although the book was not published until 1939, it expresses the dream that many writers shared in the middle of the decade, that of linking arms with the dispossessed and marching by a bridge over the gulf into the golden mountains.

At the end of the decade another mood prevailed. It was induced chiefly by events overseas: by revolutions that failed in one country after another, by the Russian purges, by the defeat of the Spanish Republic, and then by the Hitler-Stalin pact. Those events have seldom been treated effectively by American writers. No American novel in the field—with one exception—rises to the level of consciousness attained in *Man's Fate*, for example, or in Arthur Koestler's *Darkness at Noon*. By comparison Dos Passos's *Adventures of a Young Man* is bleak and simplified, while Joseph Freeman's *Never Call Retreat* is wordy and uncontrolled. But we do have one powerful and usually undervalued novel about the Spanish civil war.

*For Whom the Bell Tolls* is a much more complicated novel than it is often given credit for being. In one of its many aspects it is of course an adventure story about the blowing up of a bridge. It begins with Robert Jordan's inspection of the bridge as he lies on the pine-needled floor of the forest. It proceeds in a rigorous sequence of hours and actions, with the tension always mounting, and it ends with Jordan, his mission accomplished, waiting for death on that same pine-needled floor. The mission, however, merely provides a framework for the novel, and we must look beyond it for underlying themes.

In another aspect, *For Whom the Bell Tolls* is concerned with one man's relation to the future of society. Robert Jordan is identical in spirit—one might almost say in flesh—with Hemingway's earlier heroes. As Frederic Henry he had made his farewell not so much to arms as to armies and, in a sense, to every type of social institution. As Jake Barnes, the maimed hero (the Fisher King?), he had existed in a social wasteland. Now, having committed himself to a dream of the social future, he regains his ability to love, and he goes to his death a willing victim.

In still another aspect—an important one to the author—the novel is concerned with a victory over time. Jordan when facing the likelihood of being killed finds himself capable of living as full a life in seventy hours—sixty-eight by actual count—as he might have lived in seventy years. When he is with the woman he loves, time is transformed into an eternal present. Hemingway's working title for the novel, before he found an epigraph from John Donne, had been "The Undiscovered Country." Obviously that country is not Spain; it is the timeless region, the "Now and forever now," that Jordan enters with Maria.

A final aspect of the novel—though others might have been mentioned—depends on the earlier-noted suggestion that Jordan is a Christ figure leading a band of disciples. Among the twelve, Pablo is certainly Judas. Pilar is Mary, and there are other biblical analogies as we approach the crucifixion. Then comes a departure from the Gospel story. While Jordan is waiting alone for death, the disciples having vanished, he determines to kill a Fascist officer as his last service to the cause. "If you wait and hold them up even a little while," he tells himself while trying not to faint from the pain of a broken leg, "or just get an officer that may make all the difference."

The book appeared in the autumn of 1940. I suspect that if it had been finished two years earlier, it might have ended as another optimistic tragedy like *The Grapes of Wrath,* but Hemingway was writing in a less hopeful period. He knew that the Spanish Republic was already doomed when Jordan set out on his mission behind the Fascist lines. "If we win here we will win everywhere," the hero says to himself while waiting for death; but Hemingway knew that Jordan's exploit in blowing up a bridge would not help the Loyalists to win even a single battle, and he shows us, in fact, that the battle was lost before it started.

Then, as if twisting a knife in the wound, he tells us the name of the Fascist officer whom Jordan was waiting to kill. "The officer," we read, "was Lieutenant Berrendo . . . his thin face serious and grave." Earlier in the novel Berrendo had been introduced to us as a brave man and a Christian who served his country well, even though fighting on the wrong side. What then shall we say about Jordan's final sacrifice? Was it not only useless but evil in its result? And might the same be said of his whole service as a dynamiter and destroyer for liberty? Those inescapable questions leave us feeling that the novel has ended as did the historical 1930s, with admiration and something close to envy for the brave men who fought and died in vain, but still in a mood of disillusionment and self-questioning, a postwar mood essentially, at a time when a greater war was under way.

# VIII GEORGIA
# BOY

1 ✍ During the early Depression years I was book editor of *The New Republic* and hence was a minor source of income for young writers who were trying to keep alive in New York. Many of them had found that other sources were limited in those bleak days before the Federal Writers' Project. I felt involved in their problems, which were even worse than my own problems had been a dozen years before, when I had sat on the other side of that big, scarred desk and had tried to explain to Francis Hackett why I should be given a book for review. Now men and women younger than I were showing me their scrapbooks and making those worried explanations. I usually found a book for them if they showed intimations of having talent or if they merely looked hungry; at least they could sell the book on Fourth Avenue and buy a meal. For Erskine Caldwell, however, I didn't find a book,

even though he impressed me as having more talent than almost any of the others.

I had read some of his stories in little magazines and later when they were collected in a first book, *American Earth,* published in the spring of 1931. Clearly he had a natural gift for storytelling and he had a subject, too, in the small cotton farmers of East Georgia. He expressed the mood of those years, but expressed it better than others did because his stories seemed to be lived, not constructed according to a theory about proletarian writing. Sometimes he wrote as if he were one of the hungry farmers; as if he had dropped the plowlines that very morning, stabled the mule, and rushed to the typewriter. There were other stories about Maine country people in which the tone was that of a quizzical observer, and there was also a long prose poem in numbered paragraphs, "The Sacrilege of Alan Kent." This impressed me even more than the stories, for it revealed what seemed to be a new sensibility, with hints of remembered pain, cruelty, hunger, and savage longing. Some of the paragraphs were single sentences as tough and springy as an ax handle: "A man walked into a restaurant through the front door and ate all he wanted to eat."—"Once the sun was so hot a bird came down and walked beside me in my shadow." That sentence about the bird I kept repeating to myself, each time admiring its utter simplicity and rightness.

So I was curious about the author and pleased when he appeared at *The New Republic.* Caldwell, as I afterward learned, had lately finished *Tobacco Road,* which had been accepted by Scribners for spring publication; now he planned to spend the winter in New York while writing a second novel. He was a big young man with a square-cut head, broad shoulders, and enormous hands, but with little flesh on his bones. His orange hair was cut short and lay forward close to his scalp, so that he looked like a totem pole topped with a blob of orange paint. When we talked about his stories he complained that people thought he was a humorist. "I have never tried to be funny," he said, making a wooden gesture. His features were as solemnly inexpressive as those of a backwoods farmer.

"He's not as innocent as he seems," I said to myself—but what did I say to Caldwell? Though I can't set down the words, I remember feeling experienced and almost patriarchal. I must have told him that he had a truly exceptional gift for storytelling, but that he didn't impress me as having a critical mind. When he volunteered that he had written a lot of reviews for the Charlotte *Observer*, I brushed aside the information. "Keep away from book reviews," I must have said. "They wouldn't earn you a living and they would interfere with your real business, which is writing stories." He clumped down the stairs without a book, while I sat in the editor's chair feeling ashamed of myself for having pontificated. I didn't know until much later that he had been living mostly on rye bread and rat-trap cheese, with a ten-cent bowl of soup in the evening.

Still, I had given Caldwell sound advice, even if books for review would have been more appreciated. That winter was to be his last really hard one. *Tobacco Road* came out in February 1932 and was not a commercial success, but it had more than a few enthusiastic readers. One of them was Jack Kirkland, who later asked for permission to dramatize the book. In March Caldwell went back to Maine, where he lived with his wife and three children in a big drafty house belonging to his wife's family. He had finished his second novel, but, after some hesitation, Scribners turned it down (that book was not to be published for twenty years). Then spring came to Kennebec County and everything seemed brighter. Caldwell started a new novel for which he already had a title: *God's Little Acre*. He had acquired a literary agent, Maxim Lieber, who represented several other new authors, and Lieber was beginning to sell his stories to magazines that paid for them. This new novel had gone well in the writing; it was finished in August and was promptly accepted by the Viking Press. With the advance against royalties, Caldwell bought a new typewriter, three new dictionaries—one for each of three rooms—and the first roast of beef his family had eaten for a year. He was still poor, but he would never again go hungry for want of money.

"A man walked into a restaurant through the front door and ate all he wanted to eat." Caldwell was now the man.

The next time I remember seeing him—though there were other times now forgotten—was in the winter of 1936–37, at a meeting in a midtown hotel held to advance some worthy left-wing cause. Caldwell appeared late and in the company of a spirited young woman, the photographer Margaret Bourke-White. They had lately traveled together through the Deep South, she taking pictures and he recording conversations for a book that was to become a classical record of the Depression years: *You Have Seen Their Faces* (1937). Now, the wife in Maine forgotten, they were radiantly in love, so that their presence transformed the crowded room. Suddenly I thought of Wallace Stevens and his "Anecdote of the Jar":

> *I placed a jar in Tennessee,*
> *And round it was, upon a hill.*
> *It made the slovenly wilderness*
> *Surround that hill.*

I felt that those two, absorbed in each other, gave focus and form to the slovenly meeting, while we others had become the wilderness in which they gleamed.

Bourke-White was gallant, ambitious, and hard-working, with a habit—not displayed that afternoon—of surveying a room to pick out celebrities, then walking straight up to them. In Caldwell she had found her dearest celebrity. By that time Jack Kirkland's Broadway version of *Tobacco Road* had been running for three years—with four more years to come—and it was yielding as much as $2000 a week in royalties to each of the collaborators. One of Caldwell's stories, "Kneel to the Rising Sun," had made him a hero of the left-wing press, which extolled him as a spokesman for the dispossessed. He was praised in Russia. *God's Little Acre* had just been published in a French version by Faulkner's translator, Maurice Coindreau, with a preface by André Maurois. In this country a respected critic, Joseph Warren Beach, had written of Caldwell (or was soon to write), "He was destined to follow in the footsteps of Chaucer and Dickens, of Balzac and Gorky." That was heady praise, but, in those days, it did not seem implausible.

2 ✍ Erskine Caldwell was a preacher's boy raised in genteel poverty. His father, Ira S. Caldwell, had once been secretary of the Home Missions Board of the Associated Reformed Presbyterian Church, an imposing title with little or no income attached to it. The A.R.P., as the boy learned to call his father's church, is one of the smaller and stricter Presbyterian sects, with very few bankers or rich widows among its members, and for some years his father's occupation was to travel through the rural South, from one struggling congregation to another, and minister to each of them for a few months, perhaps for a year or more, until its rifts were healed and it could afford a minister of its own. Sometimes he caused a new rift by taking the liberal side on racial questions. His salary wasn't always paid. Even after 1919, when he accepted a permanent post with the A.R.P. church in Wrens, Georgia, his income was less than $2000 a year.

By that time his only son was a gangling boy of sixteen. Born in Coweta County, Georgia, in December 1903 (or perhaps in 1902; there is some argument about the year), Erskine had attended school intermittently—a few months in Staunton, Virginia, four years in Atoka, Tennessee—but he had also been tutored at home by his mother, who had once taught Latin and French at a fashionable school for girls. After one year at the Wrens high school, the boy was given a diploma. He wanted to attend the University of Georgia, and instead he went rebelliously to Erskine, a small denominational college named like himself for the Scottish founder of A.R.P. He was there for three years and played football on the freshman and varsity squads, but he had a miserable academic record and was often away from campus. Once he went to New Orleans and tried to get a job on a freighter bound for South America, but he was jeered off the ship. Later in the same month—it was February 1922—he was arrested for vagrancy in Bogalusa, Louisiana, then a sawmill town, and spent nine days in jail. He might have spent three months there, but he smuggled out a letter to his father, who wired money enough to pay his fine and buy a ticket back to Georgia.

In 1923 he got away from Erskine College by applying to the United Daughters of the Confederacy for a scholarship to the University of Virginia. He had four semesters at Virginia, in all, but they were scattered over four academic years. He did well in English, as one might expect, and in sociology, but indifferently in his other studies, and he took to writing stories. In March 1925 he secretly married Helen Lannigan, the daughter of an athletic coach at the university. Forgiven by the bride's parents, the Caldwells spent another semester at the university; then Erskine talked himself into a job as cub reporter on the Atlanta *Journal*. He gave up the job in the late spring, determined as he was by then to earn a living by writing fiction. With his wife he went to Maine, where the Lannigans owned a house and a hundred acres in the town of Mount Vernon, near Augusta. Erskine fell into the routine of hoeing potatoes or chopping wood all day, in preparation for winter, then writing through much of the night. His stories went out to magazines and came back with rejection slips. In 1929 he received his first letter of acceptance; it was from the poet Alfred Kreymborg, who was then helping to edit a distinguished yearbook, *The New American Caravan*.

That is a bare record of Caldwell's early years, based on information kindly supplied by Dr. William A. Sutton, the author of "Erskine," an unpublished biography. His account differs at various points from those offered by Caldwell himself, which in turn differ with each other (except in their common quality of being romanticized). I quote from a letter that Caldwell wrote to the compilers of *Twentieth Century Authors* (1942):

When I was eighteen, I enrolled at Erskine College, Due West, S.C., but remained only a short time. I went to sea on a boat that was running guns for a revolt in a Central American republic, and ended up several months later in Mexico. My next attempt to complete my education was when I entered the University of Virginia after having won a scholarship offered by the United Daughters of the Confederacy. I remained there almost a year, working nights in a poolroom for room and board. I had begun to write short stories, though, before I left, and continued writing while working in a variety store in Pennsylvania, playing professional football, managing a lecture tour for a British soldier of fortune, and selling building lots in Alabama under three feet of water. I attended the University of Pennsylvania for a short time, making my expenses, and more, as a bodyguard for a Chinaman. . . .

The article in *Twentieth Century Authors* goes on to summarize information offered by Caldwell on other occasions. It says, "Anyone who doubts Mr. Caldwell's close personal knowledge of the underdogs of whom he writes should note that in addition to the jobs he mentions he has also been a cotton-picker, a lumber-mill hand, a hack-driver, a stagehand in a burlesque theater, a soda-jerker, and a cook and waiter." Some of those jobs he really held, if briefly, while others are as improbable as his running away to Central America. Dr. Sutton said in the course of a long letter, "Perhaps I have left you with the impression that no Caldwell statement about himself can be taken as necessarily true. Exactly right. As one of his old friends told me, 'He is a put-on artist.' "

It would be more accurate to say that he is simply an artist, one who assigns some of his own adventures to a fictional character named Caldwell. That sort of yarning is not at all unusual among poets and novelists. Whitman, Sherwood Anderson, Hemingway, Faulkner, and Nathanael West—to mention only a few names—all created imaginary selves and thereby made trouble for their biographers. In Caldwell's case the process can be broken down into three stages (though I suspect that these developed almost simultaneously). *First stage:* He wrote a great number of stories (often late at night or when he was tired and hungry). Some of the stories surprised him by the feelings they revealed, which were different from those of the daytime Caldwell. *Second stage:* He therefore adopted a persona, that of the man who might logically be supposed to have written the stories.

*Third stage:* Even a persona must have a past, so Caldwell constructed it, yarned it out, using a mixture of episodes from his early life with impulses on which he had never acted.

In "The Sacrilege of Alan Kent," the early prose poem that corresponds on a lesser scale to Whitman's "Song of Myself," one notes the beginning process of self-dramatization. Here is what happens to the nine days in Bogalusa jail:

> I went to a town where lumber was planed, and lay in jail two or three years or more. There was nothing to do at any time other than listen to a Mexican file his pointed yellow teeth and to feel my growing beard.

And here is the episode of his asking for a job on a freighter docked at New Orleans:

> One night I crawled aboard a coaling tramp and begged a man for a job. He heaved a cask-bung at my head and shouted, "Get the hell off here, you God-damn rat!" Before the tramp and the man got half way across the Atlantic, they went down and no one knows where.

Perhaps Caldwell was taking a fictional revenge on the bo's'n who jeered him off the ship. By 1942, however, the episode was to grow into that mythical voyage to Central America on a gun runner. Here is another paragraph, wholly imagined and not pretending to be anything else, that foreshadows a deep feeling expressed in his later work:

> The night when he heated the iron pokers and began burning the Negro girl with them, one of the Negro men and I took two shotguns and killed him. After we had broken the chain around the girl's waist, we walked all night until we reached the town.

The feeling is that blacks and whites of the oppressed classes should join forces against the oppressors. It is a feeling mingled with dreams of miscegenation—as note the presence of a Negro girl—and the dreams become clearer in still another paragraph:

For a week on the top floor of a seven-story warehouse, a brown-limbed girl fed me every day and warmed me at night. She even helped me lick my wounds. When I threw my cigarette butts out of the window, they fell into the ocean; and I could see all the way across it. Then I went away for two years and came back to get her, but she was not there; and I can't find her now.

That "brown-limbed girl [who] fed me every day" was to reappear often in Caldwell's novels. Of course "The Sacrilege of Alan Kent" is a fantasy, not a novel, much less a factual memoir. There is, however, a similar dramatization or pure invention of episodes in Caldwell's purportedly true story of his life, *Call It Experience* (1951). I thoroughly enjoy the book, which is full of lively incidents, and have never felt an impulse to separate the fact in it from the fiction. Whether Caldwell really worked on the night shift of a cottonseed-oil mill in Wrens, Georgia, during the spring of 1920 is a question that I gladly leave to Dr. Sutton. A much more interesting subject is the persona he created for himself: its function, its nature, and its effects on his writing, which were good at first, but ultimately disastrous.

3 ✍ I should guess that the primary function of the persona was simply to make the author an interesting figure. At one time he must have told himself a continued story in which he was the hero; that is a boyhood practice of many or most authors. Now— again like many authors—he was embroidering the story for others. But the persona also had a secondary function that became always more important, and this was to validate his fiction. Caldwell was presenting himself as, in his publisher's words, "the spokesman for simple people, good or evil, vicious or oppressed," but there might be those who doubted his "close personal knowledge of the underdogs of whom he writes." The obvious answer

was that he had been one of the underdogs; that he had worked or looked for work or starved among them as a field hand, a saw-mill hand, a carnival roustabout, and a vagrant—not to mention other occupations—and that he had shared their brief pleasures of drinking, gambling, and whoring. One remembers how "Song of Myself" presented its author to the public: he was

> *Walt Whitman, an American, one of the roughs, a kosmos,*
> *Disorderly fleshy and sensual . . . . eating drinking and*
> *breeding.*

In constructing a public image, Caldwell had less to con-ceal than Whitman and stayed closer to his true self. He was truly a wanderer, truly a listener, truly used to working with those big hands. He withstood hunger and cold like an Indian brave. He truly raged against injustices to Negroes and sufferings en-dured by poor whites. On the other hand, he was less of a Deep Southern primitive than he pretended to be, had more schooling than he acknowledged, and had read more contemporary fiction, at least when he was reviewing books for the Charlotte *Observer*. His pose of gullible innocence was combined with a good deal of shrewdness in dealing with editors and in judging how long his money would last.

The public image was that of a man driven to write fic-tion by "an almost uncontrollable desire," so he tells us in *Call It Experience*, "that seeks fulfillment at any cost . . . as overpowering as the physical need for food and drink." Or warmth or sleep, he might have added. "Upstairs in an unheated room," he says in speaking of his first Maine winter,

> I wore a sweater, a leather jerkin, and an overcoat while I sat at the typewriter. I kept a blanket wrapped around my feet and stopped once in a while to blow on my numbed fingers. . . . For ten and twelve hours a day, and often through the night, I wrote story after story, revising, correct-ing, and rewriting . . . trying over and over again to make a story sound to the inner ear the way I wanted to make it sound.

Caldwell went south in January when he had burned the last of his firewood and eaten almost the last of his potatoes. He tells us:

> For several weeks I lived in a one-room cabin in the piney woods near Morgana, Edgefield County, South Carolina, eating a can of pork-and-beans three times a day and writing for sixteen or eighteen hours at a time. After a while I went to Baltimore and lived on lentils and wrote short stories in a room on Charles Street. When money gave out, it was spring. I returned to Maine.
>
> This time . . . I would cut wood during the day and hoe potatoes in the long purple twilight, and, when night came, I would sit down and work on a short story. At that time of year, in that latitude, it was broad daylight at three o'clock in the morning when I went to sleep for a few hours. Time seemed to go so swiftly and there was so much to do that some nights I would stop the clock or turn the hour hand backward while I was at the typewriter.

And what was the purpose of all this labor, beyond the gratification of his physical need for writing? On that point Caldwell has less to say, but still he makes one specific statement:

> I wanted to tell the story of the people I knew in the manner in which they actually lived their lives from day to day and year to year, and to tell it without regard for fashions in writing and traditional plots. It seemed to me that the most authentic and enduring materials of fiction were the people themselves, not crafty plots and counterplots designed to manipulate the speech and actions of human beings.

In those early days his writing was never impeded by the want of subjects to write about. He had known hundreds of persons in the Deep South, and later in Maine, whose moments were clamoring to be recorded. If memories failed him, he could always continue his travels around the country making new observations. "Often I would find myself wondering," he says, "what people might be doing at that moment elsewhere in America, in hundreds of villages and small towns." He was so busy at all times observing, experiencing, and recording that he had no leisure for reading books. "Many years ago," he was to say on various occasions, "I divided the population into two parts, those who read and those who write. I wished to belong in the latter category." The one book he carried with him on his travels—besides his typewriter and a cigarette-making machine—was a collegiate dictionary. "I not only consulted it frequently," he says, "but in my free time I read the dictionary instead of reading novels and magazines." Once he went through it striking out every word of more than four syllables.

Such is the image of *homo scribens,* the writing man, that Caldwell presents to the world, and to himself as an ideal. It is a radically simplified picture that omits the problems encountered by others who follow the trade. Caldwell's idealized writer has no problems except material ones; no doubts of himself, no hesitations, no fears of losing contact with his subliminal wealth. He is impelled to write by a physical need that makes him forget the need for sleep; turning back the clock, he goes on working without being disturbed by hunger or sexual desire. His only aim is to set down, in the simplest words, a true unplotted record of people without yesterdays. Past literature does not exist for him, and he is scarcely aware of having rivals in the present. As with Adam in the garden, every statement he makes is new. His only mentor is *Webster's Collegiate Dictionary;* his only acknowledged judge and critic is the inner ear.

So far as the author himself accepted that simplified image, he was limiting his possibilities of development. Writers learn from life, if they are lucky, but they also learn from other writers, and Caldwell was learning less than his contemporaries. In the beginning, of course, he had learned somewhat more than he confessed to himself. I suspect that most of his early stories could not have been written without the challenge offered by *Winesburg, Ohio,* which had already served as a challenge to other new talents of that age, including Hemingway and Faulkner. I also suspect that Caldwell owed a debt to Hemingway's Michigan stories, though he never wrote Hemingway prose; and he must have been affected by the experimental spirit of the little magazines that published his early work. But once he stopped reading—except for "half a dozen novels a year," as he tells us—he deprived himself of models to shape his critical sense (that "inner ear"); and he also lost what Henry James, in a passage already quoted, called "the stimulus of suggestion, comparison, emulation." There was no one he cared to emulate—not James, most certainly; not Proust or Joyce or Conrad; he never mentions them. Although he lived in an age of experiments, including his own, he refused to profit from the experiments of others, which he dismissed, in fact, as "crafty plots and counterplots designed to manipulate the speech and actions of human beings." He wanted to depend on his own technical resources. In the proud way of many American writers at the time, conscious as they were of speaking for a new age, in a new country, he wanted to be completely his own man, owing no debt to anyone else's work. All he asked was that his own work be recognized—and recognized it was, after he had served an arduous but relatively brief apprenticeship.

Early recognition—perhaps at a cost to be paid later—is not unlikely to be the fortune of those who cling to a simple image of themselves. So it was with Caldwell, and the bands were already playing in his honor during the winter of 1936–37, when I saw him at that meeting in a midtown hotel. But I wondered even then what his next literary step was to be.


4 ✍ In those days his name was very often coupled with that of William Faulkner, and we have forgotten that the two authors had many things in common. Especially in subject matter: both of them dealt with a society that appeared to be in a violent stage of decay. They came from different, but not strikingly different, sectors of that society. Caldwell's forebears were less prominent than Faulkner's and he took less pride in them, but they were educated persons some of whom had fought for the Confederacy.

The real difference here was one of election: Faulkner elected to speak for the former slaveowning class, where Caldwell made us feel his sympathy for the white and black cotton tenants. Both men, however, were intensely conscious of having roots in the Deep South.

Caldwell was outraged and Faulkner was saddened by injustices to Negroes. Both men were fascinated by the theme of miscegenation, with the difference here that Caldwell admired his quadroons and octoroons, whereas Faulkner presented most of his as damned souls. Both wrote about Southern gangsters and prostitutes. One might say that Caldwell's early novelettes *The Bastard* (1929) and *Poor Fool* (1930) are his versions of the material that Faulkner used in *Sanctuary* (1931). There is no possibility of literary influence, since *The Bastard* and the first draft of *Sanctuary* were being written at the same time, one in Maine, the other in Mississippi, but still there are curious similarities. Other parallels might be noted among short stories, again without any likelihood of literary derivation. Still, "Saturday Afternoon" is Caldwell's "Dry September," "Candy-Man Beechum" is his "Pantaloon in Black," and "Meddlesome Jack" is his "Spotted Horses." While reading novels by both men, one might think of Caldwell's Darling Jill, in *God's Little Acre,* as the sister of Faulkner's Eula Varner and might regard the people on Tobacco Road as the still more ignorant and destitute cousins of those in Frenchman's Bend.

In the early careers of the two authors, just as in their work, it is easy to find resemblances. Both were proud of having worked at odd jobs, of which they both exaggerated the number. Both had early moving-picture assignments, and in the spring of 1933 they worked successively on the same picture, never released, which had "Bride of the Bayou" for its studio title. Director Tod Browning was shooting it on the Gulf Coast a hundred miles south of New Orleans. Faulkner was fired by MGM and Caldwell took his place with so little lapse of time that both must have been bitten by the same mosquitoes. Later both men worked in Hollywood without becoming part of the movie colony.

Even in the beginning, when they were regarded by the

studios and by the public as almost interchangeable values, there were tremendous differences between them. "Faulkner's genius," one says immediately, but genius is hard to define and one has to look for its manifestations in an author's life and works. There is a clue, perhaps, in the image that Faulkner had formed of himself, which was different from Caldwell's self-image and provided more incentives to growth. Very early in his career, Faulkner showed that he wanted to be not only a writer but among the greatest writers. Shakespeare, the Bible, Dostoevski, Conrad, Joyce: he read them all intensively. He had a spirit of emulation that kept driving him ahead to study and surpass his contemporaries, then to surpass himself. Some of his good stories became great stories only on revision, as note "That Evening Sun" and *Sanctuary* and "The Bear." Caldwell, with an immense natural gift for storytelling, made fewer demands on it. He depended less on imagination and invention than Faulkner did, though both qualities were richly present in his early work. More and more he came to rely on simple observation of what people said and did.

That self-image of Caldwell's was not the best of auguries for his future as a novelist, but still he was to have an amazing career.

For nine years after the publication of his third novel, *Journeyman* (1935), he wrote comparatively little fiction. Instead he traveled to collect material, first by himself and later with Margaret Bourke-White (they were married in 1939 and divorced in 1942). They were in Moscow to do a book of photographs and text on the Soviet Union when Hitler's armies crossed the border in June 1941. For the next few months Caldwell was fantastically busy as one of the first American correspondents on the scene, then later, in Connecticut, as an author rushing books into print to record his impressions. He was summoned to Hollywood as an adviser on the film *Mission to Moscow*, with other assignments to follow. It was not until 1944 that he terminated a studio contract (at four times the salary then being paid to Faulkner) and went back to writing fiction.

Caldwell's project was to finish a series of roughly a dozen novels dealing with various aspects of the Deep South; "a

Southern cyclorama" was his name for it. Perhaps he had looked up "cyclorama" in his favorite *Webster's Collegiate,* where, in the edition he must have owned, he would have found the word defined as "a pictorial view extended circularly, so that the spectator is surrounded as if by things in nature." That came close enough to Caldwell's purpose, which was to encircle the reader with a series of accurate representations. The publisher promised that each of the novels would present a facet of Southern life "seen through the eyes of a sociologist who is also an artist and a humorist. . . . The sum total will give a picture of a society as detailed and complete as Tolstoi's panorama of Czarist Russia."

Grandiose as the project sounds when translated into publisher's talk, it was a mere extension of Caldwell's self-image as a writer. He was simply planning to tell more stories about more and more of the people he knew, "in the manner in which they actually lived their lives from day to day." He was making the most of his travels and his skill as a reporter while neglecting his subconscious resources, including his imaginative power and his talent for transforming the ordinary into the grotesque and apocryphal. He was substituting extensity for intensity, at the risk of exhausting his material and of reusing the same plots as he moved from one Southern background to another. Did he suffer, perhaps, from the same sort of fatigue, moral and imaginative, that afflicted Steinbeck and other writers who had been emotionally involved in the social dreams of the 1930s? In any case he pushed ahead with the series, and a new novel appeared each year without adding to his literary reputation. As late as 1946 Faulkner spoke of him as one of five contemporaries who were interesting to read (the others being Wolfe, Hemingway, Dos Passos, and Steinbeck). A year later Faulkner was quoted as saying to a group of students "that he had once had great hopes for Erskine Caldwell, but now he didn't know."

Great hopes were being realized at the same time, but they were of a different and unexpected nature. Caldwell was becoming a central figure in a new branch of American publishing.

Early in 1946 *God's Little Acre* had been the first of his novels to appear as a twenty-five-cent mass-market paperback. His reprint publishers, Kurt Enoch and Victor Weybright, informed him six months later that its sales had passed a million copies, then an unprecedented figure, and were expected to reach two million by the end of the year. Enoch and Weybright had started as American representatives of Penguin Books, but now they had founded their own company, Signet Books (later the New American Library). Of course they were eager to reprint Caldwell's other novels and to promote them vigorously. The rest of the story can be told in phrases and figures that appeared on the back covers of those other books as they were published in Signet editions year after year.

1949 "It is only recently, with the publication of his work in 25-cent editions, that Caldwell has emerged as one of the most influential and bestselling authors of all time. Eleven million copies of six novels have been sold in Signet editions alone (over four and a half million of *God's Little Acre*)."

1949 (There was a second book that year.) "Fifteen million copies of seven books."

1950 "Over 23,000,000 copies."

1952 "Erskine Caldwell is America's favorite author. His books have sold over 25,000,000 copies in Signet editions alone, with *God's Little Acre* topping the list with sales over 6,000,000."

1952 (Again there was a second book for the year.) "America's bestselling novelist. Almost 30,000,000 copies of his books have now been sold."

1956 "The world's most popular novelist . . . has written a brilliant succession of novels and volumes of short stories which have sold over 37,000,000 copies in their paperbound Signet editions alone and have been published in twenty-six countries and languages."

1957 ". . . the world's bestselling novelist . . . has achieved international fame as one of the greatest writers of the twentieth century. . . . His books have topped 40,000,000."

1963 "His books have been translated into 27 languages, with over 61,000,000 copies of all editions in print."

As late as 1967 Caldwell was still being advertised as "the world's bestselling novelist," but his publishers had stopped giving figures of "copies in print"; perhaps these weren't growing fast enough. The figures, incidentally, are not the same as the number of copies actually sold, since they do not allow for unsold books returned to the warehouse and shredded. Might one guess that 40 million copies would be closer to the actual sales? That is still an impressive figure, though later it was to be surpassed by the actual sales of a few other novelists. Even the unprecedented record of *God's Little Acre* was to be left behind. Caldwell's "unsparing realism" seemed less unsparing in an age of total sexual candor, and his "earthy, robust" country humor was being replaced by kinky urban humor. Still, during a period of fifteen years or more, the demand for his novels had increased the sale of paperbound books in general and had helped to establish mass-market publishing as the most flourishing branch of the industry. After being a literary force in a somewhat limited field, he became a commercial property that, for a time, had its national importance.

It should be added that those sales to a vast public were accidental at first and were not a reflection of his self-image. Unlike many of his successors in the mass market, Caldwell never became a manipulator of plots and characters for the sake of producing a sensation. He made concessions, sometimes in an awkward fashion, sometimes repetitively, to what he thought the public expected of him, but he still was telling honest stories about people he might have known. In the 1960s he resumed his efforts to write more serious books without much thought of whether they would reach a wide audience. *In Search of Bisco* (1965) is an account of how he traveled through the Deep South looking for a black playmate remembered from his childhood. The search, however, is only a framework for his reflections on race prejudice and for dramatic monologues by others. Another non-fiction book, *Deep South* (1968), is a report on fundamentalism as he observed it in various white and black congregations. The best passages of the book are tributes by a wayward son to his father's tolerant and courageous Christianity. Some of Caldwell's later novels also treat his material more seriously and even, in one or two cases, with a hint of affection. The best of them is *Weather Shelter* (1969), which is based on two themes that appeared in his earliest writing: miscegenation and the search for a lost son of mixed blood. This time they lead to a happy ending. The son will be found, will be rescued from an attempted lynching, and will inherit his white father's property.

I read those three late books with sympathy and respect for the author, but with none of the troubled surprise I had felt on reading his work in the early 1930s. It is the early books—say the first three novels and the stories up to *Georgia Boy* (1943)—on which his reputation will stand or fall. Today there is an unfortunate tendency to let it fall, to dismiss the books as having been too popular, and to forget that they made a contribution to American letters—not to mention their having added a chapter to American folklore.

In a way they continued the tradition of what used to be called Southwestern humor, though more of it was Georgian or Alabamian. What they added was a new vision, combined with new characters and a new sensibility. Caldwell was taking chances and giving rein to his subconscious feelings. The result in his work was that homely objects or events—a crushed strawberry, a sack of turnips, a crown fire in the piney woods—became charged with emotion and were remembered as symbols. There was a vein of poetry beneath the surface of his early writing; it was laid bare in "The Sacrilege of Alan Kent," but he did not try to exploit it and later it disappeared. There was also a hint that many of his "unplotted" stories fall into ritual patterns corresponding to racial memories. In *God's Little Acre*, for instance, why does Will Thompson tear the clothes from Griselda and reveal her "rising beauties" before he turns on the power in the closed-down cotton mill? There is nothing logical in the sequence of events, but still we sense that it is right. In *Tobacco Road,* when the grandmother is dying of hunger with her face in the dirt, why does Jeeter Lester feel that the soil is right for planting, and set a fire to clear his overgrown fields, and die in the flames? "All this is magic," Kenneth Burke said long ago in the best essay that anyone has written on Caldwell's early work. "... the plots are subtly guided by the logic of dreams." It is no wonder that Jeeter and Will Thompson have become figures in American folklore. The magic is there, and it must have cast a spell on the millions who bought the novels in paperback long after the critics had forgotten them.

# IX THE
# SENSE OF
# GUILT

1   I find a curious mood in myself when thinking about the second half of the 1930s. It is different from my feelings about the earlier days when writers went on missions to Harlan County or joined the League of Professional Groups for Foster and Ford. That first half of the decade seems very distant now, and I can talk about my part in it as if I were someone else—an earnest character who marched in May Day parades and sang "The International," sometimes with tears in his eyes as he dreamed of contributing his share to the future; who did crazy things (was that really I?) that seem no crazier in retrospect than what had been done, for instance, by Charles E. Mitchell in the boom years when he was president of the National City Bank, and without Mitchell's excuse or sin of doing them for his own profit. In those years he—I, not the investment bankers—did no great harm and nobody suffered much for the man's political errors.

It seems different in the second half of the decade. By that time I had acquired, at a price, a fair amount of political sophistication and had lost many, though not all, of my illusions about the Communists. I still had no political ambitions. I wanted to be a good writer and an honest man; I wanted to observe, to learn as much as possible. I had come to recognize the strict limits of my vitality, which were narrower than I had hoped to find; but within those limits, and within my proper field of activity, I wanted to do what I could to oppose the evil in the world and the advance of Hitler's legions and to prevent another world war—if it *could* be prevented; but after a time I began to feel that it was inevitable and that the best hope was to strengthen our will to resist, so that we could win the war when it came. All these seemed high motives and still seem so in retrospect. Why then, in thinking about the period, do I feel once again a sense of guilt?

Partly it comes from the fact that we failed disastrously in all our aims. "We" in this case refers to all the thousands of writers and would-be writers, of intellectuals and would-be intellectuals, in the Western countries who were moved by similar aspirations. We were the Men of Good Will, in the phrase made popular by Jules Romains's many-volumed novel; we were those of public spirit, assured of their perspicacity, who held meetings and issued statements and uttered warnings of impending catastrophe. Internationally the Russians were our friends. We had learned to be skeptical about what was happening inside Russia; about all those photographs or paintings (how tell them apart?) of grim-jawed Russian workers with immense biceps (and Stalin smiling in the background), as about the confessions of Old Bolsheviks brought to trial, of how they had conspired to overthrow the Soviet state. It hardly mattered whether or not we believed the evidence; false or true it painted a terrifying picture of the workers' fatherland. Internationally, however, the Russians seemed above reproach. They supported the League of Nations, they voted for sanctions against the aggressors, they promised to defend any Eastern country that Hitler invaded, they proclaimed that peace was indivisible, that security must be collective; in other words, they flattered us by saying exactly what we might have said if given a voice in international rivalries. We were moralists, and so, it seemed, were the Russians outside their own borders.

As a matter of fact, we were part of their calculations. They hoped, they gambled that they could change the policies of France, Britain, the United States, and thus form an alliance too strong for Hitler to attack. In order to persuade the governments of those countries, they had to create a strong base in popular sympathies, and this was not a task that could be performed by the Communist parties, which were especially weak in Britain and the United States. But perhaps—so the Russian leaders must have reckoned—the Men of Good Will could do more to convince or frighten the statesmen. We writers, professors, publicists might thereby contribute something to the defense of the Soviet Union— and hence we were solicited, importuned, published, assembled in congresses, gently admonished, wildly praised, and in general made to feel our importance.

This Russian courtship of the intellectuals, these protestations of moral purpose, and indeed the whole campaign for collective security have often been dismissed as purely hypocritical, but I suspect that the charge is an oversimplification of a type to which writers are prone. They think of Russia as a single person who said one thing while preparing to do another. But not even Russia under Stalin or Germany under Hitler was completely monolithic. It seems now that Stalin himself never had any respect for the Men of Good Will, whom he had reviled a few years before as "rotten liberals." It also seems clear that he had no striking talent, or at least no instinctive feeling of what could be achieved, in the field of foreign affairs; certainly nothing to compare with his genius for political maneuvers inside the Communist party. By 1935 he was ready to admit to himself that the policy of abusing the Socialists and liberals as "social Fascists," and of fighting harder against them than against the Fascists themselves, had failed in the West. The hope of a proletarian revolution was fading away except in Spain; the menace of fascism was growing everywhere; and meanwhile he had urgent problems in Russia. In foreign affairs his principal answer to the new situation was the People's Front, as proclaimed at the Seventh World Congress of the Communist International in August 1935; henceforth the Communist parties were to collaborate with everyone opposed to Hitler. But isn't it also possible that Stalin said to his Foreign Commissar, Maxim Litvinoff, something on this order? "Very well, see what you can do with the rotten liberals. I'll let you make the gamble."

It would mean that Litvinoff had a measure of liberty in foreign affairs from 1935 till the Munich Conference in 1938. He adopted policies that appealed to the Men of Good Will, and I do not think that he was being hypocritical; he was simply expressing his own ideas with Stalin's temporary consent. When his policies failed and the Western liberals were proved, at Munich, to have no real power, Stalin turned against them once more, and the first unmistakable sign of change was Litvinoff's resignation, in May 1939. No more flattery, no more compliments from Moscow for the Men of Good Will. They were left bewildered, but also with the suspicion that if they had done something more, had been more persuasive, more self-sacrificing, more perspicacious, perhaps the long gamble would have been a success after all. Those who fail are always guilty.

Guilty too are those who are punished, a very old principle rediscovered by Freudian psychologists. "Father sent me upstairs without my supper," the child says to himself. "I *must* have done something wrong." Men and women often react to events in the same fashion; when the volcano erupts or the earth shakes, they perform acts of penance. I think there was something penitential in the behavior of liberals from 1948, to set an arbitrary date, to the end of the McCarthy era. They were being punished for acting on what they had always regarded as the highest principles, and hence they came to feel that the actions were wrong. Some of them were being punished, I should say more accurately; they were shamed before their neighbors, discharged from posts in government or education or motion pictures, forced to make public confessions—sometimes in full-page advertisements—and led step by step into situations where they betrayed their human dignity. A few went to prison, and many more went into voluntary exile (as note Doris Lessing's picture, in *The Golden Notebook,* of an American colony in London).

Of course these were a minority among the former Men of Good Will. The majority kept their jobs, with only a little harassment, a little loss of self-confidence and earning power, and yet, in many cases, the threat of punishment hung over them. Usually it was the nightmare of being summoned before an investigating committee and given the choice of either betraying their friends—who by that time were as disillusioned with communism as everyone else—or of refusing to testify at the price for the refusal of losing their jobs or their security clearances. As long as the threat of punishment remained, they all felt guilty. If actual punishment was inflicted, they accepted it, in many cases, not like martyrs but like apprehended criminals: "The wicked flee and no man pursueth." The most disheartening feature of that era was not the aggressions against liberty by Joe McCarthy and his allies, but the lack of resistance among his threatened victims. When the attack was finally halted, it was not the liberals, but a few of the old-fashioned conservatives, easy in their consciences, who made the effective stand.

2  But something is lacking from the explanation, so that the picture it paints is more exculpatory than the complete truth would be. The Men of Good Will committed sins of a sort—of several sorts, in their individual cases—as well as those errors of judgment they have been only too eager to confess. I, for example, seem to myself a less sympathetic figure after 1935 than in the earlier period of faith and foolishness. The faith was secretly oozing away, and the foolishness was giving place, as I said, to a measure of sophistication. At the same time I was working hard for *The New Republic* and was feeling a sort of fatigue that was moral even more than physical. It had become

more difficult to establish human contacts; there was no time for them if I wanted to preserve a few hours weekly of solitude and soliloquy. Like many others at the time—as it seems in retrospect —I retreated into merely official relations. I did my job; I ordered and edited the sort of book reviews about which I wouldn't have to argue with my senior colleagues, Bruce Bliven and George Soule; I answered yes or no to requests while citing precedents— but more often yes than no, since it came easier. "Yes," I would say to an importunate visitor, "you can list my name as a member of your committee, because I agree with your general purposes— but on condition that you don't ask me to write statements or attend meetings." The meetings I did attend were either those for Spain, at which I often found myself chairman, or those called to discuss what the League of American Writers could do. I was a vice-president of the League and took the office seriously, in the few evenings I could devote to it, but I learned to address rows of faces instead of persons. Having built a house in the country, where I spent four days each week, I found a sense of relief in planting and hoeing and watching vegetables that grew according to plan, as persons refused to do.

I was becoming not so much a person as a name on letterheads, a presence behind a desk, a possible source of favors—in other words a bureaucrat, like many other writers at the time, though most of the others were bureaucrats in Washington or Hollywood or on the staffs of *Time* and *Fortune*. *The New Republic* was more casual and familial, even after it moved from Chelsea to Madison Avenue, but its opinions seemed more or less fixed after 1935, and it had lost the excitement of the earlier years. In retrospect it seems to me that I committed more than a simple error, almost a sin against myself, when I failed to resign from the paper and strike out in some new direction. By that time, however, I had a family, I was paying off a mortgage on our country house, and I was afraid of living without a salary.

I don't want to exaggerate my transgressions or beat my breast in public. No matter how far I fell short of my own standards, I wrote nothing that I did not believe to be true or that misstated my convictions. That honesty about oneself is not so much a virtue for a writer as a mere instinct and condition of his survival. Oneself is his stock in trade, and if he adulterates the self or makes false claims for it he will soon go bankrupt. Accordingly I preserved a shopkeeper's honesty about my beliefs and skepticisms, but I kept silent about some of them, out of laziness or loyalty. There were observations I confided to my notebook and did not think of publishing. That failure to publish led me into false situations, and later I would suffer for it—deservedly, I say to myself in private reckonings. When I add together these various sins of silence, self-protectiveness, inadequacy, and something close to moral cowardice, there appears to be reason for my feeling a sense of guilt about the second half of the decade.

But something more was being asked—not from me as an individual, but from the former Men of Good Will as a type, almost a social class—than this acknowledgment of sins which they honestly felt to be theirs. The inquisitors now demanded that they confess to greater sins, even though they were not conscious of having committed them. That is what I seemed to gather from two or three reviews of Arthur Miller's play *After the Fall* (1964), and especially from what Robert Brustein said about it in *The New Republic*. Brustein objected to the play for every sort of reason, but what seemed to be his central indictment was political.

> For all the talk about "truth" and "honesty," [he said] few of the insights of the play sound genuine. . . . It is difficult to ignore Miller's foggy political discussions. As the title suggests, the author thinks that he has emerged from a prelapsarian state of innocence into a state of anguished experience, but he still conceives of politics in the simple-minded language of the thirties. All of the ex-Communists in the play, for example, are merely "fighting injustice," while the friend who commits suicide is "a decent broken man that never wanted anything more but the good of the world." No wonder these men were duped when they knew so little about their own political motives. After all these terrible years, is Miller still defining Stalinism as if it were a sentiment without any reference to ideas, ideology, or power?

I turn to the text of *After the Fall* and find it hard to recognize from Mr. Brustein's excoriation. There are two ex-Communists in the play, Lou and Mickey. The hero, Quentin, has never been a Communist, but he was a close friend of Lou and Mickey and their ally in the days of the People's Front; I suppose that Mr. Brustein would include him among the Stalinists. Quentin says at one point :

> I look back at when there seemed to be a kind of plan, some duty in the sky. I had a dinner table, and a wife, a child, and the world so wonderfully threatened by injustices I was born to correct! How fine! Remember? When there were good people and bad people? And how easy it was to tell! The worst son of a bitch, if he loved Jews and Negroes and hated Hitler—he was a buddy. . . . God, when I think of what I believed, I want to hide!

Quentin's older friend, Lou, has been called before an investigating committee, has refused to testify, and has narrowly escaped losing his post on a law-school faculty. He has also been indicted for contempt of Congress, and Quentin—one of his former students, now a successful attorney—has taken his case after other former students have refused to help him. Lou makes an anguished confession:

> When I returned from Russia and published my study of Soviet law— *Breaks off*. I left out many things I saw. I . . . lied. For a good cause, I thought, but all that lasts is the lie. It's so strange to me now—I have many failings, but I have never been a liar. And I lied for the Party. Over and over, year after year. And that's why, now . . . with this [new] book of mine, I want to be true to myself. You see, it's no attack I fear, but being forced to defend my own incredible lies.

Later we learn more about Lou's study of Soviet law. He had begun by writing an honest book on the subject, but his wife, Elsie, had persuaded him to burn the manuscript and write a false book instead, for the sake of the party. At present Elsie is trying to seduce Quentin, yet she feels a sense of tenderness, a sort of half-loyalty, toward the husband she is preparing to betray. The situation becomes more complicated when a third friend, Mickey, appears; he is one of Quentin's law partners. Summoned by the investigating committee, he too has refused to testify, but he now regrets his decision.

> Lou [Mickey says], when I left the hearing room I didn't feel I had spoken. Something else had spoken, something automatic and inhuman. I asked myself what am I protecting by refusing to answer? Lou, you must let me finish! You must. The Party? But I despise the Party, and have for many years. Just like you. Yet there is something, something that closes my throat when I think of telling names. What am I defending? It's a dream, now, a dream of solidarity, but hasn't that died a long time ago? The fact is, I have no solidarity with the people I could name—excepting you. And not because we were Communists together, but because we were young together. Because we—when we talked it was like—monks probably talk, like some brotherhood opposed to all the world's injustices. It's you made my throat close, just the love whenever we saw one another. But what created that love, Lou? Wasn't it a respect for the truth, a hatred of hypocrisy? Therefore, in the name of that love, I ought to be true to myself now.

Mickey proposes to make a second appearance before the investigating committee and name all the names, including Lou's. Thus, he will satisfy his hunger for truth, and Lou will be ruined. Mickey will be ruined too—morally ruined, so the audience is led to believe—even though he keeps his law partnership and his eleven-room apartment. But Quentin feels too much guilt in himself to pass judgment on others. True, he has come to Lou's defense at a substantial risk to his own career; he will probably be voted out of the law partnership if he does not drop the case. He plans to go through with it, however, but only out of duty and with the sense of performing a disagreeable task. He has lost the feeling of human brotherhood that inspired him during the thirties. The great "we" has dissolved into separate persons all begging for love, each ready to betray the others. Quentin himself is betraying Lou by degrading him from a friend into an object of pity.

Then he hears that Lou has thrown himself under a subway train. Full of remorse for his thoughts, he makes a confession to his wife.

QUENTIN: When I saw him last week he said a dreadful thing. I tried not to hear it.

LOUISE: What?

QUENTIN: That I turned out to be the only friend he had.

LOUISE, *genuinely:* Why is that dreadful?

QUENTIN: ... It was dreadful because I was not his friend either, and he knew it. I'd have stuck it to the end but I hated the danger in it for myself, and he saw through my faithfulness; and he was not telling me what a friend I was, he was praying I would be—"Please be my friend, Quentin," is what he was saying to me, "I am drowning, throw me a rope!" Because I wanted out, to be a good American again, kosher again—and he saw it, and proved it in the joy ... the joy ... the joy I felt now that my danger had spilled out on the subway track!

I am trying to summarize the political story that is told in scattered scenes of the first act. It is not simple-minded, and neither is it appealing. One cannot identify oneself with any of these victims who grovel in their sackcloth and ashes. They are too willing to blacken their past, too much the slaves of others' opinions, too eager for a pat on the head, and above all too weak, that is, without conviction or inner resources. One thinks by immense contrast of Emerson's essay on self-reliance. "Let a man know his worth," he says, "and keep things under his feet. Let him not peep or steal, or skulk up and down with the air of a charity-boy, a bastard, or an interloper in the world which exists for him." By Emerson's standards, these prosperous lawyers afraid to leave the shelter of their eleven-room apartments are not men at all, but charity-boys and skulkers. Still, they have suffered in what Mr. Brustein calls "all these terrible years"; they are making anguished efforts to recognize the truth about themselves, and they deserve some of the pity for which they beg. Mr. Brustein is unmoved by their self-abasement. "Let them suffer and perish," he seems to say as he looks at them with the stony eyes of the Grand Inquisitor. "Let them be handed over to the secular arm for punishment. They are heretics trying to save themselves by a partial confession. They do not admit to their real crime, which was Stalinism with all it implies"—and now I can quote his actual words—with "reference to ideas, ideology, or power."

I take it that "power" is the operative word in that last phrase. "Ideas" and "ideology" can be passed over on the ground that they were less important among the Stalinists—if Mickey and Lou really belonged to that sect—than simple fears and aspirations. But "power" is a word intended to strike home. Brustein is too young to have fought the battles of the 1930s, but he has read the books, and he feels certain of knowing more than the combatants knew about their motives. For Mickey, Lou, and all the Men of Good Will, the central motive—he implies—was either greed for personal power or an abject worship of Stalin as a powerful leader.

3 ⚡ Brustein's point becomes clearer when we read a review of *The Prophet Outcast*, a study of Trotsky's last years by Isaac Deutscher, which Philip Rahv discussed at length in *The New York Review* of January 23, 1964. I think Rahv and Brustein are talking about the same thing, but Rahv is a veteran of the thirties, and his indictment is not only more detailed than Brustein's but in large part accurate and deserved.

> When [Rahv says], on August 30, 1940, an agent of Stalin's drove an ice-axe into Trotsky's skull, the news

scarcely caused a ripple of interest among intellectuals of the American Left. Except for the small group of Trotskyites—a group even then in the process of dissolution—most of them cared nothing for Trotsky and his ideas. Power is what they respected and Trotsky had none. His unique intellectual genius and his greatness as a Marxist leader and strategist of revolution was of no interest to them. . . . They had attached their loyalty to the Soviet Union and in no sense to Marxism. Insofar as they took Marxism into account at all, it meant merely what, at any given moment, Stalin said it meant.

This is what is not properly understood about the Thirties nowadays, and, by failing to stress it, most of the writing dealing with the decade is positively misleading. . . .

The Thirties was a period of radicalization, to be sure, but it was mainly a radicalization controlled and manipulated by the Stalinist party-machine. Hence one can scarcely discuss this decade without also characterizing it as a period of ideological vulgarity and opportunism, of double-think and power worship, sustained throughout by a mean and crude and unthinking kind of secular religiosity. No wonder that some of its survivors (joined, perhaps not too surprisingly, by a few ex-Trotskyites) have now turned into Cold Warriors of the "hard-nosed" variety, whose endless exposures of Communism and the Soviet state, so simplemindedly Manichaean in political content, can scarcely be said to serve any purpose except incitement to war.

Simply for the record, it would have been better for Rahv to concede that the death of Trotsky might have attracted more than a ripple of interest if Stalin's agent had murdered him in a different month and year. August 20 (not 30, probably a printer's error), 1940, was the end of a first phase in the Battle of Britain. It was the day when Winston Churchill offered his famous tribute to the Royal Air Force: "never in the field of human conflict was so much owed by so many to so few." It seemed quite possible, however, that the Luftwaffe could still destroy the RAF and make the Channel safe for the invaders. One might forgive the left-wing intellectuals for neglecting the death of a great man at a time when they feared that their whole world was dying. But Rahv is painfully right, after certain qualifications have been made, about the ideological vulgarity of what passed for Marxian criticism in the 1930s.

My principal qualification would be that his indictment does not fully apply to the first five years of the decade. They were a time of intellectual ferment when one could watch the bubbles rising as in a jug of new cider. Of course the jug itself was the Communist party, which contained and more or less controlled this working of minds. The result was that little appeared in the way of independent speculation or Marxian analyses of political crises or literary movements; there was chiefly the cider pomace that capped the jug with foam. Still, with so much ebullience and fervor, it seemed that something new must soon come forth. After 1935, however, the bubbles stopped rising. Those were the years when—to forget the cider jug—the Russians were trying to make allies in the West. They had to conceal part of the truth about their own society—a larger part, as time went on— and the writing that appeared in left-wing journals was most of it shallow or only half-sincere or based on appeals to what Marx or Lenin had said in completely different situations. Marxism had become a faith to be expounded on different levels and not a method to be applied.

Even for those last years of the decade there are qualifications to be made. I remember that among the visitors to *The New Republic* were many European Marxists, each with his own analysis of the power structure in Germany or France or Spain. Some of the analyses were exact and illuminating, but almost always in a rather limited fashion, as if made by men whose ideas were circumscribed by their loyalties. André Malraux was the only visitor from abroad who impressed me as having risen to the level of great events. Among the American Marxists who came to see me, I remember Herman Simpson with affection. He was a frail and polite old man with a sallow face, when I first met him, that had turned wood-ashen by the end of the decade. Once a month he appeared with a review written in a copperplate hand on alternate lines of ruled legal paper. The style, like the handwriting, was admirably clear, logical, and cold. Simpson had spent his youth in the movement, had known Lenin in Geneva and Trotsky in Brooklyn, had argued with both leaders, and felt no great admiration for either: Lenin was dogmatic, he said, and Trotsky was vain. As he talked, with many references to Marx and Sophocles, he conjured up a past when Marxism was a free culture concerned with everything human and not a church with archbishops to be revered.

Marxism had entered a period of inner stagnation, but so had the whole intellectual world (as opposed to the literary world, which showed vitality). There seemed to be no giants appearing to take the places of William James and Henry Adams, of Veblen and Dewey and Beard, the heroes of an earlier generation. It was not a time that encouraged original thinking, though even this rule admits to a few exceptions. In an earlier chapter on the thirties, I mentioned Lewis Mumford and Kenneth Burke, and I might also have mentioned Reinhold Niebuhr in theology, as well as the rising school of the social anthropologists. But it was hard for most of us to think abstractly in the shadow of another war. It was harder still for the English, who were more directly threatened. On a visit to London in 1937, "How can we start new projects," I heard writers complaining, "when we know there won't be time to finish them?" Even here we were learning to think in terms not of ultimate goals, but of army divisions, tanks, planes, factories, and military alliances.

That is the element of truth in Rahv's contention that the "intellectuals of the American Left" respected nothing but power, and that the period was one "of double-think and power worship, sustained throughout by a mean and crude and unthinking kind of secular religiosity." Communism was indeed a religion, but I wouldn't call it secular, considering its theocratic side—especially under Stalin—and neither would I call it mean in its vision of the future; rather, it was tragically mistaken. But when Rahv condemns the "intellectuals of the American Left," he includes a great majority among them who were non-Communists and whose religion, if any, was a sort of humanism strengthened and given a sense of urgency by their hopes for mankind, then later by their fears. The war had already begun for them—in China, in Ethiopia, in Spain—and the Communists seemed to be fighting on their side, with more discipline and farsightedness than other allies; therefore they listened with respect—often blind respect—to what the Communists were saying.

They did not desire power for themselves, or at least they desired it, as a group, no more than did average Americans. What most of them hoped to achieve in their personal careers was *status*, defined as a position of honor that does not involve public responsibilities. Many of the writers among them had a special distrust for political power, which does involve such responsibilities and which, if it was thrust upon them, would destroy their freedom as writers. While fighting for the good cause they preferred to serve as guerrillas or "partisans," to use the Russian word, or even as privates in the ranks, but not as officers.

Did they have too much respect for the power of great statesmen, notably Stalin, as Rahv implies? After a long period of hesitation, many of them came to respect and even worship another statesman, Roosevelt. Many worked for Henry Luce, who was, at the time, the great statesman of journalism, but only a few became his faithful henchmen. More of his brilliant editors and correspondents were waiting for the day when they could tell what they thought was the truth about *Time* in a corrosive novel. And Stalin? Very few intellectuals on the left regarded him as a sympathetic figure. Even when they refused to acknowledge his crimes, as most of them refused, they felt that his ideas were undistinguished, that his prose was mechanical (though it showed a genius for expressing the ominous in terms of the commonplace), and that his taste in art was worse than General Grant's. Still, he commanded the Red Army, which, for the intellectuals already at war, was a power to be respected. Other powers were the French Army, which had not yet revealed its weakness, the British Navy, and the productive capacity of the United States. But the greatest single power, by 1937, was Hitler's Wehrmacht, which, unless the others united against it, would defeat them one at a time—or, as the German exiles kept warning us, would eat the world like an artichoke, leaf by leaf.

4✍ Meanwhile another war was raging in the intellectual world. It was fought mostly with words—in America, I mean—but it left real wounds that festered for years; I am not sure that all of them have healed. What added to the bitterness was that neither side could understand the other, partly because each insisted on describing and condemning the other by the wrong name. One faction was called the Trotskyites, a form of the word that their enemies preferred to Trotskyists because the "ites" seemed to identify them as a tribe to be smitten, like the Jebusites and the Amalekites. The other was called the Stalinists—not "ites" for some reason, possibly because Stalinists was a better word to hiss. Both names when used in a broad sense were symbols of incomprehension.

The actual Trotskyites were a small group, as Rahv says, and they were always dividing into smaller groups. On the other hand, they had a high average level of intelligence, they were inspired by a brilliant leader, and their influence in the intellectual world was out of proportion with their numbers. The actual Stalinists—if we use the word in a narrow sense—were hardly more numerous than the Trotskyites. Nobody in this country worshiped Stalin in the fashion that not a few worshiped Trotsky. But the American officials of the Communist party, from the general secretary down to the unit organizers, had discovered that they could not rise in the hierarchy unless they invoked Stalin's name in speeches, followed his announced policies to the letter, and even—if they held important posts—guessed what Stalin would say before he had spoken. Those *apparatchiks* were the real Stalinists, and of course they exerted a much wider influence than the Trotskyites, through their connections with Moscow and their control of the party machinery.

In a broader sense, the term Stalinist might be applied to everyone who, in Stalin's time, regarded himself as a Communist subject to party discipline. That would include every party member in the years from 1928 to 1935, when the American Communists were like a preaching order that had lately purged itself of heretics. It might also include most of those who remained faithful to the party after 1939, in spite of the Stalin-Hitler pact. In the intervening years, however—those of the People's Front—the party was like an evangelical church, eager to accept anyone who professed faith in its doctrines. Many of the new converts had no taste for discipline. Many others were innocent people who "never wanted anything more but the good of the world," as Arthur Miller's hero says of his dead friend, and it merely confuses the issue to call them Stalinists. But the term is even more confusing when applied—as it often was in those days—to the much broader group composed of liberals who believed in the People's Front as a grand alliance that would include Stalin and everyone else opposed to Hitler. As for the term Trotskyite in the sweeping sense that was favored by Communists in the late 1930s, it was not so much a name as an exorcism.

I find myself groping for words in the effort to tell the truth about an old quarrel without reopening wounds and without offering apologies or recriminations. What makes the writing more painful is that I had taken one side of the quarrel, that I must have given some of the wounds, and that I suffered many. Today it seems to me that I could neither understand the other side, in those times, nor succeed in making myself understood; no one was willing to listen. I suggest that the real issues would become clearer if now, belatedly, we found better names for the two factions. They were not divided by the leaders that one or the other admired, but rather by the leaders that one or the other hated, feared, and opposed to the last breath. As broad factions in the intellectual world, they were not Trotskyites and Stalinists, but anti-Stalinists and anti-Hitlerites.

For one faction, Stalin was the man who had betrayed the revolution. He was the embodiment of brutal tyranny and of other bad things as well: slyness, vindictiveness, intrigue, the bureaucratic state, and personal mediocrity. His allies were either dupes or careerists greedy for power. His policies had led to the defeat of the Chinese workers in 1927, of the German workers in 1933, and would inevitably lead to the defeat of the workers in Spain, no matter which side won the civil war. Therefore the great immediate task was to expose Stalin's crimes and falsehoods, to deprive him of allies, to fight against his policies without exception, and thus to restore the purity of the revolutionary dream (or alternatively, for those who were not revolutionists, to save this republic from its most dangerous enemy). Every other problem in the world was secondary to that of defeating Stalinism.

For the other faction, Stalin was not important as a person or a set of doctrines, but chiefly as the head of the Russian state and the Communist party. The anti-Hitlerites were divided in their feelings about the party, with some moving toward it in a burst of enthusiasm, others standing aloof, and still others—including many or most of those who had been fellow travelers in 1933—slowly moving away. All members of the faction were convinced, however, that Russia was on their side—on *our* side—in the struggle against Hitler. The central problem for them was to keep Russia there while promoting a grand alliance of all the democratic parties and countries. In their devotion to that purpose, they could not understand why the anti-Stalinists insisted on denouncing and disrupting the alliance—to the sole profit of Hitler, so they felt. Meanwhile the other faction sincerely believed that the anti-Hitlerites were serving as cat's-paws for Stalin. It was a double failure in understanding that led to bitter personal quarrels; indeed, I cannot remember a time when so many friendships were broken. Words then spoken in anger might also help to explain that persistent sense of guilt.

And who was right in the mortal argument?

In one sense both sides were right, by virtue of what they opposed. In another sense both were wrong, by virtue of what one or another failed to see. The anti-Hitlerites, for their part, displayed several types of blindness about Stalin's real purposes, as about the tyranny and terror he had imposed on Russia. It is always tempting to believe the best about one's allies, or at least to conceal their crimes from oneself in order to maintain a precarious sincerity when making public statements. That explains why many of the anti-Hitlerites adopted a tone of bluster in their political writing, as if they were trying to shout down their private questions. They had no one who spoke as candidly about political subjects as George Orwell on the other side, or as his nearest American analogue, Dwight Macdonald.

The anti-Stalinists, however, fell into a different type of error. They were not tempted to form an alliance with Hitler or to conceal his crimes, but, with their eyes fixed on another danger, they forgot that he was bent on conquering Europe and the world. "After Spain it will be Austria," I said to one of them in 1937. "That may be true enough," he answered, "but Hitler would never have come to power except for Stalin's blunders in 1932." He explained the blunders at length and was right about them; but I remembered that in 1932 his friends had talked less about the German crisis than about Stalin's blunders in China, in 1927. It seemed to me that they lived in the past, like defeated generals forever planning strategies that might have won the last war instead of trying to defeat the present enemy.

I was sharp at discerning other people's errors in those days, and slower in recognizing my own. But even after forty years, and even while trying to be completely fair about the time, I still cannot believe that the errors were equally distributed on the two sides, that is, as regards the choice of whom to oppose.

Stalin was evil, Hitler was evil, and there will be no end to the arguments about which was worse. "Stalin was to blame for everything," a writer said to me some years ago. She and I had been on opposite sides in the late 1930s, but now I could sympathize with what she said. Stalin was the enemy of ideals. Besides condemning millions on millions to death, in the famine of 1932–33 and the later purges, he betrayed the dream of those other millions who had died for the revolution in Russia, China, Germany, and Spain. There was something hypocritical in the double position he occupied, as leader of a movement aimed at humanizing the world and as head of the Russian state. While pretending to advance the movement, he clung to the state as his true property. He was like an avaricious Norman peasant guarding his land, cruel to his family, attacking by force or fraud anyone who threatened his ownership, and eager to degrade his neighbors (that is, the Communists of other countries) into spies or constables. Hitler was not that sort of hypocrite. Representing evil absolute and unashamed, he played the part of Satan, not of the vindictive but wily and cautious Beelzebub. But he was also more powerful than the other tyrant and offered a more immediate threat to the world. It would have been impossible for the West to have overthrown both tyrants at once. After forty years I am still convinced—as Winston Churchill was at the time—that the only sound policy was to check Hitler by any possible means and with the greatest possible number of allies, including Beelzebub.

# X A PERSONAL RECORD

After the preceding chapter, something is needed in the way of personal narrative to explain the subjects and sequence of the chapters that follow.

I had been less surprised than others by the Hitler-Stalin pact of August 1939. During the spring of that year there had been many indications that Russian policy was about to change once again, this time to the disadvantage of the West. I had noted already that the Russians seldom changed their policies just a little; more often they made an about-face (though without ever breaking ranks). Something drastic was to be expected, but still I was shocked by the pact with Hitler and shocked once more by the events that followed it. In the mythology of the 1930s there had been a "good" country and a "bad" country; now the two had linked arms. Hitler invaded Poland, then Stalin invaded Poland. Stalin invaded Finland, then a few months later Hitler invaded Denmark and Norway (with Stalin providing a tankerload of oil for the expedition). Those events had their repercussions in New York, where dismay, dissension, and that private sense of guilt were spreading on the literary left; it was the time of resignations. I too wanted to resign from everything, but quietly, without offering public indictments or apologies. I did, however, write many private letters in the effort to explain how I felt. From the longest, which was to Edmund Wilson, I quote the closing paragraphs.[1]

"As for my own attitude toward Russia, communism, and all the etceteras," I said, "it is a little hard to define as of February 4, 1940. We have a little time now for thinking, and I don't want to rush into any position that I shall have to desert in a few months. I am profoundly disturbed by what has happened in the Soviet Union—as who isn't? I think that the Communists here are tied to the apron strings of Russian foreign policy. They have ceased to play the vitalizing part in the American labor movement that they played in 1937, and they are at this moment willing to destroy the united-front organizations they founded rather than lose control of them. You think that I should now frankly discard my illusions—but granted for the sake of argument that they are illusions, what is the good of discarding them if I have to adopt another set of illusions to the effect that Krivitsky, for example, is really a sterling character and Ben Stolberg a pure-hearted defender of labor unions?"

Krivitsky was a high official of the Russian secret service who had defected to the West and had written his memoirs, a book that I reviewed unfavorably in *The New Republic*. Ben Stolberg was a witty labor journalist, formerly a radical, who later attacked labor unions and the New Deal. My letter to Wilson continued with other rhetorical questions. "And must I

---

1. I was answering a severe letter from Wilson, in which he had accused me of having "given hostages to the Stalinists in some terrible incomprehensible way." See his *Letters on Literature and Politics*, pp. 357–58.

believe," it asked, "that Communists I saw working hard and sacrificing themselves are really, without a single exception, unprincipled careerists?

"What I believe as of February 4 is that the situation makes necessary a much more fundamental change in attitude than simply deciding that what used to be white is now black and vice versa. *Why* did the Russian revolution get into its present situation? Is it Stalinism or Leninism or Marxism that is essentially at fault? What is the essential element that was left out of all those directions for making a better society? Was it democracy that was omitted? That seems to me a rather simple-minded answer—since it involves the further question why democracy had to be omitted—and I am inclined to look for something else. The Marxist theories are based on history and economics, among the social studies. Would anthropology give us a clue to their misreading of the human animal? What are the faults of communism as a religion? That it has become a religion in fact, there isn't much doubt, considering that all those heresies and inquisitions and excommunications remind one of nothing so much as the history of the Christian church during the first three centuries.

"I am left standing pretty much alone, in the air, unsupported, a situation that is much more uncomfortable for me than it would be for you, since my normal instinct is toward cooperation. For the moment I want to get out of every God damned thing. These quarrels leave me with a sense of having touched something unclean. They remind me of a night a dozen years ago when I went on a bat with a lot of noisy and lecherous people I thoroughly despised, while realizing that I was one of them. We stayed a long time in a Harlem speakeasy, down in a cellar. When I came up the stairs at last, I saw the doorman standing in the light of morning with his hands the color of cold ashes, and that is how I felt I was inside. Sometimes I feel a little like that today. Getting involved in these feuds and vendettas of the intelligentsia is like being an unwilling participant in a Harlem orgy.

"It makes me wonder what the world would be like if it were ruled by the intellectuals. Some of them we know are admirable people, humble and conscientious, but intellectuals in the mass are not like that. A world run by them would be a very unpleasant place, considering all the naked egos that would be continually wounding and getting wounded, all the gossip, the spies at cocktail parties, the informers, the careerists, the turncoats. Remember too that the character assassinations now so much in vogue (and even you are succumbing to the fashion, with your open letters to the *NR*) are nothing less than symbolic murders. They would be real murders if the intellectuals controlled the state apparatus. Maybe that is part of the trouble in Russia.

"(Note that nothing I said about the intellectuals is to be construed as an attack on the *intelligence,* which remains our best and almost our only tool for making this country a better place to live in. I am thinking about the customs and folkways of the intellectuals as a class—which compare pretty unfavorably with the folkways of coal miners and dairy farmers.)

"Meanwhile I can't forget that all this business started with high purposes and dreams of a better society. Not many people, intellectuals or workers, go into the radical movement to make a career for themselves—some do, I suppose, but they are damned fools because there are much brighter and easier careers to be found elsewhere. No, the best of the radicals start out with a willingness to sacrifice themselves—and even when they betray their ideals I tend to forgive them in their bastardy. Once I wrote in a poem addressed to the people of tomorrow:

> *Think back on us, the martyrs and the cowards,*
> *the traitors even, swept by the same flood*
> *of passion toward the morning that is yours:*
> *O children born from, nourished with our blood.*

"Well, we're all in a pretty pickle now, and I wonder how it happened. As a sequel to your present book describing the evolution of an idea to the moment of Lenin's arrival in the Finland Station, you ought to write another describing the devolution of an idea from Marx to *The New Leader* and from Lenin to the latest editorial in *Pravda* on exterminating the Finnish bandits."

That letter to Edmund Wilson was a statement, as accurate as I could make it, of my bruised feelings in the winter of 1940. I was appalled by the march of Hitler's armies, disheartened by the short-visioned cynicism of Russian policy, and revolted by the bickering of the American left. I wanted to get out of "the movement," as it was vaguely called, and take no further part in public arguments until I had made peace with my inner convictions. I wanted to think things out, but for this there was to be little time. By the middle of June France had fallen, the country I loved next to my own, and Hitler was in command of Western Europe. I was certain by then that the United States would have to enter the war—the sooner the better if anything was to be salvaged—and this belief brought me into open conflict with the Communists, who were then shouting for peace at any price: "The Yanks aren't coming." Soon I was being excoriated in *The Daily Worker* and caricatured in *The New Masses* (as a soldier with a whisky flask in his hip pocket and a chamberpot on his head, offering a fascist salute to J. P. Morgan), and meanwhile I was still under fire from the Trotskyites and the Red-hunters. It was a new experience to be attacked simultaneously as a lackey of capitalism and a tool of Stalin. Cannonaded from the left, the right, and the center, "Storm'd at with shot and shell," I felt like a retreating soldier who had lost his weapons.

Weapons I never had except my typewriter, and I couldn't use it for self-defense without involving *The New Republic* in my personal difficulties. That was something I did not propose to do. Moreover, in the winter of 1940–41 there was a crisis at *The New Republic* that changed my situation there. After the crisis Bruce Bliven was in charge of the paper, Edmund Wilson had severed connections with it, and George Soule (that friendly, intelligent, unaggressive man) and I had been given writing assignments without editorial responsibility. Ruminating at home in the country, I became more and more disturbed by the possible effects that war, when it surely came, would have on a still divided country. I wrote long letters on the subject to Archibald MacLeish and others close to the President. A week before Pearl Harbor MacLeish had me come to Washington and join his newly formed government agency, the Office of Facts and Figures.

That was to be an unhappy and enlightening experience. The OFF—sad acronym—was a short-lived agency soon to be absorbed into the Office of War Information. Staffed with writers and editors, all eager to play a part in the war effort, it was regarded by congressmen as a haven for impractical people with dangerous opinions. The Dies Committee went to work on it. Since I had once permitted my name to be used on the letterheads of a great many radical organizations, I was chosen from the staff as the most vulnerable target. For two months or more I was presented in almost every issue of *The Congressional Record* as a horrible example; then I resigned in order to stop the attacks and let the OFF get on with its work. That ended the worst two years of my life, and it also ended my direct participation in the war against Hitler, since I was by then too middle-aged and deaf for the armed services.

By the first of April I was back in Connecticut, writing book reviews for *The New Republic* and spading up my garden. I made a number of resolutions between spadefuls of cold brown earth. Not to join anything in the future. Not to write statements. Not to sign statements written by others. Not to let my name appear on letterheads. Not to attend meetings, much less take the chair as I had often done in the past. "Not," I grunted, stepping hard on the spade. "Not...Not." I remembered something that Whittaker Chambers had said to me in 1940: "The counter-revolutionary purge is still to come." After the months in Washington I was ready to believe him on that point. Vaguely I foresaw the inquisitions of the McCarthy years and was preparing to survive them in obscurity, as regards political issues, but with self-respect, not beating my breast or turning informer. I felt politically amputated, emasculated, but then I had never been happy among politicians. Now, with a sense of release and opportunity, I could get back to my proper field of interest.

That field was and had always been the contemporary history of American letters, though I also liked to trace lines of descent by making incursions into the literary past. It was not at all a crowded field at the time. In the academic world Melville, Hawthorne, and Whitman showed signs of becoming growth industries, but contemporary writing was still a disputed area in which discoveries could be made. It was the time when the New Critics were coming forward with their "close readings" of masterpieces. While admiring their acute interpretations, I was distressed by their ignorance of the writing profession. They insisted on brushing aside everything social, economic, historical, or biographical, including the hopes and plans of the author. I too believed that the work itself should be the focus of the critic's attention, but I was also deeply interested in authors: how they got started, how they kept going, how they pictured themselves, and the myths that they embodied in their work. I was interested in their social backgrounds and in the question of whom they were thinking about when they said "we." I liked to speculate on the relation between an author and his audience. Perhaps from the 1930s, I had retained the stubborn belief that literature, while having it own laws, is also part of history.

Being a literary historian is a rewarding but not a lucrative profession. After 1948 I supplemented my income by doing a good deal of knockabout teaching and lecturing at various universities, but never for more than a quarter or at most a semester in a given year. Allen Tate and I used to joke about our playing the same role as wandering scholars in the Middle Ages. More of my time, though, was spent at home in the country, writing, reading, and gardening. I was able to write at some length about individual authors and groups of authors, among them Faulkner, Fitzgerald, Hemingway, Hawthorne, Whitman, the American Naturalists and the Lost Generation. I wrote about changes in the audience and in the language, about fashions in criticism, and at one time I put together "A Natural History of the American Writer." Those studies and many more have appeared in previous books.

The present volume has been concerned with other aspects of the literary life. Much of it, as I said in the Foreword, has dealt with the nature of literary generations, or age groups, and has described some of the conflicts that arise when each new group asserts its own standards of the good life and good writing. Another theme has been the more or less deliberate refusal of some gifted writers to pay the price they thought was demanded for becoming famous (as note what Robert M. Coates had to say about his friends Hemingway and Thurber). The chapters that follow will deal with such additional topics as how writers write, particularly if they write fiction, and why most of them write best when telling stories, rather than when taking snapshots, parading their egos, or constructing models of spatial architecture. A chapter on Faulkner ends by discussing the limitations of meta-Freudian criticism, with its obsessive search for Oedipal conflicts. Another, on Conrad Aiken, is partly concerned with Transcendentalism as a surviving habit of mind in New England writing. After a digression on the 1960s and the Love Generation, the book ends with some observations on ethics in the arts and the special code that good writers still try to follow.

The chapter called "Sir: I Have the Honor," printed just after this personal interlude, requires a further introduction. In 1949 I was elected to the National Institute of Arts and Letters. By accepting membership I was breaking my own rule "Not to join anything," but the Institute was nonpolitical and I thought it helped to maintain standards in the arts. Later I was president of the Institute for six years and still later I was elected to the Academy, which serves it as a sort of upper house or council of elders. I began digging into the files of both organizations, which, as I learned, were a seldom-used source of information about the literary life and the climate of opinion from 1900 down to yesterday. In particular they told the story of a battle that raged in the Academy during the year 1940 while Hitler was overrunning western Europe. The American battle had its comic side, but also had serious implications, since it ended with a defeat for the genteel tradition in its last stronghold. There would never again be a secretary of the Academy, or of any other literary group, who announced his election in a letter to himself beginning "Sir: I have the honor."

# XI "SIR:
# I HAVE
# THE HONOR"

1 ✍ The National Institute of Arts and Letters was founded
in 1898, toward the end of what then appeared to be a brilliant
period in American culture. There were famous Americans in all
the arts, most of them trained in Europe, and it was felt that they
should have an organization of their own, something that would
correspond to the Institut de France. The original suggestion came
from the American Social Science Association, which named a
committee to draw up a constitution for the new body and carefully select its members. When the Institute held its first meeting,
in February 1899, there were a hundred and fifty of these, in
the three departments of Art, Literature, and Music. Some
esteemed figures had been overlooked, however, and it was soon
decided to fix the limit of membership at two hundred and fifty,
where it has remained.

By then the Institute was a corporate body with its own

president, the familiar essayist Charles Dudley Warner (until he died in 1900 and was succeeded by William Dean Howells). The corporate body has kept its records from the beginning, and they are a source that has been neglected by literary historians. They are rich in material that casts light on forgotten and well-remembered figures, on changing standards of literary conduct, and on arguments that sometimes became wars of faith and continued till the death of the last survivor.[1]

One of the first arguments was occasioned by the size of the Institute: wasn't it too large to confer enough dignity on its individual members? "Dignity" was a great word in those days of gray-bearded, frock-coated worthies. It was felt—felt by whom? first by Edmund Clarence Stedman, the stockbroker poet, then by the composer Edward MacDowell, by Robert Underwood Johnson, assistant editor of the dignified *Century* magazine, and by a number of others—that there should be a smaller and more exalted body, this time on the model of the French Academy. Its object would be "to give greater definiteness to the work of the Institute in protecting and furthering the interests of literature and the fine arts"—that was the orotund phrase.

The proposal was submitted to the annual meeting of the Institute in January 1904. At another meeting three months later, it was formally accepted, together with a scheme for choosing members devised by Johnson, who was a master and slave of protocol. The first seven members of the Academy were to be elected by the Institute, each of whose members would cast a secret ballot. Those seven were to elect eight more, the fifteen were to elect five, and the twenty were to elect ten, all chosen from the membership of the Institute. The intention was to stop after choosing thirty academicians, on the principle that the fewer they were, the greater honor devolved on each of them, but soon a difficulty came to light. Thirty members, most of them

---

1. After this account of the Academy and Institute was published, Geoffrey T. Hellman wrote a long and entertaining article for *The New Yorker* ("Some Splendid and Admirable People," February 23, 1976) based largely on those records. "A good job," I said to myself. But the records still contain an unexplored wealth of material.

hoary and some of them living abroad, were not enough to supply a quorum at meetings. But they could ballot by mail, and in 1907–08 they elected twenty additional members, bringing the Academy to its permanent limit of fifty.

That series of choices established a sort of pecking order in literature and the fine arts. Especially the first list of seven academicians was revealing. They were, in order of votes received, William Dean Howells, Augustus Saint-Gaudens, Edmund Clarence Stedman, John La Farge, Mark Twain, John Hay, and Edward MacDowell. It was the judgment of the establishment, less flagrantly mistaken than a popular judgment would have been in 1904, but different from that of posterity. Howells' position as dean of American letters was then unquestioned. Stedman's appearance in third place seems more surprising, but he was then immensely popular with his colleagues. They were a little less confident about Mark Twain—after all, he was a humorist—and they ranked him just above John Hay, who was secretary of state and had collaborated in writing the standard life of Lincoln.

Among the well-remembered names on the second list (again in order of votes received) were those of Henry James (8), Henry Adams (10), and Theodore Roosevelt (14). On the final list of twenty—or rather of twenty-five, since the places of five defunct members had to be filled—the second name was that of the dignified Robert Underwood Johnson (32). He stood well above Julia Ward Howe (41), the only woman elected—but she was eighty-nine years old, not so much a woman as a national institution—and Woodrow Wilson (42). Johnson was secretary of the Institute, and now he was made permanent secretary of the Academy. With his high sense of protocol, he wrote a letter to himself formally announcing the new secretaryship— "Sir: I have the honor to inform you"—and then another letter to himself in which the office was accepted by "Very respectfully yours, Robert Underwood Johnson."

Pompous as he was, even to himself, and utterly conventional as a poet, Johnson still made a useful secretary. He was devoted body and soul to the well-being of the Institute—no, it must never open its doors to rebel poets or cubist painters—and the growth in dignity of the Academy. One of his first efforts was to obtain congressional charters for both organizations. He lobbied in Washington, he wrote hundreds of letters—not to mention articles and pamphlets—and eventually he pushed both bills through Congress against some opposition and more indifference. The Institute was chartered in 1913, during the last days of the Taft administration, and the Academy in 1916 under Wilson, who was still one of its members. Meanwhile Johnson was trying to procure endowments for both the chartered bodies, and he had already found a possible benefactor in Archer M. Huntington.

Huntington had been elected to the Institute in 1911 as an authority on Spanish literature, though he was also a philanthropist, the stepson and principal legatee of a railroad magnate, Collis P. Huntington. In 1915 he gave the Academy a plot of land —in the center for the arts that he dreamed of establishing on Washington Heights—as well as a contribution to the building fund. In 1919 he was "elevated to the Academy," in the phrase of the time. His benefactions increased and soon McKim, Mead and White could be commissioned to design a stately building. Its cornerstone was laid with a silver trowel by Marshal Foch of the French Academy. Johnson had written a sonnet, "The Temple," which he read to the distinguished guests. It proclaimed that the Academy building must be something more than a house—

> No, 'tis a temple—where the mind may kneel
> And worship Beauty changeless and divine;
> Where the sage Past may consecrate the stole
> Of Truth's new priest, the Future; where the peal
> Of organ voices down the human line
> Shall sound the diapason of the soul.

To that high organ peal the guests dispersed. Old Marshal Foch, in a fit of absentmindedness, limped off with the silver trowel in his hip pocket.

When Johnson's temple, Venetian Renaissance style, was opened with another ceremony in 1923, it seemed that the Institute and the Academy might grow old together in wealth and honor. Instead they were weakened by a struggle, both internal

and external, that was to end with the disappearance of a generation and the final defeat of gentility in American arts and letters.
The struggle was one that could hardly have been avoided. Both
the Institute and the Academy had been founded by the genteel
establishment, which had chosen as its representatives men in their
sixties or older. By exception Hamlin Garland, a repentant idol-
smasher, was in his early fifties. I forget in which volume of his
interminable memoirs, he describes the Institute dinner in January 1902, with Howells in the president's chair.

"He looked old and sad that night," Garland says, "tragically sad it seemed to me, so instant in humor he had been
through all the years of our acquaintance. Stedman also looked
his age. In truth nearly every man present was gray-haired.
Hopkinson Smith was almost white—so was Cable; only Brander
Matthews remained much the same as when I first saw him.
Edward MacDowell and I were the youngest men in the room
and we were not so very young even by contrast. 'I cannot claim
to be one of the younger writers any longer,' I said to him, and
with a chuckle he replied, 'Nor I to being a promising young
composer.' "

Howells, Stedman, and the others had first come forward
during the 1860s or 1870s; even Garland and MacDowell were
men of the 1880s. Normally their places would have been taken
by the new generation of the 1890s, but this had been wiped out
by one of those cataclysms that sometimes take place in a culture.
Almost all the promising new men died at an early age—Stephen
Crane, Frank Norris, and Trumbull Stickney among many others
—and for some years they had very few talented successors. The
gap between literary generations was becoming an abyss. When
the successors finally appeared after 1912, most of them were so
objectionable by genteel standards that the Institute ignored them.
There were a few exceptions such as E. A. Robinson, elected to
membership in 1908 after President Theodore Roosevelt had
discovered his work, and Robert Frost, elected in 1916 when he
already showed signs of becoming a classic, and Edgar Lee
Masters, elected two years later, but almost all the other new
members were either aged or conventional, or both. The Academy

for its part had fallen into the dignified habit of electing public figures (that is, if they had published books and were already members of the Institute). Among the academicians of 1920 were two senators, a former secretary of state, five ministers or ambassadors, the presidents of Harvard, Yale, and Columbia, and the President of the United States.

Fortunately not all the old codgers in both organizations—not even a majority—were old fogeys too, but the fogeys (or stalwarts) were more vociferous than the liberals (or locofocos). They were loudest, perhaps, in objecting to the election of women, of whom there had been not one in the Institute since the death of Julia Ward Howe in 1910. Every year the locofocos suggested to the Council, or governing body, that women's names be placed on the ballot; every year the stalwarts raised their voices and the motion was tabled. The stalwarts never surrendered, but they were dying off like the French Guard at Waterloo, and finally the motion carried. In 1926 Margaret Deland, Mary Wilkins Freeman, Agnes Repplier, and Edith Wharton entered the Institute together, and in 1930, after further argument, Mrs. Wharton was elected to the Academy.

In December of the same year there was another engagement, this time reported widely in the press. The Nobel Prize for Literature had just been awarded to Sinclair Lewis, the first American to receive the honor. Some of the stalwarts detested his work. Speaking as a member of the American Academy, Henry Van Dyke told the world and the Swedish Academy that an award to a man who had scoffed so much at American institutions was an insult to our country. Lewis had an international audience for his reply, which he made in Stockholm, in the course of a lively address accepting the prize. After poking fun at Van Dyke as a writer "chiefly known for his pleasant little essays on the joys of fishing," Lewis turned his attention to the Academy and condemned it for not electing the living giants of American literature. "It does not represent literary America of today—it represents only Henry Wadsworth Longfellow," he said. The stalwarts in the Academy never quite recovered from Lewis's attack.

Although our friend Mr. Johnson had served on the

liberal side in the controversy about admitting women, that seems to have been his only defection from the stalwarts. Devoted as he was to Beauty changeless and divine, he abhorred any novel —and still more, any poem—in which there was even a faint smell of blood, sweat, or imagism. He thought he detected such a smell in *John Brown's Body,* and in 1929 he had fought hard and vainly to keep its author out of the Institute. But Stephen Vincent Benét was almost admirable in his eyes compared with others who were soon assaulting the citadel. In 1933 Johnson wrote to his brother-in-arms Harrison S. Morris, a minor poet and industrialist who flourished in Philadelphia, "Dear Harrison me boy: I have just discovered that Carl Sandborg"—Johnson disdained to spell the name correctly—"is proposed for the Institute. Ye Gods! What a quartet—Eliot, Jeffers, Sandborg and M——!" "M——" was H. L. Mencken, and Johnson couldn't bring himself even to speak his name. The letter continues: "Surely the radicals will soon have control. I think the only thing for me to do is to resign.

"I have written more than 40 letters against H. L. M., but my fight for the old standards is a lone one so far. I can not keep it up and I shall not be able to go to the Inst. Meeting. Three physicians have told me that the one thing I *must* avoid is excitement, including indignation. So my life is at stake and I need what is left of it for other work."

Sandburg was elected to the Institute that year, in spite of his being opposed by still other stalwarts. Two years later Sinclair Lewis joined the Institute, to everyone's astonishment. He had been elected in the 1920s, years before making his Nobel Prize address, but had politely declined membership. Now the Council invited him to reconsider his refusal, and Lewis consented; in fact he became a fairly active member, speaking picturesquely at dinner meetings against candidates he regarded as timid or genteel. In 1936 he was nominated for the Academy, but narrowly failed of election. In 1937 he was nominated again, and this time he was almost certain to be voted in. Johnson, then eighty-three years old, fought a last battle to keep him out. He offered an amendment to the by-laws of the Academy providing that any candidate with ten or more votes against him would be ineligible for membership. There was no doubt, Johnson believed, that ten stalwarts would blackball Lewis.

The directors of the Academy considered his proposal at a meeting on October 8. Nobody favored it, and the motion was laid on the table—"so as not to hurt the old man," one of the directors explained. Johnson died six days later, too soon to read the announcement of Lewis's election. Johnson's place in the Academy, where he had succeeded John Hay in Chair 6, would next be occupied by Stephen Vincent Benét.

The ranks of the stalwarts were thinning and still the struggle continued. By this time, however, the more conservative members of the Academy had decided that the Institute was a lost territory already controlled by the rabble and that they might as well surrender it. Since the Academy had most of Archer Huntington's endowment, why not cut it loose from the Institute? Why not maintain it as a dignified public organization with members chosen by itself from the most respected leaders of American culture? Those questions led to a new battle, in this case fought over the by-laws of the Academy. It was to last for more than a year, and it led to the complete victory of the liberals in both organizations.

2 ⬧ Nicholas Murray Butler, then president of the Academy (as well as of Columbia University), presided at a meeting of the directors on October 13, 1939. Most of the directors were conservative, and one of them was Huntington himself. According to the account that Butler gave afterward to Walter Damrosch, his principal opponent, there was not much business to transact and conversation languished. Huntington thereupon volunteered the opinion that the Academy should have absolute power to choose its own members, whether or not they were already members of the Institute. Butler concurred, as did most of the other directors.

Of course Huntington's opinion was not casual, nor was it merely "volunteered." His benefactions had been based on a vision of the Academy as a body whose members should enjoy the widest popular esteem. Like the Académie Française, he believed, it should include not only men of literary distinction but also statesmen, prelates, and generals—Black Jack Pershing, to give a specific example. Wasn't he the American counterpart of those French academicians Marshals Joffre and Foch? Not highly endowed with literary talents, Pershing would never be elected to the Institute—but if the Academy had absolute power to choose its own members, who would vote Pershing down?

At this particular meeting, someone remarked that the power could be assumed by a simple change in the Academy's by-laws. Nothing was needed except the striking out of Article IV, Section 2, a paragraph that read:

> Only members of the National Institute of Arts and Letters shall be eligible for election to the Academy.

Someone else remarked that the present by-laws permitted the directors themselves to adopt such an amendment, after duly warning the membership and after a delay of thirty days. He offered a resolution to that effect. Judge Robert Grant of Boston, a respected but not very exciting novelist, spoke against the proposed amendment. After reminding his fellow directors that the Academy had been created by the Institute, he told them that extending the choice of members to persons outside the Institute might destroy the existing harmony between the two bodies. Huntington said that freedom of choosing its own members was essential "for the dignity of the Academy," and let it be understood that, if the amendment failed of passage, he would resign and make no further benefactions to the Academy or the Institute, "now or hereafter." The resolution passed after some discussion, with only Judge Grant voting against it. A few days later all the members of the Academy—there were forty-five at the time—were informed by mail of the proposed amendment.

Walter Damrosch, the conductor and composer, was one of the forty-five, and he was also president of the Institute. He was determined to combat any measure that would separate the two bodies. Writing urgently to the other academicians, he asked them to express their opposition to the amendment. Letters and telegrams passed back and forth, an enormous sheaf of them, and it soon became apparent that a majority of the members supported Damrosch and Grant, not Butler and Huntington. Nevertheless, a majority of the directors persisted in their intention of adopting the amendment. There was a moment when it seemed possible that a compromise would be reached. Having finally consented to meeting with Damrosch and Arthur Train, as representatives of the Institute, Butler proposed that the Academy should confine itself to electing Institute members except in the case of one new member each year (would the first exception be Black Jack Pershing?). It transpired that Huntington would be satisfied with this arrangement if it was approved by the Council of the Institute, which would have to make a parallel change in its by-laws. Such a change was indeed brought forward at a meeting of the Council in January 1940, but it was unanimously voted down, and the battle resumed in all its polite fury.

One cannot read the records of the Academy for the winter and spring of 1940 without a feeling of excitement. There was a war in Europe, but great things were also at stake in the American world of the arts, or so it seemed to the insurgents. The great things included the recognition of new forces, the independence of the Academy, its survival as a body representing the arts, and even its mere survival, since Huntington had been paying its bills. Huntington was a man of vision, but uncommunicative and lacking in tact. He seems to have felt that the Institute could be dominated and dismissed, much in the fashion that his stepfather, the Southern Pacific magnate, had treated the California state assembly. Once he offered to give the Institute a million dollars and a fine building of its own if it would separate itself from the Academy. The offer was refused, much to the indignation of Nicholas Murray Butler, who had a deep respect for wealth. Butler made things worse by talking down to his colleagues as if they were recalcitrant members of his Columbia faculty. The insurgents also respected wealth, but they clung to their principles. Some of them hoped to achieve peace by flattery, as Charles Dana Gibson, a blunt man, revealed at a meeting on January 17:

"You know what endowments mean," Gibson said. "You know what Butler means. We have all accepted a great deal. It has been very useful to have these material things. We don't know what happens to a man when he gets very rich. Humor the old man. Pat him on the back, if there is a way to do that. We do not have to worry about our dignity. This Academy is not the greatest thing in your life. You would have been great men if you had not been elected. We have accepted his gifts. Say he is sick. I am sure if you cajole him a little, he'll be as happy as a child with a toy."

Huntington, "the old man," was then sixty-nine, and he was the youngest of those deeply engaged in the fight. Gibson himself was seventy-two; Damrosch and Butler were seventy-seven —as was Ex-Governor Wilbur L. Cross of Connecticut, who took Butler's side—and Judge Grant was just a week from his eighty-eighth birthday. Many years earlier he had come to the defense of Hemingway's first novel, even though it offended his sense of the proprieties. "You *must* publish the book, Charles," he had written to his old friend Mr. Scribner, who had sent him the manuscript, "but I hope the young man will live to regret it." Now he was plunging into a last struggle. It was a battle among septuagenarians and octogenarians, but most of them, like Grant, were fighting on the side of youth.[2]

On April 12, three days after the invasion of Denmark and Norway, there was another meeting of the Academy directors. This time they formally adopted the amendment that separated the Academy from the Institute. Judge Grant being ill in Boston, only Gibson voted against it. The other academicians were duly informed of the directors' action, their feelings exploded, and thirty

---

2. But Grant had taken the other side in some political issues. With President Lowell of Harvard and President Stratton of M.I.T., he had served (1927) on the committee that reviewed the evidence in the Sacco-Vanzetti case. The committee reported that the two "anarchist bastards," as Judge Webster Thayer called them in one of his remarks off the bench, had received a fair trial.

of them—two-thirds of the membership—signed letters or sent telegrams requesting that the amendment be rescinded. The directors were perturbed and voted to meet again on May 14; it was the day after Hitler's armies outflanked the Maginot Line. In the Academy building, it was a day of surrender. Damrosch and Stephen Vincent Benét, then the youngest academician, had been invited to a conference before the meeting, and they presented the signed protests. After they left, the board went into session, and Huntington presented a resolution that was unanimously carried: "The Directors, acting for the Academy, for the time being, waive the right to elect members outside the Institute."

The battle wasn't over. As long as the right had merely been waived "for the time being," it could be exercised on some future occasion. The insurgents were determined to have the amendment repealed and to restore the close relation of the Academy and the Institute. That would be done only by a new board of directors, and a new board might be elected at the annual meeting of the Academy, to be held in November. Plans for the meeting were already being laid when the insurgents heard that Judge Grant had died on May 19, after supporting their efforts to the end.

There was a truce during the summer while the champions of both sides rested in their country places, but hostilities resumed at the end of September. It was a question first of choosing candidates. In recognition of past services, the insurgents decided to retain Butler as president of the Academy, Cross as chancellor, and Huntington as a director, but they would bring forward six additional candidates strongly opposed to the amendment. These, if elected, would give them two-thirds of the board. Another tactical problem was that of persuading all their supporters to attend the meeting, including those who were infirm or occupied in Washington with affairs of state. Once more the telegraph wires were busy.

The meeting on November 14 was the best attended since the Academy had received its charter, and the insurgents were present in a clear majority. Damrosch had consulted a lawyer and had been given written instructions on how to present his slate—this to forestall parliamentary moves by Butler, who was known as a wily and autocratic chairman. Butler surprised everyone, however, by announcing that he and Huntington accepted the insurgent slate, which was thereupon elected by a unanimous vote.

3 ⟨ That was the moment of capitulation, but there were to be two more meetings before the revolution was complete. The new board of directors met November 19 and voted to restore the old by-laws, after the membership had been duly warned. Huntington then resigned as a director and said—though not for the minutes—that he would never enter the Academy building again. Butler resigned as president and Cross as chancellor. At another meeting, on January 14, 1941, their places were filled by Damrosch as president, James Truslow Adams as chancellor and treasurer, and Deems Taylor as a director. Their election was announced in the newspapers, but otherwise, and for thirty years, not a word about the struggle appeared in print.

"We found affairs in the Academy in quite a mess when we took hold," Damrosch reported to the secretary, William Lyon Phelps, a few weeks later. He might have gone on to explain that Mrs. Grace Vanamee, the assistant to the former president, had been reigning there as chatelaine and had overstaffed the Academy building with her retainers. "But things have become brighter," Damrosch continued, without adding that Mrs. Vanamee had retired to Florida on the day that the new officers took over. "Our affairs are in good order and I hope the Academy will prosper peacefully for some time to come."

It has prospered after a modest fashion, even though Huntington held to his word. He lived to be eighty-five, but he never again entered the Academy building. The endowment he had already given to the Academy proved to be fairly substantial, and it was well managed by Adams, the new treasurer, who had been a member of the New York Stock Exchange before he became a historian. After the staff had been reduced and reorganized by Felicia Geffen, a capable new assistant to the president, the Academy found that it had enough income to carry on all past activities and even to undertake new ones: such, for example, as contributing to the expenses of the Institute, which was not so well endowed, then joining with the Institute to present more and more annual awards for achievement in the arts. It has never tried to fulfill Huntington's vision of its becoming a Hall of Fame for the living like the Académie Française; in fact it has moved in the opposite direction. Today there are no senators and no college presidents among its members, let alone a President and an ex-President of the United States. There are only professional writers, artists, and composers, all chosen from the equally professional membership of the Institute.

An incidental result of the long struggle was the defeat of the Ancients in both organizations. Of course the Ancients are always defeated, by time if by nothing else, though the Moderns who drive them from the field usually end by finding that they have become Ancients in their turn; that is why the war is always resumed in different forms, with new armies. The row, the ruckus, the battle over the by-laws was merely an episode in the war, but it had a few special features, one of which I have mentioned already: that the champions on both sides were old men. The Ancients, no older in years, were nevertheless older in spirit, since they represented the vanishing standards of the genteel tradition. It must be remembered that the standards were social as well as literary. The genteel writers, including those stalwarts of the Academy, were spokesmen for the educated and prosperous middle classes of the Eastern seaboard, mostly of English descent. They were bent on excluding the new writers not only as literary rebels but also as outlanders, immigrants, and social or sexual interlopers. The Moderns in the Academy were just as genteel in their personal lives as the Ancients, but they placed aesthetic above social standards, talent above tradition, and they were determined to be hospitable to the new men and women. Their attitude prevailed, and in this respect the defeat of the Ancients was final.

Sandburg (or Sandborg or Sandbag), old Mr. Johnson's favorite example of barbarism, was elected to the Academy in 1940, the year of the battle, and so was Edna Millay. Robinson Jeffers, whom the stalwarts equally detested, was elected in 1945, and he was followed by Marianne Moore (1947), E. E. Cummings (1949), and William Carlos Williams (1950). With the exception of Wallace Stevens, an Institute member overlooked for I don't know what reason, all the rebel poets of talent entered the Academy if they lived long enough, and so did the rebel painters and composers. Meanwhile the Academy and the Institute were drawing closer together, and in 1976, after discussions that had lasted more than a year, they separately agreed to a complete financial merger. The larger endowment of one and the smaller endowment of the other are now jointly administered by a new corporate body, the American Academy *and* Institute of Arts and Letters.

The merger is less than complete in other respects, and the Institute, like the Academy, continues to elect its own members. In the years since the battle of the by-laws, it has become even more eager to welcome new talents. Today its membership represents many of the new as well as the old schools in art, literature, and music, while its awards have gone to younger men and women representing most of the others. It acts on the principle that there is such a thing as personal distinction in the arts, something independent of all the schools—and of course independent of color, sex, geography, national origin, or position in society. One can imagine what Robert Underwood Johnson or his still more conservative friend Harrison Morris would say about the election to the Institute of Henry Miller (1957), John Cage (1968), Duke Ellington (1970), Allen Ginsberg (1973), Anaïs Nin (1974), or Claes Oldenburg (1975). They would say—peace to their angry shades—that the forces of degeneracy in all the arts had captured the whole shebang.

# XII HOW
# WRITERS
# WRITE

✒ I was asked to edit and write an introduction to *Writers at Work: The Paris Review Interviews* (1958), a book that proved to be the first in a series. That first volume contained sixteen interviews with writers all of whom were internationally known for their novels or short stories. In the introduction, based largely on what they said about themselves, I tried to offer some generalities about the actual writing of fiction. I haven't found it necessary to revise those statements. Still, as a matter of history, it should be noted that this volume and later ones selected from *The Paris Review* had a perceptible effect on the general standards of literary interviewing. In other magazines as well, more attention was paid to the form in itself and more care was taken in asking the right questions, so that some of the remarks in my original first paragraph—the one that follows—would no longer apply.

1 ✍ This is the best series of interviews with writers of our time that I have read in English. The statement, though sweeping, isn't quite so eulogistic as it sounds. As compared with Continental Europeans, the English since Boswell, who was Scottish, and Americans from the beginning have seldom been good at literary interviews. Everything in their background has been against the development of the form. Editors haven't been willing to give it much space because of a probably justified feeling that their public was not interested in literary problems. Authors have been embarrassed or reticent, often at the wrong places, and interviewers by and large have been incompetent. I can think of recent exceptions, but most of the interviewers either have had no serious interest in literature or else have been too serious about themselves. Either they have been reporters with little knowledge of the author's work and a desire to entrap him into making scandalous remarks about sex, politics, and God, or else they have been ambitious writers trying to display their own sophistication, usually at the expense of the author, and listening chiefly to their own voices.

In this book the literary conversations are of a different order, perhaps because of changing times. The interviewers belong to the new generation of the 1950s, the one that used to be called "silent," though a better word for it would have been "waiting" or "listening" or "inquiring." They have done their assigned reading, they have asked the right questions, or most of them, and have listened carefully to the answers. The authors, more conscious of their craft than authors used to be, have talked about it with an engaging lack of stuffiness. The editors of *The Paris Review* have been generous with their time and space, and the result is a series that seems to me livelier and more revealing than others of its kind. Unlike most of the others it is concerned primarily with the craft of fiction. It tells us what fiction writers are as persons, where they get their material, how they work from day to day, and what they dream of writing.

The series started with the first issue of *The Paris Review* in the spring of 1953. The new quarterly had been founded by young men lately out of college who were in Europe working on their first novels or books of poems. Their dream of having a magazine of their own must have been more luminous than their picture of what it should be, yet they did have a picture of sorts. They didn't want their magazine to be "little" or opinionated (*engagé*, in the slang of that year) or academic. Instead of printing what were then the obligatory essays on *Moby Dick* and Henry James's major phase, they would print stories and poems by new authors—and pay for them too, as long as the magazine kept going. They wanted to keep it going for a long time, even if its capital was only a thousand dollars, with no subventions in sight. They dreamed that energy and ingenuity might take the place of missing resources.

At this point *The Paris Review* took a different direction from that of other magazines published by Americans in Europe. Like them it wanted to present material that was new, uncommercial, "making no compromise with the public taste," in the phrase sanctified by *The Little Review*, but unlike the others it was willing to use commercial devices in getting the material printed and talked about. "Enterprise in the service of art" might have been its motto. The editors compiled a list, running to thousands of names, of Americans living in Paris and sent volunteer salesmen to ring their doorbells. Posters were printed by hundreds and flying squadrons of three went out by night to paste them in likely and unlikely places all over the city. In June 1957 the frayed remnants of one poster were still legible on the ceiling of the washroom in the Café du Dôme.

The series of interviews was at first regarded as another device—more dignified and perhaps more effective too—for building circulation. The magazine needed famous names on the cover, but couldn't afford to pay for the contributions of famous authors. "So let's talk to them," somebody ventured—it must have been Peter Matthiessen or Harold Humes, since they laid the earliest plans for the *Review*—"and print what they say." The idea was discussed with George Plimpton, late of *The Harvard Lampoon,* who agreed to be editor. Plimpton was then at King's College,

Cambridge, and he suggested E. M. Forster, an honorary fellow of King's, as the first author to be interviewed. It was Forster himself who gave a new direction to the series, making it a more thoughtful discussion of the craft of fiction than had at first been planned. Forster began by saying that he would answer questions if they were given to him in advance so that he could brood over them. The questions were submitted, and a few days later when the interviewers appeared, Forster gave his answers so methodically and slowly that his guests had no trouble keeping up with him. It was a simple interview to transcribe, and it furnished the best of patterns for the series that followed.

Interviewers usually worked in pairs, like FBI agents. Since no recording equipment was available for the early interviews, they both jotted down answers to their questions at top speed and matched the two versions afterward. With two men writing, the pace could be kept almost at the level of natural conversation. Some of the later interviews—with Frank O'Connor, for example—were done with a tape recorder. After two or three sessions the interviewers typed up their material; then it was cut to length, arranged in logical order, and sent to the author for his approval. Sometimes he took a special interest in the text and expanded it with new questions of his own. There were important additions to some interviews, including those with Mauriac, Faulkner, and Moravia, while this volume was being edited.

It seems strange that famous authors should have devoted so much of their time to a project from which they had nothing to gain. Some of them disliked the idea of being interviewed but consented anyway, either out of friendship for someone on the *Review* or because they wanted to help a struggling magazine of the arts, perhaps in memory of their own early struggles to get published. Others—notably Simenon, Cary, Warren, and O'Connor—were interested in the creative process and glad to talk about it. Not one of the interviewers had any professional experience in the field, but perhaps their inexperience and youth were positive advantages. Authors are sometimes like tomcats: they distrust all the other toms, but they are kind to kittens.

"Kind" in this case means honest and painstaking in one's

own fashion. Rereading the interviews, this time as a group, I was impressed by the extreme diversity of the characters and talents they present. The sixteen authors have come from the ruling class, the middle class, or the working class of five different countries. They are Catholic, Protestant, Jewish, or agnostic; old or young; married, single, or divorced; and they have had all sorts of education, from those who never finished secondary school (Simenon, Faulkner) to those who are university professors or fellows. One started life as a gunman, another as a bindle stiff, another as a soldier and government official; several went straight into professional writing. All have strongly marked personalities which are revealed—asserted, one might say—in their simplest remarks, and no personality resembles any other. Yet in spite of their diversity, what emerges from the interviews is a composite picture of the fiction writer. He has no face, no nationality, no particular background, and I say "he" by grammatical convention, since two of the authors are women; but they all have something in common, some attitude toward life and art, some fund of common experience. Let us see how they go about their daily task of inventing stories and putting them on paper.

2 ✍ There would seem to be four stages in the composition of a story. First comes the germ of the story, then a period of more or less conscious meditation, then the first draft, and finally the revision, which may be simply "pencil work," as John O'Hara calls it—that is, minor changes in wording—or may lead to writing several drafts and what amounts to a new work.

The germ of a story is something seen or heard, or heard about, or suddenly remembered; it may be a remark casually dropped at the dinner table (as in the case of Henry James's story, *The Spoils of Poynton*), or again it may be the look on a stranger's face. Almost always it is a new and simple element introduced into an existing situation or mood; something that expresses the mood in one sharp detail; something that serves as a focal point for a hitherto disorganized mass of remembered material in the author's mind. James describes it as "the precious particle . . . the stray suggestion, the wandering word, the vague echo, at a touch of which the novelist's imagination winces as at the prick of some sharp point," and he adds that "its virtue is all in its needle-like quality, the power to penetrate as finely as possible."

In the case of one story by the late Joyce Cary, the "precious particle" was the wrinkles on a young woman's forehead. He had seen her on the little boat that goes around Manhattan Island, "a girl of about thirty," he says, "wearing a shabby skirt. She was enjoying herself. A nice expression, with a wrinkled forehead, a good many wrinkles. I said to my friend, 'I could write about that girl . . .'" but then he forgot her. Three weeks later, in San Francisco, Cary woke up at four in the morning with a story in his head—a purely English story with an English heroine. When he came to revise the story he kept wondering, "Why all these wrinkles? That's the third time they come in. And I suddenly realized," he says, "that my English heroine was the girl on the Manhattan boat. Somehow she had gone down into my subconscious, and came up again with a full-sized story."

The woman with the wrinkled forehead could hardly have served as the germ of anything by Frank O'Connor, for his imagination is auditory, not visual. "If you're the sort of person," he says, "that meets a girl in the street and instantly notices the color of her eyes and of her hair and the sort of dress she's wearing, then you're not in the least like me. . . . I have terribly sensitive hearing and I'm terribly aware of voices." Often his stories develop from a remark he has overheard. That may also be the case with Dorothy Parker, who says, "I haven't got a visual mind. I hear things." Faulkner does have a visual mind, and he says that *The Sound and the Fury* "began with a mental picture. I didn't realize at the time it was symbolical. The picture was of the muddy seat of a little girl's drawers in a pear tree, where she could see through a window where her grandmother's funeral was taking place and report what was happening to her brothers on the ground below. By the time I explained who they were and what they were doing and how her pants got muddy, I realized it would be impossible to get all of it into a short story and it would have to be a book." At other times the precious particle is something the author has read—preferably a book of memoirs or history or travel, one that lies outside his own field of writing. Robert Penn Warren says, "I always remember the date, the place, the room, the road, when I first was struck. For instance, *World Enough and Time*. Katherine Anne Porter and I were both in the Library of Congress as fellows. We were in the same pew, had offices next to each other. She came in one day with an old pamphlet, the trial of Beauchamp for killing Colonel Sharp. She said, 'Well, Red, you better read this.' There it was. I read it in five minutes. But I was six years making the book. Any book I write starts with a flash, but takes a long time to shape up."

The book or story shapes up—assumes its own specific form, that is—during a process of meditation that is the second stage in composition. Angus Wilson calls it "the gestatory period" and says that it is "very important to me. That's when I'm persuading myself of the truth of what I want to say, and I don't think I could persuade my readers unless I'd persuaded myself first." The period may last for years, as with Warren's novels (and most of Henry James's), or it may last exactly two days, as in the extraordinary case of Georges Simenon. "As soon as I have the beginning," Simenon explains, "I can't bear it very long. . . . And two days later I begin writing." The meditation may be, or seem to be, wholly conscious. The writer asks himself questions—"What should the characters do at this point? How can I build to a climax?"—and answers them in various fashions before choosing the final answers. Or most of the process, including all the early steps, may be carried on without the writer's volition. He wakes before daybreak with the whole story in his head, as Joyce Cary did in San Francisco, and hastily writes it down. Or again—and I think most frequently—the meditation is a mixture of conscious and unconscious elements, as if a cry from the depths of sleep were being heard and revised by the waking mind.

Often the meditation continues while the writer is engaged in other occupations: gardening, driving his wife to town (as Walter Mitty did), or going out to dinner. "I never quite know when I'm not writing," says James Thurber. "Sometimes my wife comes up to me at a dinner party and says, 'Dammit, Thurber, stop writing.' She usually catches me in the middle of a paragraph. Or my daughter will look up from the dinner table and ask, 'Is he sick?' 'No,' my wife says, 'he's writing.' I have to do it that way on account of my eyes." When Thurber had better vision, he used to do his meditating at the typewriter, as many other writers do. Nelson Algren, for example, finds his plots simply by writing page after page, night after night. "I always figured," he says, "the only way I could finish a book and get a plot was just to keep making it longer and longer until something happens."

The first draft of a story is often written at top speed; probably that is the best way to write it. Dorothy Canfield Fisher, who is not among the authors interviewed, once compared the writing of a first draft with skiing down a steep slope that she wasn't sure she was clever enough to manage. "Sitting at my desk one morning," she says, "I 'pushed off' and with a tingle of not altogether pleasurable excitement and alarm, felt myself 'going.' I 'went' almost as precipitately as skis go down a long white slope, scribbling as rapidly as my pencil could go, indicating whole words with a dash and a jiggle, filling page after page with scrawls." Frank O'Connor explains the need for haste in his own case. "Get black on white," he says, "used to be Maupassant's advice—that's what I always do. I don't give a hoot what the writing's like, I write any sort of rubbish which will cover the main outlines of the story, then I can begin to see it." There are other writers, however, who work ahead laboriously, revising as they go. William Styron says, "I seem to have some neurotic need to perfect each paragraph—each sentence, even—as I go along." Dorothy Parker reports that it takes her six months to do a story: "I think it out and then write it sentence by sentence—no first draft. I can't write five words but that I change seven."

O'Connor doesn't start changing words until the first draft is finished, but then he rewrites, so he says, "endlessly, endlessly, endlessly." There is no stage of composition at which these authors differ more from one another than in this final stage of preparing a manuscript for the printer. Even that isn't a final stage for O'Connor. "I keep on rewriting," he says, "and after it's published, and then after it's published in book form, I usually rewrite it again. I've rewritten versions of most of my early stories, and one of these days, God help, I'll publish these as well." Françoise Sagan, on the other hand, spends "very little" time in revision. Simenon spends exactly three days in revising each of his short novels. Most of that time is devoted to tracking down and crossing out the literary touches—"adjectives, adverbs, and every word which is there just to make an effect. Every sentence which is there just for the sentence. You know, you have a beautiful sentence—cut it." Joyce Cary was another deletionist. Many of the passages he crossed out of his first drafts were those dealing explicitly with ideas. "I work over the whole book," he says, "and cut out anything that does not belong to the emotional development, the texture of feeling." Thurber revises his stories by rewriting them from the beginning, time and again. "A story I've been working on," he says, "...was written fifteen complete times. There must have been close to two hundred and forty thousand words in all the manuscripts put together, and I must have spent two thousand hours working at it. Yet the finished story can't be more than twenty thousand words." That would make it about the longest piece of fiction he has written. Men like Thurber and O'Connor, who rewrite "endlessly, endlessly," find it hard to face the interminable prospect of writing a full-length novel.

For short-story writers the four stages of composition are usually distinct, and there may even be a fifth, or rather a first, stage. Before seizing upon the germ of a story, the writer may find himself in a state of "generally intensified emotional sensitivity ...when events that usually pass unnoticed suddenly move you deeply, when a sunset lifts you to exaltation, when a squeaking door throws you into a fit of exasperation, when a clear look of trust in a child's eyes moves you to tears." I am quoting again from Dorothy Canfield Fisher, who "cannot conceive," she says, "of any creative fiction written from any other beginning." There is not much doubt, in any case, that the germ is precious largely because it serves to crystallize a prior state of feeling. Then comes the brooding or meditation, then the rapidly written first draft, then the slow revision; for the story writer everything is likely to happen in more or less its proper order. For the novelist, however, the stages are often confused. The meditation may have to be repeated for each new episode. The revision of one chapter may precede or follow the first draft of the next.

That is not the only difference between writing a short story and writing a novel. Reading the interviews together, I was confirmed in an old belief that the two forms are separate and that mere length is not their distinguishing feature. A long short story —say of forty thousand words—is not the same as a novel of forty thousand words, nor is it likely to be written by the same person. Among the authors interviewed, the division that goes deepest is not between older and younger writers, or men and women writers, or French and English writers; it is the division between those who think in terms of the short story and those who are essentially novelists.

Truman Capote might stand for those who think in terms of the short story, since he tells us that his "more unswerving ambitions still revolve around this form." A moment later he says, "I invariably have the illusion that the whole play of a story, its start and middle and finish, occur in my mind simultaneously— that I'm seeing it in one flash." He likes to know the end of a story before writing the first word of it. Indeed, he doesn't start writing until he has brooded over the story long enough to exhaust his emotional response to the material. "I seem to remember reading," he says, "that Dickens, as he wrote, choked with laughter over his own humor and dripped tears all over the page when one of his characters died. My own theory is that the writer should have considered his wit and dried his tears long, long before setting out to evoke similar reactions in a reader." The reactions of the reader, not of the writer, are Capote's principal concern.

For contrast take the interview with Simenon, who is a true novelist even if his separate works, written and revised in about two weeks, are not much longer than some short stories.

Each of them starts in the same fashion. "It is almost a geometrical problem," he says. "I have such a man, such a woman, in such surroundings. What can happen to them to oblige them to go to their limit? That's the question. It will be sometimes a very simple incident, anything which will change their lives. Then I write my novel chapter by chapter." Before setting to work Simenon has scrawled a few notes on a big manila envelope. The interviewer asks whether these are an outline of the action. "No, no," Simenon answers. "...On the envelope I put only the names of the characters, their ages, their families. I know nothing whatever about the events which will occur later. Otherwise"—and I can't help putting the statement in italics—"*it would not be interesting to me.*"

Unlike Capote, who says that he is physically incapable of writing anything he doesn't think will be paid for (though I take it that payment is, for him, merely a necessary token of public admiration), Simenon would "certainly," he says, continue writing novels if they were never published. But he wouldn't bother to write them if he knew what the end of each novel would be, for then *it would not be interesting.* He discovers his fable not in one flash, but chapter by chapter, as if he were telling a continued story to himself. "On the eve of the first day," he says, "I know what will happen in the first chapter. Then day after day, chapter after chapter, I find what comes later. After I have started a novel I write a chapter each day, without ever missing a day. Because it is a strain, I have to keep pace with the novel. If, for example, I am ill for forty-eight hours I have to throw away the previous chapters. And I never return to that novel." Like Dickens he lets himself be moved, even shattered, by what he is writing. "All the day," he says, "I am one of my characters"—always the one who is driven to his limit. "I feel what he feels.... And it's almost unbearable after five or six days. That is one of the reasons why my novels are so short; after eleven days I can't—it's impossible. I have to— It's physical. I am too tired."

Nobody else writes in quite the same fashion as Simenon. He carries a certain attitude toward fiction to the furthest point that it can be carried by anyone who writes books to be published and read. But the attitude in itself is not unusual, and in fact it is shared to some extent by all the true novelists who explain their methods in this book. Not one of them starts by making a scene-by-scene outline, as Henry James did before writing each of his later novels. James had discovered what he called the "divine principle of the Scenario" after writing several unsuccessful plays, and in essence the principle, or method, seems to be dramatistic rather than novelistic. The dramatist, like the short-story writer, has to know where he is going and how he will get there, scene by scene, whereas all the novelists interviewed by *The Paris Review* are accustomed to making voyages of exploration with only the roughest of maps. Mauriac says, "There is a point of departure, and there are some characters. It often happens that the first characters don't go any further and, on the other hand, vaguer, more inconsistent characters show new possibilities as the story goes on and assume a place we hadn't foreseen." Françoise Sagan says that she has to start writing to have ideas. In the beginning she has "a character, or a few characters, and perhaps an idea for a few of the scenes up to the middle of the book, but it all changes in the writing. For me writing is a question of finding a certain rhythm." (One thinks of Simenon and his feeling that he has to keep pace with the novel.) "My work," says Moravia, "...is not prepared beforehand in any way. I might add, too, that when I'm not working I don't think of my work at all." Forster does lay plans for his work, but they are subject to change. "The novelist," he says, "should, I think, always settle when he starts what is going to happen, what his major event is to be. He may alter this event as he approaches it, indeed he probably will, indeed he probably had better, or the novel becomes tied up and tight. But the sense of a solid mass ahead, a mountain round or over which or through which the story must go, is most valuable and, for the novels I've tried to write, essential.... When I began *A Passage to India* I knew that something important happened in the Malabar Caves, and that it would have a central place in the novel—but I didn't know what it would be."

Most novelists, one might generalize on this evidence, are like the chiefs of exploring expeditions. They know who their companions are (and keep learning more about them); they know what sort of territory they will have to traverse on the following day or week; they know the general object of the expedition, the mountain they are trying to reach, the river of which they are trying to discover the source. But they don't know exactly what their route will be, or what adventures they will meet along the way, or how their companions will act when pushed to the limit. They don't even know whether the continent they are trying to map exists in space or only within themselves. "I think that if a man has the urge to be an artist," Simenon muses, "it is because he needs to find himself. Every writer tries to find himself through his characters, through all his writing." He is speaking for the novelist in particular. Short-story writers come back from their briefer explorations to brood over the meaning of their discoveries; then they perfect the stories for an audience. The short story is an *exposition;* the novel is often and perhaps at its best an *inquisition* into the unknown depths of the novelist's mind.


3 ✍ Apparently the hardest problem for almost any writer, whatever his medium, is getting to work in the morning (or in the afternoon, if he is a late riser like Styron, or even at night). Thornton Wilder says, "Many writers have told me that they have built up mnemonic devices to start them off on each day's writing task. Hemingway once told me he sharpened twenty pencils; Willa Cather that she read a passage from the Bible—not from piety, she was quick to add, but to get in touch with fine prose; she also regretted that she had formed this habit, for the prose rhythms of 1611 were not those she was in search of. My springboard has always been long walks." Those long walks alone are a fairly common device; Thomas Wolfe would sometimes roam through the streets of Brooklyn all night. Reading the Bible before writing is a much less common practice, and, in spite of Cather's disclaimer, I suspect that it did involve a touch of piety. Dependent for success on forces partly beyond his control, an author may

try to propitiate the unknown powers. I knew one novelist, an agnostic, who said he often got down on his knees and started the working day with prayer.

The usual working day is three or four hours. Whether these authors write with pencils, with a pen, or at a typewriter—and some do all three in the course of completing a manuscript—an important point seems to be that they all work with their hands; the only exception is Thurber in his sixties. I have often heard it said by psychiatrists that writers belong to the "oral type." The truth seems to be that most of them are manual types. Words are not merely sounds for them, but magical designs that their hands make on paper. "I always think of writing as a physical thing," Nelson Algren says. "I am an artisan," Simenon explains. "I need to work with my hands. I would like to carve my novel in a piece of wood." Hemingway used to have the feeling that his fingers did much of his thinking for him. After an automobile accident in Montana, when the doctors said he might lose the use of his right arm, he was afraid he would have to stop writing. Thurber used to have the sense of thinking with his fingers on the keyboard of a typewriter. When they were working together on their play *The Male Animal,* Elliott Nugent used to say to him, "Well, Thurber, we've got our problem, we've got all these people in the living room. What are we going to do with them?" Thurber would answer that he didn't know and couldn't tell him until he'd sat down at the typewriter and found out. After his vision became too weak for the typewriter, he wrote very little for a number of years (using black crayon on yellow paper, about twenty scrawled words to the page); then painfully he taught himself to compose stories in his head and dictate them to a stenographer.

Dictation, for most authors, is a craft which, if acquired at all, is learned rather late in life—and I think with a sense of jumping over one step in the process of composition. Instead of giving dictation, many writers seem to themselves to be taking it. Mauriac says, "During a creative period I write every day; a novel should not be interrupted. When I cease to be carried along, when I no longer feel as though I were taking down dictation, I stop." Listening as they do to an inner voice that speaks or falls silent as if by caprice, many writers from the beginning have personified the voice as a benign or evil spirit. For Hawthorne it was evil or at least frightening. "The Devil himself always seems to get into my inkstand," he said in a letter to his publisher, "and I can only exorcise him by pensful at a time." For Kipling the Daemon that lived in his pen was tyrannical but well-meaning. "When your Daemon is in charge," he said, "do not try to think consciously. Drift, wait, and obey."

Objects on the writing table, which is the altar of the Daemon, are sometimes chosen with the same religious care as if they were chalices and patens. Kipling said, "For my ink I demanded the blackest, and had I been in my Father's house, as once I was, would have kept an ink-boy to grind me Indian-ink. All 'blue-blacks' were an abomination to my Daemon.... My writing-blocks were built for me to an unchanged pattern of large, off-white, blue sheets, of which I was most wasteful." Often we hear of taboos that must be observed—even by Angus Wilson, although he is as coolly rational as any fiction writer who ever set pen to paper (the pen in his case is medium and the paper is, by preference, a grammar-school exercise book). "Fiction writing is a kind of magic," Wilson says, "and I don't care to talk about a novel I'm doing because if I communicate the magic spell, even in an abbreviated form, it loses its force for me." One of the interviewed authors—only one, but I suspect there are others like him—makes a boast of his being superstitious. "I will not tolerate the presence of yellow roses," Capote says—"which is sad because they're my favorite flower. I can't allow three cigarette butts in the same ashtray. Won't travel on a plane with two nuns. Won't begin or end anything on a Friday. It's endless, the things I can't and won't. But I derive some curious comfort from these primitive concepts." Perhaps they are not only comforting but of practical service in helping him to weave his incantations. I can't help thinking of the drunk who always carried a ventilated satchel. "What's in it?" said his neighbor on a bus. "Just a mongoose. To kill snakes." The neighbor peered into the satchel and said, "There's nothing in it. That's an imaginary mongoose." The drunk said, "What about the snakes?"

**4** ✒︎ At a summer conference on the novel, at Harvard, one of the invited speakers gave a rather portentous address on the Responsibilities of the Novelist. Frank O'Connor, on the platform, found himself giggling at each new solemnity. After the address he walked to the lectern and said, "All right, if there are any of my students here I'd like them to remember that writing is fun." On that point most of these authors would agree. "I have always found writing pleasant," Forster says, "and don't understand what people mean by 'throes of creation.'" "I write simply to amuse myself," says Moravia. Angus Wilson "started writing as a hobby." Thurber tells us that the act of writing "is either something the writer dreads or something he actually likes, and I actually like it. Even rewriting's fun." At another point he says, "When I'm not writing, as my wife knows, I'm miserable."

The professional writers who dread writing, as many do, are usually those whose critical sense is not only strong but unsleeping, so that it won't allow them to do even a first draft at top speed. They are in most cases the "bleeders" who write one sentence at a time, and can't write it until the sentence before has been revised. William Styron, one of the bleeders, is asked if he enjoys writing. "I certainly don't," he says. "I get a fine warm feeling when I'm doing well, but that pleasure is pretty much negated by the pain of getting started each day. Let's face it, writing is hell." But a moment later he says without any sense of contradiction, "I find that I'm simply the happiest, the placidest, *when* I'm writing...it's the only time that I feel completely self-possessed, even when the writing itself is not going too well." Not writing is the genuine hell for Styron and others in his predicament; writing is at worst a purgatory.

Whatever the original impulse that drives them to write—self-expression, self-discovery, self-aggrandizement, or the pain of not writing—most authors with a body of work behind them end by developing new purposes. Simenon, for example, would like to create the pure novel, without description, exposition, or argument: a book that will do only what a novel can do. "In a pure novel," he says, "you wouldn't take sixty pages to describe the South or Arizona or some country in Europe. Just the drama with only what is absolutely part of this drama ... almost a translation of the laws of tragedy into the novel. I think the novel is the tragedy of our day." Critics have always advised him to write a *big* novel, one with twenty or thirty characters. His answer is, "I will never write a big novel. My big novel is the mosaic of all my small novels."

At this point Simenon suggests still another purpose, or dream, that is shared by almost all the writers who were interviewed. They want to write the new book, climb the new mountain, which they hope will be the highest of all, but still they regard it as only one conquest in a chain of mountains. The whole chain, the shelf of books, the Collected Works, is their ultimate goal. Moravia says, "In the works of every writer with any body of work to show for his effort, you will find recurrent themes. I view the novel, a single novel as well as a writer's entire corpus, as a musical composition in which the characters are themes." Faulkner says, "With *Soldier's Pay* I found out that writing was fun. But I found out afterward that not only each book had to have a design, but the whole output or sum of a writer's work had to have a design." Graham Greene says, in *The Lost Childhood,* "A ruling passion gives to a shelf of books the unity of a system." Each of these novelists wants to produce not a random succession of books, like discrete events for critics to study one by one, without reference to earlier or later events, but a complete system unified by his ruling passion, a system of words on paper that is also a world of living persons created in his likeness by the author. This dream must have had a beginning quite early in the author's life; perhaps it goes back to what Thornton Wilder calls "the Nero in the bassinet," the child wanting to be omnipotent in a world he has made for himself; but later it is elaborated with all the wisdom and fire and patient workmanship that the grown man can bring to bear on it. Particle after particle of the living self is transferred into the creation, until at last it is an external world that corresponds to the inner world and has the power of outlasting the author's life.

I suspect that some such dream is shared by many authors, but among those interviewed it is Faulkner who has come closest to achieving it, and he is also the author who reveals it most candidly. "Beginning with *Sartoris*," he says, "I discovered that my own little postage stamp of native soil was worth writing about and that I would never live long enough to exhaust it, and that by sublimating the actual into the apocryphal I would have complete liberty to use whatever talent I might have to its absolute top. It opened up a mine of other people, so I created a cosmos of my own. I can move these people around like God, not only in space but in time." And then he says, looking back on his work as if on the seventh day, "I like to think of the world I created as being a kind of keystone in the universe; that, small as that keystone is, if it were ever taken away the universe itself would collapse. My last book will be the Doomsday Book, the Golden Book, of Yoknapatawpha County. Then I shall break the pencil and I'll have to stop."

# XIII A DEFENSE OF STORYTELLING

1 ⚓ There is no doubt whatever that storytelling has lost the privileged place it used to occupy in the literary world and much of the attention it used to receive from critics as well as readers. In the 1960s there was hardly a book reviewer who had not announced that the novel was dead. If the novel survived, it was in altered forms and with a different audience. Shorter fiction had almost disappeared from the more popular magazines. Somehow the idea had gotten around that storytelling was a primitive skill, a little easy, a little to be despised; that a book or a long poem that told a story was not quite "serious," did not "speak to the age"; and that plot, which is the story element, was a rather shameful concession to the audience.

At times plot was rejected—is still being rejected—in favor of "immediacy," that is, of plunging the reader into the midst of events—no, not of events, since these might imply a story, but rather into a welter of sense impressions. At other times plot is rejected on the ground of a higher reality and the notion that there are no plots in the chaos and absurdity of contemporary life. Often it is given away to the ragman, or the television camera, as if it were last year's fashion. "Here, I have no use for this peasant blouse."

Extreme statements of this attitude toward storytelling are easy to find. One of them goes back to 1951; it occurs in a book published that year by Hugh Kenner: *The Poetry of Ezra Pound.* Among modern authors, Pound is the one who most clearly lacks a feeling for sequence, in either the temporal or the logical meaning of the word. He is interested chiefly in images that are sharp, accurate, evocative, but that stand alone. He insists that his major work, the *Cantos,* is an epic poem, but it has neither a hero nor a central action. Kenner's book explains that these deficiencies are virtues of a high order. It says that "Pound's principal achievement" has been to dispense with "a subject matter, a plot, a line of philosophical development.... In the *Cantos* the place of a plot is taken by interlocking large-scale rhythms of recurrence." After comparing this technique to the use of montage in moving pictures, Kenner passes on to Mallarmé. "The fragmentation of the aesthetic idea into allotropic images," he says, "as first theorized by Mallarmé, was a discovery whose importance for the artist corresponds to that of nuclear fission for the physicist. Plot, in the Dickensian sense, is obsolete."

The obsolescence of plot or story or mere sequence in the Dickensian or any other sense is a notion that many writers, mostly younger ones, have clutched to their minds. Perhaps the notion was most firmly clutched during the later 1960s, as a reaction against the well-made and usually timid stories of the preceding decade.[1] There is a college anthology called *Anti-Story*

---

1. Afterward there was to be another reaction, not toward realism, which continued to be disdained, but in favor of fictions that dealt with a recognizable series of events. Another college anthology, *Superfiction,* edited by Joe David Bellamy (1975), is divided into five categories: Fantasy/Fabulation/Irrealism; Neo-Gothic; Myth/Parable; Metafiction (Technique as Subject); and Parody and Put-on. These, Bellamy says, are "the dominant

(1971) that brings together various manifestations of the effort to achieve absolute insequentiality. The editor, Philip Stevick, says in his combative introduction: "Characters in the works that follow do not learn. There are no insights. Relationships are not grasped in an instant. Structurally the stories are flat, or circular, or cyclic, or mosaic constructions, or finally indeterminate or incomprehensible in their shape—they are not climactic. What they start with is pretty much what they have at the end. No epiphanies."

If there is no development in an anti-story; if there are no insights along the way and if everything ends pretty much where it began, why should we start at the beginning and why plod to the end? Mr. Stevick, in praising those negative qualities of the anti-story, is likely to increase the number of anti-readers. Fortunately, some of the "pieces," "fictions," "sketches," or "fables," as he calls the short prose works assembled in his book, are vastly better than his introduction leads us to expect. Some are savage portraits or wild conceits, and some, in spite of what he says, are truly stories with living characters involved in situations that have the plausibility of nightmares. Ionesco's "The Rhinoceros" is a masterly example.

Other "pieces" in the book are truly anti-stories, including some that are mere collections of events, with each event meaningless in itself and the collection doubly meaningless because no event is the cause or effect of any other. Such "fables" have an obvious moral—namely, that life as a whole is meaningless and absurd—but why should the author keep repeating his moral on page after page? One of the anti-heroes says to himself after being subjected to an interminable series of insults and mutilations, "How much longer must this go on?" and the reader echoes, "How much longer?" Still more objectionable, to me, are the anti-

---

inward-turning modes of the present." One notes in his collection and elsewhere that effective works have been produced in all five modes (except perhaps in Metafiction) and that they include stories in the true sense of the word.

stories that have no characters except the author himself, whose subject, or theme, is the extreme difficulty he finds in writing fiction when he knows a hell of a lot about technique and has nothing but that knowledge to offer us: no epiphanies. In effect, such authors are proudly announcing that they are sterile. The reader starts by admiring them as virtuosos, then feels embarrassed for them—can't they stop showing off?—and finally yawns in their faces. Sometimes the author himself is the first to yawn, as note John Barth in "Life Story":

> What a dreary way to begin a story, he said to himself upon reviewing his long introduction. Not only is there no "ground-situation," but the prose style is heavy and somewhat old-fashioned, like an English translation of Thomas Mann, and the so-called "vehicle" itself is at least questionable: self-conscious, vertiginously arch, fashionably solipsistic, unoriginal—in fact a convention of twentieth-century literature. Another story about a writer writing a story! Another regressus in infinitum! . . .
>
> By Jove he exclaimed to himself. It's particularly disquieting to suspect not only that one is a fictional character but that the fiction one's in—the fiction one is—is quite the sort one least prefers.

Why write it then?—or why inflict one's fictional self on readers?

Still another variety of anti-story has been represented by the New Wave novelists in Paris and especially by Alain Robbe-Grillet, who founded what he calls the School of the Look. He advocates the doctrine that writers should represent what the eye sees, that and nothing else: no characters, no comments, no emotions. Stevick's book includes one of his shorter pieces, taken from a translated collection called *Snapshots* (1968), which I was not tempted to read in full. *Snapshots* was discussed, however, in *The New York Times Book Review* (January 12, 1969) by Professor Henri Peyre of Yale, who explained the author's intentions without at all endorsing them:

In a snapshot the eye fixes the world in an instant of flux. Snapshot photography is a technique that attempts to retain the totality and diversity of the world in space while neglecting the diversity and the movement of the world in time, in consciousness, and in history. And so the title summarizes reasonably well the program or intention of the New Novel according to Robbe-Grillet.

The writing aims for the greatest possible clarity; it is pure objective observation, a simple list of particulars.

A final type of anti-story is best represented by a volume that I doubt whether anyone but the typist and the proofreader (if any) has resolutely plowed through to the end. It is a non-book, so to speak, non-written by Andy Warhol, and it is called *a*, simply the lower-case first letter of the alphabet, which I suppose might pass for a non-title. An account of it appeared in the same issue of *The Times Book Review* as did Henri Peyre's notice of *Snapshots*:

> It consists of twenty-four hours of talk—there are strangely few silences—taperecorded from the life of Ondine, a Warhol sidekick who is homosexual, high on amphetamines, and loquacious.
>
> *a* is not ultimately even realistic. Most of it—I suspect because the tape didn't pick up connecting pieces of conversation—is incomprehensible snippets and gobbets of talk. Because Ondine's brain seems irretrievably addled with amphetamines, most of what he says takes the form of grunts, squeals, and bad puns.

So here we have various examples of the recent effort not to tell a story. Almost all the examples are lacking in observed or imagined characters and in events that lead to other events so as to grasp and hold the reader's attention. To serve as a substitute for events in sequence, we have in some cases fiction about the author's inability to write fiction; in some cases fragmented and allotropic images (to borrow Kenner's logotropic phrase); in some cases mere collections of events or objects, like warehouse inventories; and in a final case nothing much more than grunts, squeals, and bad puns.

These last are tokens of a failed experiment, though I rather think that Andy Warhol was making a serious effort to apply a theory sometimes advanced in literary arguments held late at night. The theory is that form of any sort is a convention to be defied, and that the only valid type of literature—now, today—is the raw confession torn from the subconscious and slapped before the reader like a piece of butcher's meat, boneless and quivering and quick to decay if exposed to light. As for the other experiments, they are usually efforts, in the words of Henri Peyre, "to retain the totality and diversity of the world in space" —or merely in the Freudian id—"while neglecting the diversity and the movement of the world in time."

The same efforts are being made in other arts that used to depend on temporal sequence. One reads about playwrights who have abandoned story, character, and event; their only concern is with "image, metaphor, essence, and layers of consciousness." They are praised as "poets of the theater." There has been a movement called "structural cinema," whose leaders explain, "We're doing away with narrations—it's poetic cinema." Here the doctrine seems to be that images and structures are poetical, whereas motion in time is prosaic.

Of course the emphasis on space to the neglect of time has antecedents in modern fiction. An influential essay on spatial form by Joseph Frank contends that some of the greatest twentieth-century novels, including *Ulysses* and *Remembrance of Things Past,* are really exercises in the organization of space. Frank says that in *Ulysses,* for example, the reader is expected to bear in mind the whole city of Dublin as a spatial entity. He is right on this point, but he might have added that *Ulysses* also tells how Stephen Dedalus, alone in the world, found a second father, and how Leopold Bloom found a foster son to take the place of the boy he had lost; it has a temporal plot as well as a spatial structure. *Remembrance of Things Past* has a plot or story too, one that is best summarized by Ramon Guthrie in a paragraph he contributed to a fiction anthology, *The Lesson of the Masters* (1971):

> Proust himself [Guthrie says] saw his work as concerned primarily with downfall and redemption. The hero is damned by his self-indulgence and inertia as well as by the shallowness of the society in which he has chosen to live. Through most of the book he keeps sinking deeper into a slough of monotonous futility. After spending several blank years in a nursing home where he is cut off from life, he returns to Paris resigned to living out the remainder of a shallow and meaningless existence. Suddenly he has an intimation of reality, not unlike other momentary awakenings that have come to him on several occasions. This time he heeds the call and, transformed by the mystical experience, sets about "recomposing" his wasted life, by means of art, into one of glorious achievement.

The spatial elements are also present, as Frank makes clear, but he neglects to add that this temporal—and therefore irreversible—sequence of events is what holds the enormous novel together. There is another point on which I might differ with him—that is, if he followed his argument to its logical conclusion. The argument seems to imply—though Frank never says—that because spatial form is newer in fiction than temporal form, it can be recommended to contemporary novelists as a superior model. I do not like to argue such questions of better and worse; every novelist has to decide what is best for himself. It ought to be clear, however, that the author who attempts to organize space while neglecting time is venturing into a field in which materials and tools—paint, canvas, stone, metal, wood, and camera lenses—are more effective than language. He is working in two or three dimensions instead of four and is thus evading what seems to me a more difficult challenge and a greater opportunity for innovation.

2  ✍ The present disparagement of storytelling is directed against a very ancient art, perhaps the most ancient of all. When our remote ancestors gathered round the fire in a cave, some of them looked for walls on which to draw pictures of the animals they hoped to kill—such pictures survive in the caves of Lascaux and Altamira—but I like to think that even earlier, by generations and millenniums, the cavemen or their predecessors listened while someone told hunting stories, broken at rhythmic intervals by incantations for success and by the praise of tribal heroes. There were also priests among the cavemen, we have reason to surmise, and they must have found words to picture the beginnings of this pleasant earth and of the wholly admirable tribe to which they belonged. Those words must have taken the form of myths, that is, essentially, of stories.

All this would accord with a fundamental operation of thought, to be distinguished from conceptual thinking. Conceptually, we say that one thing is so *because* another thing is so *because* still another thing is so. We observe a phenomenon, then look for its cause inductively, then for the cause of that cause, until we reach the first or highest Cause. Or, reversing the process, we start with a general principle and reason deductively to particular results, all of which exist timelessly in a world of essences. But since we live in a world of time that is filled with events, we are less moved by conceptual thinking than by a storyteller who says, "This happened . . . and *then* this happened . . . and *afterward* this happened," as if each event were the direct cause of the one following it.

*Post hoc, ergo propter hoc* is a logical fallacy, but it is also an essential form of human thought, embodied in the mythology of every culture. A myth might be defined as a doctrine presented in terms of successive events; in other words, as doctrine transformed into story. To borrow a phrase from Kenneth Burke, a myth is the temporization of essence. A familiar example is the biblical myth of Creation:

In the beginning God created the heaven and the earth.

And the earth was without form, and void; and darkness was upon the face of the deep. And the Spirit of God moved upon the face of the waters.

And God said, Let there be light, and there was light.

And God saw the light, that it was good, and God divided the light from the darkness.

And God called the light Day, and the darkness he called Night. And the evening and the morning were the first day.

Here is the creation of the world in terms of story, in terms of events that follow one another in sequence. Here, too, the events are combined with a *naming* that forms part of the narrative process—"And God called the light Day"—as well as with a phrase about the evening and the morning that will be repeated to mark elapsed time, in the same way that poets use rhymes and refrains:

And God called the firmament Heaven. And the evening and the morning were the second day.

\* \* \*

And the earth brought forth grass, and herb yielding seed after his kind, and the tree yielding fruit, whose seed was in itself, after his kind: and God saw that it was good.

And the evening and the morning were the third day.

And so to the seventh day, when "God ended his work which he had made; and he rested on the seventh day from all his work which he had made." In Kenneth Burke's illuminating comment on the first three chapters of Genesis (see *The Rhetoric of Religion*, 1961), he sets forth the doctrines implicit in the story they tell. These, as he explains at length, include Original Sin, Redemption, and the coming of a Redeemer. At this point, a process is being reversed: Just as essence had been temporized into myth or story, so myth can be conceptualized into timeless doctrine, with the *post hoc* of narrative transformed into the *propter hoc* of logical relation. It is indeed a question which came first, the doctrine or the story.

I have been talking about the story in very ancient times, but I do not mean to imply that it belongs to the past or will ever become "obsolete," to repeat Kenner's word. In one important respect it seems peculiarly suited to modern society. Narrative deals with a sequence of events, that is, with a becoming, with a process rather than a pattern, and process thinking is an essential trait of the modern mind. Living as we do in unstable situations, we try to recognize the forces of change: How fast are they moving and in which directions? What seems obsolete in the light of such questions is the image thinking and pattern thinking of many contemporary authors. They might all be disciples of Zeno the Eleatic as they try, in effect, to demonstrate once again that Achilles could never overtake the tortoise and that an arrow is motionless at every instant of its flight. Because they present the world as a spatial concept, a stasis instead of a process, they offer misleading pictures of the world in which we live.

It seems to me that the real adventure for writers of each new generation lies in a different field. Instead of pasting snapshots into albums, they might look hard for new stories and new ways of telling them. They would then be helping to create the myths of what is always, and for each of them, a new age.

3 ✍ The function of the story in itself and the challenge it offers to the writer's inventiveness have usually been neglected by critics. Even novelists, when they write about their art, are likely to disparage the narrative element—as E. M. Forster does in *Aspects of the Novel* (1927), where he says that the story is a "low atavistic form" on which a good writer should rely as little as possible, his merit depending rather on what he has to say about the narrated events. As for professional critics, when they praise a novel it is usually—and for three centuries has almost always been—by describing it as something else than a novel: for example, as an object lesson in manners or morals, a much-needed sermon, a sweeping social panorama, a portrait gallery, a searching inquiry

into the human psyche, an allegory, or a re-creation of the Orestes myth. Of course it can be any of those things or others, including a clinical report, if that is what the author was truly impelled to write; but unless it also tells a story, it ceases to be a novel.

Because critics do not often concern themselves with narrative as a challenging art in itself, they have reached no agreement on the terms used to describe its various features: one man's "theme" is another man's "subject" and still another's "ground-situation." Even the key word "story" has several different meanings. Forster defines it as "a narrative of events arranged in their time sequence," thus including all sorts of factual reports, but apparently excluding fictions in which the time sequence is fragmented or in which the author works backward toward the hidden meaning of some event in the past. A lesser English novelist, Margaret Kennedy, offers what seems to me a more accurate definition. In her useful but neglected book *The Outlaws on Parnassus* (1960), she says that a story is "a pattern of events so narrated as to evoke an intended response." That has the advantage of bringing in the reader or listener, without whose hoped-for response the story would not be told; but still her definition leaves us wondering about the difference between a story properly speaking and, let us say, the newspaper account of a disaster by land or sea.

As a basis for that distinction, I might suggest that the story proper, if it is complete, will include four elements. A *person* (or group of persons) is involved in a *situation* and performs an *act* (or series of acts, or merely undergoes an experience) as a result of which *something is changed*.[2] Person, situation, action, something changed: all four elements are present in a complete story, but of course they assume a diversity of forms. Instead of being a person, the protagonist may be a wild animal, or a tame one like Black Beauty, or a big fish, or anything else personified—even a storm or a forest fire, as in two of George R. Stewart's

---

2. A similar statement of the elements, not in a story, but in a drama, was offered by Francis Ferguson in his *Idea of a Theatre* (1949). I am especially indebted to his emphasis on the "something is changed."

novels; even a spermatazoon moving with thousands of others toward union with an ovum, as in John Barth's brief and memorable "Night Journey." The situation may lie in the future, or in some imaginary world (I am not arguing here for realism); or again it may lie in the past and the present action may include a search for its true meaning; one example is Faulkner's *Absalom, Absalom!* The action may be simple or extremely complicated. Often it results from a decision by the central character, but in naturalistic novels its course is determined by natural laws, not by persons. These merely suffer the effects of natural laws, with the result in many cases that nature (or society) becomes the real protagonist.

As for the fourth element, the "something changed" that makes the action irreversible, it is often hard to recognize. In novels of sensibility such as those by Virginia Woolf and in stories such as those by Sherwood Anderson and his army of successors, there may be little change—or none whatever—in the objective situation; but the protagonist, who is most often a woman or an adolescent boy or girl, will have achieved a higher degree of self-awareness. It is this change in the protagonist during a moment of insight—an "epiphany," to use Joyce's word—that transforms a random series of impressions into a story. The device was used so often in the 1950s that it became one of the idols to be smashed in the 1960s.

I feel that the "something changed" is the most important of the four elements. Since it results from an interplay of the other three, it unites them into a single action marked off in time and set apart from the confusion of daily life. Here I am thinking of Aristotle, who said that stories "should be based on a single action, one that is a complete whole in itself, with a beginning, middle, and end, so as to enable the work to produce its own proper pleasure with all the organic unity of a living creature." I have to concede, however, that there are many true stories from which the fourth element is omitted, and wisely so, if it is present by implication. Person, situation, and action have all been so vividly presented that the author feels no need to tell his readers how the story ended; they can picture the change for themselves. I think of an early Hemingway story, "Cat in the Rain." It starts with a young American couple spending a rainy day in their hotel room on the Italian Riviera. The husband is sprawled on the bed reading a book. The wife looks out across the empty square and sees a cat trying to shelter itself under an iron table. "I'm going to get that kitty," she says. The husband goes on reading. The wife ventures into the rain after greeting the hotelkeeper, who sends a maid after her with an umbrella. She finds the iron table, but the cat has disappeared. Back in their room, the young wife says, "I wanted it so much. I wanted that poor kitty. It isn't any fun to be a poor kitty out in the rain." The husband goes on reading. There is a knock at the door and the maid appears, this time with a big tortoise-shell cat in her arms. "Excuse me," she says, "but the padrone asked me to bring this for the signora." End of the story. Apparently nothing has changed, but the reader knows that the wife is a kitten in the rain and feels that she may some day seek refuge with the hotel-keeper or someone else of the same big, paternal sort. The first Mrs. Hemingway was to do so in her second marriage, thus rein-forcing one's feeling that good stories have a predictive quality.

There is another fairly numerous group of stories in which the point seems to be made that nothing has changed in reality; the end circles back to the beginning. A beggar is invited into a wealthy merchant's house; he is bathed, given rich clothes to wear, and ushered into a feast at which he is guest of honor. He drinks too much, insults his host, falls asleep, and wakes in the street dressed in his familiar rags. Stories like these, older than *The Arabian Nights,* faintly echo the myth of eternal recurrence. In other forms of the myth, a hero spends a season in hell or paradise, then reappears among his own people. But he is never the same hero as he was before he entered the earth, just as the beggar carried out of the rich merchant's house is the same only in out-ward appearance as he was before he entered it. Something has changed for him.

There is still another group of stories—if we call them stories—in which the author's purpose is to present a wholly typi-cal day in the life of some character, usually one with a low degree of self-awareness. An example is "Mr. Reginald Peacock's Day," by Katherine Mansfield. I had forgotten Mr. Peacock and have absolutely no desire to reread the account of his day, but I might quote the clear summary that Edith Mirrielees gives in her book *Story Writing* (1947).

> The very point of the story [she says] is our certainty that the day before and the day after exhibit Mr. Peacock exactly as does the day described. Whether it is Mr. Peacock's response to his wife's waking him ... or his singing in his bath; whether it is the Duke's addressing him as "Peacock" —"quite as if he were one of themselves"—or the titled music pupil leaving her violets in his vase, the happening effects neither a change in, nor an added revelation of, Mr. Peacock's attitudes and emotions, nor does it show him meeting any crisis. The purpose of each is to display one foible, which same foible any hour of his life except a sleeping one would display with equal fidelity.

A feature that irritates me in such a narrative is the tone of condescension announced in the title. The "Mr.," standing before Reginald Peacock—in itself an emblematic name—is a nudge from the author warning us that we are not to identify ourselves with this person, but instead to thank God that our days are more varied than his and that something unexpected will happen to us tomorrow. But let us forget Mr. Reginald Peacock, who represents the weaker side of Katherine Mansfield's great talent, the sniffing attitude of revulsion into which she was always in danger of falling. Let us think about slice-of-life narratives in general and ask a simple question: Are they stories properly speaking? Whether they deal with peasants or people in the slums or middle-class snobs like Mr. Peacock, don't they belong to a type best described as fictionized sociology? Being fiction they have less authority than reports by genuine sociologists. Lacking an essential element, a something changed, they afford less pleasure to the reader than a story in which the action is a complete whole in itself. The true story is an organized period of time, much as a sculpture is organized three-dimensional space. Time, as we learn again at every moment, is irreversible. The quality of any moment in life, or in a good story, depends on the moments that preceded it in irreversible sequence. It is true that slice-of-life narratives usually deal with given periods of time, an hour, a day, a week, but since they do not embody changes in quality, they are not organized in time; they are merely sliced out of it.

4 𝒦 At this point, having denied the name of story to such narratives—as I should also deny it to character sketches, mood pieces, newspaper reports (or most of them), and mere bombardments of images, startling in themselves, but arranged in no particular sequence—I might seem to be dogmatic and restrictive. On the contrary, I am trying to broaden the field of study. As soon as we learn to recognize stories in the proper sense of the word, we find them almost anywhere: not only in novels, novellas, short stories, plays, and heroic poems, where they are to be expected, but also in many other types of writing, including essays and even very short lyric poems. The lyric too is an organized period of time. Usually the organizing principle is repetition: that is, the poet establishes a pattern in the first stanza, then repeats it with variations in the stanzas that follow. Meter and rhyme and refrain, if any, serve to mark the passing moments; the poem marches as if to music. Usually the poet's images and statements are presented in an ascending order of intensity, so that the band plays loudest before the music dies away. There is no need for telling a story in poems of this type, which include most of those in Elizabethan songbooks and their successors down to our own time. Many other lyrics, however, are enhanced by the stories they tell, which give them a progressive as well as a repetitive form. I think of a poem by Wordsworth, very short and very famous:

> A slumber did my spirit seal;
>   I had no human fears;
> She seemed a thing that could not feel
>   The touch of earthly years.

> *No motion has she now, no force;*
> *She neither hears nor sees;*
> *Rolled round in earth's diurnal course,*
> *With rocks, and stones, and trees.*

In two brief stanzas Wordsworth has told a complete story; he has given us persons involved in a situation and undergoing an action—the death of Lucy—as a result of which something is changed. One stanza follows another in narrative sequence and their order is irreversible.[3] Lyrics by many other poets might be quoted to make the same point. Blake, Heine, Tennyson, Baudelaire, Apollinaire, Yeats, even Eliot, all used the device of telling stories in their lyric poems. Ezra Pound, with his extraordinary lack of feeling for the sequence of events—indeed, for any sort of sequence—and his extraordinary emphasis on disconnected images, has been almost the only prominent exception.

Stories also abound in more popular types of writing, for example in "subject books" (as publishers call one type of nonfiction), in magazine articles, and in newspaper columns by such familiar figures as Art Buchwald and Russell Baker (as earlier in those by Ring Lardner and Damon Runyon). Not always, but on occasion, these offer us persons involved in a situation and following a course of action that leads to something changed. A few years ago Truman Capote put forward the claim that *In Cold Blood*, his factual narrative of the two young men who were executed for murdering the Clutter family, was a nonfiction novel. I was ready to agree that *In Cold Blood* is a complete story, a shape in time, and one set forth with impressive skill. In some respects, though not in others, it is as much a novel as Dreiser's *An American Tragedy*, which is also based on an actual murder

---

3. I was amused to find that Hugh Kenner, in his book on Ezra Pound, uses the same poem to illustrate the fragmentation of an idea into allotropic images. He says, "The speaker's insentience to temporal ravages, evoked, like a spell, by the girl's animal vitality, is juxtaposed with the emotions implied by her mortality. The connection [between the two stanzas] is not syllogistic." Of course the connection is supplied by an event in time, the death of Lucy.

and execution. But Capote made another claim at which I demurred: he said that he had invented the form. In simple truth the nonfiction novel was never invented; it developed over a period of many years. To name a familiar example, *The Education of Henry Adams*, privately printed in 1907, is an autobiography based on selected details, carefully arranged, and it can be read as a naturalistic novel, a better one than Dreiser's autobiographical *The "Genius."*

*Green Hills of Africa* (1935) was undertaken as an experiment in presenting factual material by means of fictional techniques. Hemingway says in his foreword, "The writer has attempted to write an absolutely true book to see whether the shape of a country and the pattern of a month's action can, if truly presented, compete with a work of the imagination." The experiment was moderately successful, and it has been replicated by many other writers. For the last three decades publishers' lists have been full of "subject books" that are really nonfiction novels. Indeed, the growing popularity of nonfiction is partly owed to the fact that trained novelists less famous than Capote, but still with an instinct for their craft, have been writing so much of it.

Of course its appeal is also owed to an almost universal hunger for stories—myths, fables, true accounts—that help to explain or illuminate one's own life in terms of successive events. Call that hunger atavistic if you will; trace it back to the Babylonians or the Australian aborigines; still it persists today at almost every level of culture—even among avant-garde writers such as John Barth, who says when speaking of his writing persona: "... in his heart of hearts he disliked literature of an experimental, self-regarding, or overtly metaphysical character, like Samuel Beckett's, Marian Cutler's, Jorge Borges's. The logical fantasies of Lewis Carroll pleased him less than straightforward tales of adventure, subtly sentimental romances, even closely circumstantial realisms like Tolstoy's."

When such authors read avant-garde fiction, it is not for pleasure, but chiefly to learn what a rival is up to, or, if they teach writing in colleges—as most of them do—to keep a running broad jump ahead of their bright students. For pleasure they read adventure novels or nonfiction.——At this point in revising my "Defense," I consulted a list of best sellers for the year 1976 that appeared in *The Times Book Review;* it was confined to hardbound fiction and nonfiction sold in bookstores. What impressed me about the annual list, which includes sales figures, was the immensely greater popularity of nonfiction. The ten best-selling novels had a total sale (as reported by their publishers, sometimes with a little optimism) of 1,605,174 copies. This was to be compared with 3,390,717 copies, or more than twice as many, for the ten leading nonfiction titles.[4] Among these "general" books, five were in the broad field of self-knowledge or self-improvement. The other five were "subject books," and they included *Roots,* by Alex Haley, which is truly a nonfiction novel and which, after its success on television, promised to be among the most widely read books of the decade. But all five had a strong narrative element and presented their factual material as "a pattern of events so narrated as to evoke an intended response."

That phrase, as may be remembered, is Margaret Kennedy's definition of a story, and I said that it had the advantage of bringing in the reader or listener and his response. The listener is always present, if only in the storyteller's imagination or on the subconscious level of his mind; if not for the listener, why should the story be *told?* One might answer that children tell stories to themselves, but at such times the child plays a double role: he is

---

4. *The Times Book Review* also publishes a weekly list of paperback best sellers. Although the list does not include sales figures, it is strikingly different from the bookstore list in what it reveals about the demand for novels. For a typical week in the spring of 1977, the mass-market paperback list included fifteen titles, of which only three were nonfiction. Among the twelve novels on the list, two had been widely and favorably reviewed when they first appeared in hard covers. The other ten were "category fiction"—that is, Hollywood scandals (called euphemistically romans à clef), thrillers, "gothics" with persecuted heroines, or science fiction. Most of the category books were pure trash, but others, especially among the thrillers and science fictions, were more imaginative and in a few cases better written than the bookstore favorites. An incidental result of the hunger for stories in the mass audience is that it sometimes encourages purely commercial authors to produce good books; to let their imaginations run riot and damn the book reviewers.

both the teller and the listener, the artist and his audience, and if the listening side of him gets bored, the story is never finished. As for adult storytellers, they are not compulsive talkers or writers bent merely on expressing themselves and having their say. They don't say, they tell or render or, to be more accurate, they use the medium of words to show us persons acting or being acted upon, while arranging the acts in a sequence calculated to grasp and reward our attention. Form, Kenneth Burke said long ago in *Counter-Statement* (1931), is "the psychology of the audience. Or, seen from another angle, form is the creation of an appetite in the mind of an auditor and the adequate satisfying of that appetite." The revolt against form and "stories" is, in one of its aspects, an effort to abolish the audience.

When the story ends something has changed, as I emphasized, and the change is for better or worse. It follows that in the broad sense every story is a fable with a moral concealed, sometimes deeply, in the texture of events. That concealed moral transforms the *post hoc* of narrative into the *propter hoc* of conceptual thought. Usually the good or prudent characters are rewarded after a fashion, if only in their hearts, and the wicked are somehow punished. Often, however, the process is reversed, with the good punished by malign forces or simply by accident, in which case the storyteller implies that there is no justice or reason in this chaotic world. That too is a sort of moral, or anti-moral, and one that may express his inmost feelings with force and brilliance. Kurt Vonnegut, to mention one of the "black" novelists, was twenty-two years old and a prisoner of war in Dresden when the city was destroyed by a firestorm in which 135,000 persons lost their lives. With other surviving prisoners he was detailed to gather and burn the corpses, which he remembers as those of "babies, old people, zoo animals, and thousands upon thousands of rabid Nazis, of course." It was an experience that confirmed his atheism and shaped his future novels. Joseph Heller, another "black" writer, was a lieutenant in the Air Force; he didn't bomb Dresden, but he had his fill of a murderous bureaucracy. Most readers, however, live out their relatively peaceful lives without being sentenced to death by the Air Force, or by Hitler or Stalin.

They would rather not accept the anti-moral, even when they bear in mind the crimes and follies of the years since 1914.

They also feel uncomfortable about a story in which the heroine is killed by accident when, for example, she steps in front of a bus. Accidents, they feel with Aristotle, should be placed at the beginning of a story, not at the end. No matter how sophisticated they may be, they still prefer a pattern or sequence of events that implies some general scheme of rewards and punishments. Shaped as I was by the confident years before the Great War, I confess to sharing, with reservations, that innocent preference. I also confess to feeling that life is the ultimate source of all fictions, even the most fantastic, and that, in its blundering, dilatory, often secret way, it provides an infinite number of fables, renewed in substance and form for each new generation.

# XIV FAULKNER
## The Etiology
## of His Art

1 ✍ If asked to name the central quality in Faulkner's work, one is likely to give the quick answer "Imagination." In respect to that quality, however it may be defined or undefined, no other prose writer of our century has equaled him. Its results as manifested in his novels have been interpreted in an extensive and still growing library of critical writing. But curiously—or so it seems to me—hardly anyone has tried to describe the nature of Faulkner's imagination in itself or to set forth the largely unconscious laws by which it operated. It did have laws—of that we can be certain—and one thing led to another by some inner design, but what was the design? What was the process by which a homely picture—"the muddy seat of a little girl's drawers in a pear tree, where she could see through a window where her grandmother's funeral was taking place and report what was happening to her brothers on the ground below"—could be elaborated into an

extraordinary novel, told in four sections by four different narrators, and leading into other novels, told by still other narrators from their different points of view, but most of them dealing with Faulkner's "own little postage stamp of native soil"? What was the imaginative pattern that held them all together?

It is questions like these that John T. Irwin has tried to answer in *Doubling and Incest—Repetition and Revenge* (1975), a "speculative reading," as he calls it, that is by far the most widely discussed and stimulating of later Faulkner studies. It is the most troubling, too, partly because of its insights, which will persuade many Faulkner students, including myself, to change some of their judgments, and partly because of its omissions and simplifications. Irwin thinks he has found "a key to the structure"—or pattern or design or psychological conformation—"out of which Faulkner's best work is written." That key is the figure of Quentin Compson as presented in the second section of *The Sound and the Fury* and again, more objectively, in *Absalom, Absalom!* By "oscillating," as Irwin says, from one novel to the other, and by interpreting the fall of Colonel Sutpen's house as a "repetition"—but fifty years in advance—of events in the Compson family, the critic recasts Quentin's story as a paradigm of Faulkner's work in general.

Irwin's book, with its insights and omissions, is an example of what might be called meta-Freudian criticism, an increasingly popular school. Here it is seasoned with more than a dash of Structuralism. After Irwin has restructured Quentin's story, however, this becomes a somber psychodrama of the sort that might have been offered as a case history by Freud's early disciple, Otto Rank, or might possibly be filmed by Ingmar Bergman.

We are told that Quentin, at some unspecified stage in his early life, wants to have sexual relations with his mother. He fears, however, that his father will punish the guilty impulse by castrating him. (One notes that "castrating" is being used here in its ambiguous Freudian sense, not in its dictionary meaning. What the child fears, in the Freudian scheme, is not castration, about which he knows and imagines nothing, but amputation of the offending member.) Repressing his first desire, but holding fast to incest, Quentin transfers the cathexis to his sister, Candace or Caddy, as a substitute for the mother. What he really wishes, however, is to be resorbed into his mother's womb.

Infantilely regressed, fixated in secondary narcissism, unable to feel real affection for others, Quentin doubles or triples his beloved self into various persons. One of them is Sister Caddy, his mirror image; another is Quentin's "bright" or paternal self, bent on acting as a brother avenger; and still another is his shadow self or brother seducer. But the brother seducer cannot seduce, and the brother avenger cannot take vengeance when Caddy is seduced by Dalton Ames. Disheartened by this double failure, Quentin falsely confesses to his father that he has committed incest with Caddy. He wants to be punished—to be castrated, that is—so that Mr. Compson will be forced to acknowledge that Quentin had once been virile enough to act as his father's rival.

All this has been reinterpreted, and at points misinterpreted, from Quentin's reveries on the day of his suicide. I must add that Irwin casts light on passages neglected by other interpreters, and that he makes a strong case for some—not all—of his suppositions. He is especially good on Quentin's feelings for Caddy and on his effort to escape from time and his shadow. Soon the critic's attention swings over to *Absalom, Absalom!* He pictures Quentin and Shreve McCannon in their freezing room at Harvard as they puzzle out the details of Colonel Sutpen's story. Quentin is fascinated by the Sutpen children because they anticipate his own tripled self: the brother seducer (Charles Bon), the brother avenger (Henry Sutpen), and their sister Judith, the mirror image of both. Quentin and Shreve, who are doubles of a sort, identify themselves with Henry and Charles. Here again Irwin casts light on the structure of the novel, as well as on Quentin's frenzy.

After a detour through Guy Rosolato's *Essais sur le Symbolique,* with its hazardous theories about the meaning of religious sacrifices, Irwin's narrative swings back to Quentin's last day on earth. Quentin has reviewed the events of his inner life and has repeated some of them symbolically. Now he plunges into the Charles River, holding two flatirons so that his body won't rise again. Quentin's suicide is a double action, so Irwin explains. "As the murder of the brother seducer by the brother avenger (the drowning of the shadow self), [it] is obviously the killing of the son by the father, but as the merging of the shadow with the mirror image in the water, the image of his sister Candace, it is the son's reentry into his mother's womb, a supplanting of the father that amounts to a 'killing' of the father." But it has other meanings as well, being somehow identified with Christ's sacrifice "on the phallic tree." Since it abolishes future generations of Compsons, it also represents a triumph over time and over the "doom"—to use Faulkner's word—of having to repeat the errors of past generations.

And what would Faulkner have said to this elaborate restructuring of Quentin's psyche? He was not hostile to reinterpreters, since his novels were there, detached from the novelist and open to various readings. Perhaps, if he had gone no farther in Irwin's book, Faulkner might have written him to point out some errors, but also to compliment Irwin on his astuteness. He might even have used much the same terms as in a 1941 letter to Warren Beck. "You found implications," Faulkner had said there, "which I had missed. I wish that I had consciously intended them; I will certainly believe that I did it subconsciously and not by accident." But Irwin still has other things to say, further conclusions to draw as he approaches the end of his book, and to some of these Faulkner would have raised violent objections.

"It is tempting," Irwin tells us, "to see in Quentin a surrogate of Faulkner." Yes, the temptation is strongly present, considering that Faulkner makes more use of Quentin—at least in the early work—than he does of other narrators, and that Quentin's perceptions often seem close to those of the author. But Irwin yields to the temptation a little too easily. "It is as if," he concludes, "in the character of Quentin, Faulkner embodied, and perhaps tried to exorcise, certain elements present in himself and in his need to be a writer." What were those elements? Is

Irwin at least faintly implying that Faulkner was infantilely regressed, fixated in secondary narcissism, seized with fears of castration, and unable to feel affection except for shadows? Is he implying more clearly that Faulkner escaped Quentin's fate only by writing novels? "Writing a book," Irwin says, "creating a work of art, is not so much an alternative to suicide as a kind of alternative suicide: writing as an act of autoerotic self- destruction."

I don't want to be tender-minded about Faulkner, for all the vast debt we owe to his work. It had better be admitted that even the greatest members of the literary community are open to aberrations that often include hatred of the fathers (whether familial or literary), obsessive narcissism (which used to be called self-centeredness), and manic-depressive tendencies. But Irwin ventures into dangerous ground when he analyzes Quentin as the author's surrogate. He should remind himself at every moment that Quentin, though he embodied elements of the author's self, probably more of them than any other character, was finally as much a dramatized figure as Hamlet was (or Rosa Coldfield or Mink Snopes). That need to dramatize everyone in his world, and himself along with the others, was among the fixed laws of Faulkner's imagination. He even spoke of himself in the third person—"Faulkner might have thought," he was heard to say—as if Faulkner-who-wrote-the-novels was another dramatized character, to be sharply distinguished from Faulkner-in-the-flesh. Yes, he doubled or tripled or centupled himself, but the doubles, even Quentin, were not mere self-images. He used scores of fictional narrators in telling his stories, but he made them something more than substitutes or surrogates or spokesmen for the author; each was given a life of his own. Thus, when I showed him an early interpretation of *Absalom, Absalom!* in 1944, he accepted most of it, but at one point he called me to order. "I think Quentin, not Faulkner, is the correct yardstick here," he said in a letter. "I was writing the story, but he not I was brooding over a situation. I mean, I was creating him as a character, as well as Sutpen et al." The letter (reprinted in *The Faulkner-Cowley File*) went on to discuss some of Quentin's judgments where they differed from his own: "Quentin *probably* contemplated Sutpen . . ." he said (my italics). It was as if Faulkner were speaking of a dead friend, possibly a cousin.

Irwin does not make this necessary distinction between author and character, though I grant that he is generally discreet in ascribing Quentin's traits to Faulkner-in-the-flesh. He is talking about the novelist, not directly about the man. Thus, he does not make an error which many others have made, that of trying to identify the Compson family with the Falkners (not Faulkners) of Mississippi. Those others should be reminded firmly that the novelist's parents bore no resemblance to Mr. and Mrs. Compson and that the four Compson children were imagined, not copied from life. There were four Falkner children too, but they did not include a Quentin, a Caddy (or any other sister to arouse incestuous dreams), a mean-spirited Jason, or an idiot boy.

But Irwin, while confining himself to the Compsons as an imagined family, often seems to strain the text, or neglect parts of the text, in order to stress an Oedipal situation. He says, for example, that "there is present in Quentin's section [of *The Sound and the Fury*] a thinly veiled hatred of the father." Hatred? If present it is too thickly veiled for most readers to perceive it. Quentin has cause to resent his father's weakness and cynicism, but the resentment, if truly felt, is mingled with trust and affection (as can be noted in the first half of *Absalom, Absalom!*, which Irwin hardly considers at all). Quentin appears as narrator elsewhere in Faulkner's work—that is, in two collected stories and in early magazine or manuscript versions of three or four others —and these give us no indication of hostility between son and father. In "That Evening Sun," which is one of the great stories —and why doesn't Irwin mention it?—Quentin and Caddy as children are allied with Mr. Compson in a tacit conspiracy against the detested mother. "I stood silent," Quentin tells us, "because father and I both knew that mother would want him to make me stay with her if she just thought of it in time. So father didn't look at me." Even as a very young child, Quentin had been neglected by his mother, who loved and spoiled only Jason. Their black servant Dilsey, not Mrs. Compson, was the familiar figure in the nursery. This is not the usual Oedipal situation.

It is hard to imagine that Quentin at any age had felt the wish
—not to mention a need for repressing the wish—to re-enter
Mrs. Compson's inhospitable womb.

Irwin is always eager to find evidence of Oedipal desires
or hatreds or, failing that, of the castration complex. Thus, he
says that Miss Quentin's theft of money—most of it her own—
from her uncle Jason "is presented as a symbolic castration of
Jason (who is his father's namesake and who has had his younger
brother Benjy gelded) by the dead Quentin's namesake. . . . Since
Jason's friend Lorraine is a prostitute, the theft of Jason's money
is a castration of his power to buy sex, and since the money that
was stolen was in part money that Jason had stolen from his
niece, Jason is rendered impotent, he is powerless to gain any
legal redress. Jason dies a childless bachelor." Here Irwin, with
that grand meta-Freudian disregard for the dictionary, is confusing childlessness with impotence, and impotence with being
balked by the law, and this in turn with castration. What we learn
from Faulkner's Epilogue to *The Sound and the Fury* is that
Jason continued his affair with Lorraine (or another Memphis
prostitute) for at least fifteen years after losing his hoard, and that
he was seen with her every Sunday morning "mounting the apartment stairs with paper bags from the grocer's . . . domestic, uxorious,
connubial." A connubial eunuch? Only a very speculative critic
would ask us to accept that reading.


2 ✍ *A Digression:* Irwin is one of the critics who, in their
effort to find and elaborate symbols, give Faulkner credit for
scholarly information that one very much doubts whether he
possessed. Thus, in discussing the Quentin section of *The Sound
and the Fury*, Irwin asserts that its date—June 2, 1910—has a
"liturgical significance" resembling that of the dates for the other
three sections. "June 2, the day of Quentin's drowning," he says,
"is the feast day of St. Erasmus (also known as St. Elmo), who is
the patron saint of sailors, particularly of sailors caught in a

storm, and thus the saint whose special care it is to prevent drownings." A footnote refers us to Lucy Menzies, *The Saints in Italy*, pp. 153–54. But it is highly improbable that Faulkner had read Lucy Menzies' book. With his Protestant background he read the Bible, but he showed no interest in the lives of Catholic saints. His reason for the assigned date of Quentin's death is still a puzzling question. "It is the eve of Jefferson Davis's birthday," another critic explains with assurance. Davis was not one of Faulkner's heroes. Isn't it possible that the date was chosen arbitrarily, within the limits provided by the text? It had to be a weekday near the end of the academic year. June 2, 1910, was a Thursday and that might help to explain the choice, considering that the other three sections take place respectively on Holy Saturday, Good Friday, and Easter Sunday.

At another point Irwin uses the killing of Colonel Sutpen as preface to a rather long discussion. Wash Jones, the killer with a rusty scythe, has been taken by some critics as symbolizing Father Time. Irwin not only agrees with the interpretation but carries it back into antiquity. He says, "It is more than likely that Faulkner intends that this allusion to the figure of Father Time should remind us of the genesis of that figure in mythology, for Father Time is an ancient conflation, based in part on a similarity of two names, of two figures—Kronos, Zeus's father, and Chronos, the personification of Time. As we know,"—but did Faulkner, who was not a student of Greek mythology?—"that conflation ultimately led to the attachment of at least two of the major legends of Kronos to Father Time—first, that Kronos is a man who castrated his father, Ouranos, and was in turn castrated by his own son Zeus, and second, that Kronos is a father who devours his children." The discussion continues for two pages or more, bringing in Nietzsche's conception of the revenge against time, then circling back to Quentin Compson on the day of his suicide. All this is pertinent to Irwin's thesis about parricide, filicide, and castration, but not at all pertinent to what Faulkner actually wrote from his private store of experience and knowledge.

It is, moreover, a serious question whether Wash Jones and his rusty scythe were intended to symbolize Time the Destroyer. They might suggest another scythe-bearing figure, that of the Grim Reaper, but that would be chiefly a metaphor used to dignify Sutpen's death. Against Irwin's interpretation there is something close to substantive evidence, in the shape of the short story "Wash," written and published nearly three years before *Absalom, Absalom!* and later revised as part of the novel. The revisions were less in substance than in narrative point of view. It is clearer in the story, however, that Wash Jones does not symbolize Time, which in fact plays a minor part in the action as compared with a class conflict. An intensely human figure, Wash *represents* (which is something different from symbolizing) the class of shiftless whites out of which Colonel Sutpen had risen (in the novel but not the story) before he won a place in the planter class. Wash rebels when Sutpen treats him and his granddaughter Milly as subhuman creatures. He cuts down the Colonel with a scythe because it is the only weapon at hand. *"Better,"* he thinks, *"if his kind and mine too had never drawn the breath of life on this earth. Better that all who remain of us be blasted from the face of earth than that another Wash Jones should see his whole life shredded from him and shrivel away like a dried shuck thrown onto the fire."* Those lines from the story are repeated in the novel, where Wash once again is an individual who speaks for his kind. To interpret him as a symbol of Time—I came near saying "a mere symbol"—is to weaken his human qualities for the reader and almost to obliterate his social meaning.

The interpretation, though, is tidy and tempting and I suspect that Faulkner himself might have accepted it, once it was pointed out to him. He might even have said, as in his letter to Warren Beck, "I wish that I had consciously intended [it]; I will certainly believe that I did it subconsciously and not by accident." He made similar remarks in other letters, about the meaning of other situations. One gains the impression that he regarded his subconscious as a mysterious ally, a shadowy force making suggestions that he didn't always understand, but one capable of producing bold effects "not by accident." He was proud of its feats and, as a writing man, proud of having found means to keep in touch with it.

Those means may never be fully explored. Possibly one of them was the dangerous expedient of drinking whisky while he wrote, at least in the early years (though he seldom mentioned drinking and writing together). There were other means, however, that he sometimes revealed in conversation. "Get it down," he said to me. "Take chances. It may be bad, but that's the only way you can do anything really good." It was as if he had learned how and when to suspend the operation of his keen critical sense. Again he said, "There are some kinds of writing that you have to do very fast, like riding a bicycle on a tightrope." The remark suggested something close to experiments in automatic writing, but I did not pursue the subject. Instead I mentioned Hawthorne's complaint that the Devil got into his inkpot. Faulkner said, "I listen to the voices, and when I put down what the voices say, it's right. Sometimes I don't like what they say, but I don't change it." We learn from his manuscripts that he did change it on occasion, or at least that he rearranged it into different sequences, since he was an habitual and gifted revisionist. One might say of him that he combined the greatest possible use of his subconscious resources (the side of him that we call his genius) with highly conscious control of the written material (the side that we call his talent). In the course of those often masterful revisions, the voices might speak to him again, as notably—one might say miraculously—during the last months of 1941 when he was recasting "The Bear." He tried at all times to preserve the integrity of what the voices said.

In later years I remembered Faulkner's mention of "the voices" when I read a statement by William Carlos Williams in his essay "How to Write." There Williams asserts, "The demonic power of the mind is the racial and individual past, it is the rhythmic ebb and flow of the mysterious life process and unless this is tapped by the writer nothing of moment can result.... [Poets] are in touch with voices, but this is the very essence of their power, the voices are the past, the depths of our very beings." I suspect that for Faulkner too the voices were the past as it lived convulsively in the present. Often they suggest something close to the Jungian notion of a racial or collective unconscious.

"Red Leaves," for example—another of the great stories—carries us back to a prelogical stage of culture. Is it a true picture of customs that prevailed among the Chickasaws about the year 1820? Ethnologists could answer that question—in the negative, I surmise—but we feel that the ritualized pursuit of Issetibbeha's body servant and his ritual death on The Man's grave belong to a pattern surviving deep in the psyche.

In "The Bear" as a hunting story, everything happens at the right, the inevitable moment as if by enchantment. A single episode might stand for many others. The orphan boy apprenticed to the wilderness, Ike McCaslin, has determined to see Old Ben, the legendary bear. He searches alone for him on the first day, the second day, the third day, obeying the rule of three that prevails in fairy stories. On the evening of the third day, old Sam Fathers tells him, "It's the gun." He takes the mage's advice and leaves his gun behind on the fourth day, carrying with him only a stick against snakes, a watch, and a compass. Still the search is vain, so he puts aside every man-made instrument, hanging the watch and the compass on a bush and leaning his stick beside them. He has lost himself in the wilderness, made himself part of it. "Then he saw the bear. It did not emerge, appear: it was just there, immobile, fixed in the green and windless noon's hot dappling, not so big as he had dreamed it, but as big as he had expected, bigger, dimensionless against the dappled obscurity, looking at him." That goes beyond Freud's perceptive but somewhat narrow concept of "the uncanny." To the reader—to this reader—it is the work of a magician, real, undeniable, but also an apparition that evokes ancestral nightmares. I fail to see any connection with the Oedipus complex that Irwin finds almost everywhere in Faulkner's novels. Is Old Ben a father symbol? Does Ike McCaslin face him as an active-passive candidate for emasculation? The answer is that Faulkner's best work contains many situations besides those that Irwin presents. As revealed in "The Bear" and elsewhere, Faulkner's imagination was a treasure house stored with many sorts of images, persons, events, not to mention patterns, motives, dreams, and compulsions. Irwin ransacks the treasure house, but the booty he carries back is disappointing: it consists of symbols, some of gold, some of britannia metal, and a "structure" based solely on interpersonal relations, always sexual, in the patrilinear family. Faulkner's work is much more than that.


3 ✍ Irwin's work is more than that, too. After presenting Quentin Compson's story as a paradigm of Faulkner's novels (or at least of his "best" novels), Irwin extends the paradigm; he makes it apply to the creation of imaginative works in general: not only novels but plays, poems, paintings, and sculptures. The extension comes near the end of the book, in a discussion of Faulkner's second novel, *Mosquitoes* (1927), hardly one of the best. A character in the novel, Gordon the sculptor, has been looking down at his own image in the water. "In Gordon's thoughts," Irwin tells us,

> . . . the three major elements of the artist's relation to his work are apparent—incest, autoeroticism, and self-destruction. The artist's reflection of himself conjoined with the work of art is "as a woman who conceives without pleasure bears without pain," [Irwin is quoting the sculptor] yet this psychic incest of the masculine self with the feminine-masculine work is also an autoerotic act, the self making love to the self, a kind of creative onanism in which, through the use of the phallic pen on the "pure space" of the virgin page or the chisel on the virgin marble, the self is continually spent and wasted in an act of progressive self-destruction. Indeed, when Gordon looks at his image and thinks, "christ by his own hand an autogethsemane," the phrase "by his own hand" simultaneously suggests a self-portrait, self-destruction, and self-abuse.

That comes close to being an X-rated movie of the artist at work. I surmise that there is truth in the picture, underneath the garish images, but the truth is a partial one that reduces the creative process to its sexual elements. Where are those other elements that generations of aestheticians and artists have argued about: art as mimesis, art as poiesis or making (which Irwin regards as an autoerotic act), art as persuasion (or rhetoric or simple communication), art as catharsis, art in relation to the tribe, art and the sense of play? Irwin's picture is ultimately based on Freud (and Otto Rank), but here again he is reductive. Where do we find in it anything corresponding to Freud's statement that the artist is exposed to more than the usual strains, that these are a constant source of fantasies, but that, with his special gifts, he knows how to find his way back to reality and how to mold his fantasies into something that the world is forced to accept as valid and a source of joy? That statement, which I have roughly paraphrased, has the virtue of including the "special gifts" of the artist, his sense of "reality," and a relation to "the world," his audience. Irwin is not concerned with any of these, but only with the artist's neuroses.

Poor artist, poor novelist, poor poet! In recent works of meta-Freudian criticism, he stands accused of every familiar aberration: not only incest, parricide, self-mutilation, and self-abuse but also petty sins like womb hunger, sado-masochism, fetishism, voyeurism, exhibitionism, and injustice collecting, all of which are said to be part of his professional character. All have in common the fact of being regressions, although their source is ascribed by different authorities to different moments in the artist's early life: the birth trauma, the oral stage, the anal stage (for pedantic writers), the first Oedipal confrontation, and secondary narcissism. "The writer," said the late Dr. Edmund Bergler, himself a voluminous writer, "is an orally regressed psychic masochist." Bergler traced the regression back to the moment when the artist's mother first denied him her breast. Irwin isn't guilty of that particular silliness, but for him, too, creating works of art is a sad activity, aberrant, regressive, and self-destroying. It is a psychic disease, to put it bluntly, and Irwin is bent on tracking down its causes, on defining its etiology.

Of course the imaginative writer suffers from being made

the subject of a clinical report, but his books suffer too when they are placed on the analyst's couch; their scope is narrowed, their meaning distorted. Irwin's "structure" does not apply to all of Faulkner's writing, nor even to all of the "best work." Notably it does not apply to the "daylight" books, those in which Faulkner is dealing with nature, or with character and class in a rural society, or is telling tall tales in the Southwestern manner (and with a quiet chuckle). It applies somewhat more to the "midnight" or obsessed novels, including two of the greatest, but even there it results in deformations.

Thus, Irwin's discussion of *The Sound and the Fury* is based on the second or Quentin section, which has seemed to many readers the weakest of the four. Irwin makes the section stronger and deeper, but still his treatment diminishes the effect of the novel as a whole. In simple truth the novel is concerned only in part with Quentin's inner conflicts and how he resolved them by suicide. Its principal theme is the decline of the Compson family, which stands by synecdoche (not symbolism) for the Old South. When we read the other three sections, many of the characters assume different values from those which Irwin assigns to them. Mr. Compson is a victim, not a rival who helped to destroy his oldest son. Mrs. Compson, stupid and selfish, is largely responsible for the ruin of her children. Black Dilsey, never once mentioned by Irwin, is the surviving heroine: "I seed de first en de last."

When Irwin "oscillates" to *Absalom, Absalom!*, he makes Quentin, not Colonel Sutpen, the center of the story, and thus transforms it into a private drama of doubling and revenge. It thereby gains something in psychological depth (although I begin to be dubious about that "depth" now that so many critics have plumbed it at no inconvenience to themselves), but the gain is made at the cost of denying that the novel is also a tragic fable of Southern history. That suggests my central grievance against the meta-Freudian method as applied to fiction. It rules out everything historical or regional or communal or merely public; it rules out the whole kingdom of nature (except for yin-and-yang symbols); and it leaves us with nothing but the naked self fantasizing self-images or doubles and striving for vengeance against the father.

It is true that Irwin tries to smuggle back at least a shadow of historical meaning. "For Faulkner," he says, "doubling and incest are both images of the self-enclosed . . . and as such, both appear in his novels as symbols of the state of the South after the Civil War, symbols of a region turned in upon itself." Does that make the South a mere shadow of the situation in the Compson family? Or does it make the Compsons a mere projection of Southern history? Which came first in Faulkner's imagination—which seemed more real to him—the region and its tragic history or the persons in the foreground of each novel?

I suggest that both were real and existed together almost from the beginning; that Faulkner's imagination was communal and historical as well as being occupied with solipsisms and closed family circles. For many of his heroes "father" soon became "the fathers," that is, all the generations of Compsons and Sartorises and McCaslins, but especially the men of "was," of the days before the Civil War. With their families they composed a social order that included those who rode off, "arrogant and proud on the fine horses," to teach the Yankees a lesson. Mr. Compson says of the fathers—and Quentin agrees with him—that they were "people too as we are, and victims too as we are, but victims of a different circumstance, simpler and therefore, integer for integer, larger, more heroic and the figures therefore more heroic too." But they had tragic flaws that led to their defeat by the Yankees and doomed their sons and grandsons both—here again Quentin agrees—to be "diffused and scattered creatures drawn blindly limb from limb from a grab bag." One notes how very soon, for Faulkner's protagonists, "he" becomes "they" and "I" is socialized into "we."

The figure of the mother also becomes transformed for Faulkner, but in a mistier fashion; it is not so much socialized as naturalized into the spirit of the land itself, for which he feels (or some of his characters feel) a more than filial affection. One remembers Ike McCaslin's great reverie in "Delta Autumn," the lines that begin: "This Delta, he thought. This Delta. *This land that man has deswamped and denuded and derivered in two generations. . . .*" For "deswamped and denuded and derivered" should one read "deflowered"? This Delta is also the land where *"usury and mortgage and bankruptcy and measureless wealth, Chinese and African and Aryan and Jew, all breed and spawn together until no man has time to say which one is which nor cares."* The reader wonders, without finding an easy answer, why images of the land are often followed, in Faulkner's work, by images of miscegenation. The land bears children of many races. Its maternal quality—or rather that of the wilderness—is more precisely named in another of Ike McCaslin's reveries, this one in the last section of "The Bear." "—; summer, and fall, and snow," he thinks, "and wet and saprife spring in their ordered immortal sequence, the deathless and immemorial phases of the mother who had shaped him if any had toward the man he almost was." In other novels Faulkner sometimes presents the fruitful land (not the wilderness) in the shape of a pregnant earth goddess such as Dewey Dell Bundren or Eula Varner or Lena Grove.

But he doesn't bother to be consistent. Old Ben the he-bear is also the spirit and totem of the wilderness; when he dies a ritual death, the wilderness is destroyed. Mink Snopes, at the end of *The Mansion,* thinks of the earth as "it," an impersonal force: "a man had to spend not just all his life but all the time of Man too guarding against it." One might waste yearlong efforts in trying to accommodate all the images—male and female, social, natural, compulsive—in a coherent system. And yet, contradictory as they sometimes are, based largely on the subconscious or on the accidents of writing, they reinforce one another in Faulkner's work. Irwin is denying the scope and complexity of the work, and of Faulkner's imagination, when he tries to reduce them both to a single Oedipal structure.

—And a final word about Irwin's scheme as applied to the creation of imaginative works in general. The scheme is sexist, to use the cant word, in a rather naïve fashion. For Irwin the artist is always "he," the male who lusts after his mother, who fears that he will be castrated by his father, and who later indulges in "psychic incest of the masculine self with the feminine-masculine work . . . through the use of the phallic pen on the 'pure space' of the virgin page." What about the great women writers who were denied those fruitful aberrations by mere facts of anatomy? If producing works of art is a psychic disease, as Irwin seems to believe, it must have had a different etiology in the cases of Jane Austen, George Eliot, Virginia Woolf. Will Irwin explain to us how they contracted the disease and why they exhibited almost the same symptoms as their great male contemporaries?

# XV CONRAD AIKEN
## From Savannah
## to Emerson

1 ✍  Rereading Conrad Aiken's work, one is impressed again by
the unity that underlies its real mass and apparent diversity. He
published some fifty books, all told, and they include novels,
stories, criticism, a play, an autobiography, and thirty or more
books of poems that were finally brought together in *Collected
Poems: Second Edition,* a volume of more than a thousand closely
printed pages. He was a poet essentially, but he was also the
complete man of letters, distinguished for his work in many forms
of verse and prose. The unity was there, however, and in every
form he spoke with the same candid, scrupulous, self-deprecatory,
yet reckless and fanciful New England voice. Yes, the voice was
that of his ancestors, not of his birthplace. Aiken says of himself
in his last poem, "Obituary in Bitcherel,"

*Born in beautiful Savannah*
*to which he daily sang hosanna*
*yet not of southern blood was he*
*he was in fact a damned Yankee.*

I remember first meeting him in 1918, when I was a junior at Harvard. Not long before I had read *The Jig of Forslin,* a long poem that impressed and a little frightened the apprentice poet by what it had done to achieve a symphonic form. I went to see its publisher, Edmund Brown, who ran a little bookstore near the Back Bay station, and he gave me the author's address. There was an exchange of letters and Aiken suggested that we meet in the lobby of the Hotel Touraine. I was to look for a man in an orange necktie who wasn't a fairy.

Aiken was then twenty-eight years old, was six years out of college, and was already the author of two red-haired children and four published volumes of post-Romantic poetry, besides two others waiting to appear. On that mild February evening I saw the necktie as he came in the door; it was brighter than his Valencia-orange hair. For the rest he wore the Harvard uniform of the period: white button-down oxford shirt and brown suit. His forehead was broad, his jaw was square, and his blue eyes were set wide apart. Short and solidly built, a block of a man, he had a look of mingled shyness and pugnacity

I remember that our conversation was broken at first, but that later, over seidels of beer, we found many common interests in spite of my callowness and our nine years' difference in age. We both liked Boston in decay, we had notions about the French Symbolists, we spoke of achieving architectural and musical effects in verse (such as Aiken in fact had achieved), and we were fascinated by the political maneuvers of the poetry world without wishing to take part in them. Soon we were talking without pauses, talking with such excitement—at least on my part—that I didn't notice the streets through which we wandered before parting at the door of Aiken's lodging house, on the unfashionable side of Beacon Hill.

I was right to be excited, and elated too, since I found

afterward that Aiken seldom opened himself to literary strangers. There were years when he stayed away from almost all writers and editors as a matter of principle, and I was lucky to be one of the few exceptions. He refused to attend literary dinners and could seldom be inveigled into cocktail parties. In some ways the shyest man I knew, he was also one of the best talkers. The shyness kept him from talking in company except for an occasional pun: thus, he would describe his friend Tom Eliot's notes to *The Waste Land* as a "verbiform appendix," or Frost's less successful poems as having "the artlessness that conceals artlessness"; but such phrases were spoken in a voice so low that most of the company missed them. Only quite late at night, or earlier over martinis with one or two friends, would he launch into one of those monologues that ought to be famous for their mixture of flagrant wit and complete unself-protective candor.

In the course of time I discovered that candor was close to being his central principle as a man and a writer, particularly as a poet. The principle evolved into a system of aesthetics and literary ethics that unified his work, a system based on the private and public value of self-revelation. No matter what sort of person the poet might be, healthy or neurotic, Aiken believed that his real business was "to give the lowdown on himself, and through himself on humanity." If he was sick in mind, candor might be his only means of curing himself. "Out of your sickness let your sickness speak," Aiken says in one of his Preludes—

> the bile must have his way—the blood his froth—
> poison will come to the tongue. Is hell your kingdom?
> you know its privies and its purlieus? keep
> sad record of its filth? Why this is health.

"Look within thyself to find the truth" might have been his Emersonian motto; and it had the corollary that inner truth corresponds to outer truth, as self or microcosm does to macrocosm. Aiken believed that the writer should be a surgeon performing an exploratory operation on himself, at whatever cost to his self-esteem, and penetrating as with a scalpel through layer after layer of the semiconscious. That process of achieving self-knowledge might well become a self-inflicted torture. At times the writer might feel—so Aiken reports from experience—"the shock of an enormous exposure: as if he had been placed on a cosmic table, *en plein soleil,* for a cosmic operation, a cosmic intrusion." Let him persist, however, and he will be rewarded by finding—here I quote from a letter—"what you think or feel that is secretly you—shamefully you—intoxicatingly you." Then, having laid bare this secret self, which is also a universal self, the writer must find words for it, accurate and honest words, but poured forth—Aiken says in a Prelude—without reckoning the consequences:

> *Let us be reckless of our words and worlds,*
> *And spend them freely as the tree his leaves.*

Here enters the public as opposed to the merely private value of complete self-revelation. By finding words for his inmost truth, the writer—especially the poet—has made it part of the world, part of human consciousness. He has become a soldier, so to speak, in the agelong war that mankind has been waging against the subliminal and the merely instinctive.

But service in that war involves much that lies beyond the simple process of discovering and revealing one's secret self. The writer must divide himself into two persons, one the observer, the other a subject to be observed, and the first must approach the second "with relentless and unsleeping objectivity." The observer-and-narrator must face what Aiken calls "That eternal problem of language, language extending consciousness and then consciousness extending language, in circular or spiral ascent"; and he must also face the many problems of architectural and sequential form. The words that depict the observed self must not only be honest; they must be "twisted around," in Aiken's phrase, until they have a shape and structure of their own; until they become an "artifact" (a favorite word of his) and if possible a masterpiece that will have a lasting echo in other minds. The "supreme task" performed by a masterpiece—as well as by lesser works and deeds in a more temporary fashion—is that of broadening, deepening, and subtilizing the human consciousness. Any man who devotes himself to that evolving task will find in it, Aiken says, "all that he could possibly require in the way of a religious credo."

His name for the credo was "the religion of consciousness."[1] It is a doctrine—no, more than that, a system of belief—to which he gave many refinements and ramifications. Some of these are set forth, with an impressive density of thought and feeling, in two long series of philosophical lyrics, *Preludes for Memnon* (1931) and *Time in the Rock* (1936); Aiken regarded these as his finest work. But the doctrine is a unifying theme in almost all the poetry of his middle years, say from 1925 to 1956, and in the prose as well. It is clearly exemplified in his novels, especially in *Blue Voyage* (1927), which brought young Malcolm Lowry from England to sit at the author's feet, and *Great Circle* (1933), which contains a brilliant, drunken, self-revealing monologue that Freud admired; he kept the book in his Vienna waiting room. Self-discovery is often the climax of Aiken's stories, and it is, moreover, the true theme of his autobiography, *Ushant* (1952). At the end of the book he says of his shipmates on a postwar voyage to England, "They were all heroes, every one of them; they were all soldiers; as now, and always, all mankind were soldiers; all of them engaged in the endless and desperate war on the unconscious."

---

1. The phrase "religion of consciousness" was I think first used in print by F. O. Matthiessen in *Henry James: The Major Phase* (New York: Oxford University Press, 1944); it serves as title for the last chapter. But the chapter has less to say about James's consciousness than one expects of such a fruitful critic as Matthiessen. Long after reading the book, I learned that he had discussed it with Aiken and had borrowed the phrase from him, after receiving Aiken's permission.

2 🖋 Aiken's life had an intricate unity almost like that of his poetry and his fiction. Such is one's impression after reading *Ushant,* which deserves a place among the great autobiographies. In American literature there is nothing to compare with it except *The Education of Henry Adams,* which is equally well composed, equally an artifact—to use Aiken's word again—but which gives us only one side of the author. In *Ushant* the author writes in the third person, like Adams, and maintains the same objective tone, while recording not only his "education" but also his faults and obsessions, his infidelities, his recurrent dreams, his uproarious or shabby adventures: in short, while trying "to give the lowdown on himself, and through himself on humanity."

His pursuit of the essential self leads him back to his childhood in Savannah, spent in a house with a high front stoop and a chinaberry tree in the back yard. He tells of two experiences in the Savannah house that were to shape the rest of his life. One of these was lying on the carpeted floor of the nursery and reading the epigraph to the first chapter of *Tom Brown's School Days:*

> *I'm the poet of White Horse Vale, Sir,*
> *With liberal notions under my cap.*

Not understanding the word "poet," Conrad asked his father what it meant, and learned that the admired father had also written poems. From that moment the boy determined to be a poet himself, with liberal notions, and to live in England somewhere near White Horse Vale. Indeed he was to live there for many years, in a house with a big room in which he tried to re-create the parlor of the Savannah house. "The entire life," he says, "had thus in a sense annihilated time, and remained, as it were, in a capsule or in a phrase." It was the second experience, however, that confirmed the first and froze it into an enduring pattern. Since it was the last and grisliest scene of the poet's childhood in Savannah, it should be presented in his own words:

"... after the desultory early-morning quarrel came the half-stifled scream, and then the sound of his father's voice counting three, and the two loud pistol shots; and he had tiptoed into the dark room, where the two bodies lay motionless, and apart, and, finding them dead, found himself possessed of them forever."

Perhaps it would be more accurate to say that the dead New England parents took possession of their son. Conrad was brought north to live with relatives in New Bedford, but still he was to spend the rest of his life coming to terms with his father and his mother. There was to be a third experience, however, that also helped to shape his career, though it was partly a sequel to what happened in Savannah. Conrad had spent happy years at Harvard and had made some lifelong friends, including Tom Eliot. When he was about to be graduated, in 1911, he was elected class poet. He refused the honor, resigned from college in something close to panic, and fled to Italy. "He had known, instantly," he says in *Ushant*, "that this kind of public appearance, and for such an occasion, was precisely what the flaw in his inheritance would not, in all likelihood, be strong enough to bear.... It was his decision that his life was to be lived *off-stage*, behind the scenes, out of view." In the next sixty years he did not change his mind. Aiken never, to my knowledge, gave a public lecture, read his poems to a women's club (or any other live audience), or appeared on a platform to accept an honorary degree.

Partly as a result of his obstinately remaining off-stage, he has been more neglected by the public than any other major American poet since Herman Melville, who was privately published, and Emily Dickinson, who didn't bother to put her poems into books. Aiken had those fifty published titles, but not one of them was a booksellers' choice. In 1934 I asked him for nominations to a list that was going to be printed in *The New Republic*, of "Good Books That Almost Nobody Has Read." He nominated Kafka's *The Castle*—that was long before the Kafka boom—then added in a postscript: "Might I also suggest for your list of Neglected Books a novel by c. aiken called Great Circle, of which the royalty report, to hand this morning, chronicles a sale of 26 copies in the second half year? and Preludes for Memnon, which I think is my best book, and which has sold about seven hundred copies in three years."

In 1946 I had the notion of trying to persuade some quarterly to publish a Conrad Aiken number. What should go into it? I asked him in a letter. He answered from England, making no suggestions whatever. "Appraisals of my work," he said, "have been rare or brief or nonexistent whether in periodicals or books on contemporary poetry: in me you behold an almost unique phenomenon, a poet who has acquired a Reputation, or a Position, or what have you, without ever having been caught in the act—as it were, by a process of auto-osmosis. At any given moment in the Pegasus Sweepstakes, in whatever Selling Plate or for whatever year, this dubious horse has always been the last in the list of the also-ran,—he never even placed, much less won, nor, I regret, have the offers to put him out to stud been either remunerative or very attractive. Odd. Very odd."

A few years later he began to receive a series of official honors,

*And Awards and Prizes of various sizes*
*among them a few quite delightful surprises. . . .*

as he said in his "Obituary in Bitcherel." He accepted the honors gladly, on condition that they didn't involve a public appearance. Thus, from 1950 to 1952 he served as Consultant in Poetry at the Library of Congress. He received the Bryher Award in 1952, a National Book Award in 1954, the Bollingen Award in 1956, the Fellowship of the National Academy of Poets in 1957, the Gold Medal for Poetry of the National Institute in 1958, and finally the National Medal for Literature in 1969. Meanwhile his position with the public (and with the booksellers) had improved scarcely at all; perhaps it had deteriorated. He reported in 1971 that his *Collected Poems: Second Edition,* containing the work of a lifetime, had a sale for its first half-year of 430 copies.

It is hardly surprising that some developments in his later poems went unnoticed by poetry readers, and by critics too.

3 ✍ Without in the least abandoning his religion of consciousness, Aiken's poems of the 1950s and 1960s introduced some new or partially new elements. One of these was a note of ancestral piety, with allusions to earlier Aikens, but more to his mother's connections, the Potters (who had started as New Bedford Quakers) and the Delanos. The note is already audible in "Mayflower," written in 1945. It is a poem partly about the ship (on which two of the poet's ancestors had been passengers), partly about the flower, and partly about the sandy shores of Cape Cod, where the Pilgrims had landed before sailing on to Plymouth. In other poems there is frequent mention of what might be called ancestral scenes: New Bedford and its whaling ships; the Quaker graveyard at South Yarmouth, on the Cape, where Cousin Abiel lies buried; Sheepfold Hill, also on the Cape; and Stony Brook, where the herring used to spawn by myriads. There is also talk of godfathers and tutelary spirits: among the poets Ben Jonson, Shakespeare, Li Po, and among historical figures Pythagoras and William Blackstone, the scholar and gentle heretic who built a house on the site of Boston before the Puritans came, then moved away from them into the wilderness. Blackstone becomes the hero of Aiken's cycle of poems about America, *The Kid* (1947). In "A Letter from Li Po" (1955), the Chinese maker of timeless artifacts is set beside the scoffing Quaker, Cousin Abiel:

> *In this small mute democracy of stones*
> *is it Abiel or Li Po who lies*
> *and lends us against death our speech?*

Another new or newly emphasized feature of the later poems is something very close to New England Transcendentalism. Its appearance should be no surprise, except to those who have fallen into the habit of regarding Transcendentalism as a purely historical phenomenon, a movement that flourished from 1830 to 1860, then disappeared at the beginning of the Civil War. On the contrary, it has been a durable property of New England thinking, a home place, one might say, to which some poets return as they grow older. In one or another of many aspects, the Transcendental mood is manifested in Robinson, in Frost, to some extent in Eliot, perhaps in Millay—see "Renascence" and some of the very late poems—then in Cummings, Wilder, S. Foster Damon, John Wheelwright, and most clearly in Conrad Aiken.

A complete definition of Transcendentalism would comprise most of Emerson's essays, beginning with *Nature*. As a shorter definition, the best I have found is a paragraph in the article "Transcendentalism" in *The Oxford Companion to American Literature*. One is grateful to the editor, James D. Hart, for bringing almost everything together in a few sentences. He says:

> . . . the belief had as its fundamental base a monism holding to the unity of the world and God and the immanence of God in the world. Because of this indwelling of divinity, everything in the world is a microcosm containing within itself all the laws and meaning of existence. Likewise the soul of each individual is identical with the soul of the world, and latently contains all that the world contains. Man may fulfill his divine potentialities either through a rapt mystical state, in which the divine is infused into the human, or through coming into contact with the truth, beauty, and goodness embodied in nature and originating in the Over-Soul. Thus occurs the doctrine of the correspondence between the tangible world and the human mind, and the identity of moral and physical laws. Through belief in the divine authority of the soul's intuitions and impulses, based on the identification of the individual soul with God, there developed the doctrine of self-reliance and individualism, the disregard of external authority, tradition, and logical demonstration, and the absolute optimism of the movement.

For a brief statement of Transcendental doctrines, James Hart's paragraph—from which I have omitted a few introductory phrases—seems to me almost complete. It does omit, however, two doctrines of some importance. One is the rejection of history—

at least of history conceived as an irreversible process, a causally linked series of events in which the masses as well as the "representative men" play their part. For this rejection, see Emerson's essay "History" and also many of Cummings' later poems. Thornton Wilder, a New Englander by descent and residence—though born in Wisconsin—tells us that history is not a sequence but a tapestry or carpet in which various patterns are repeated at intervals. Having spatialized time in this fashion, Wilder could never have become a social or a political historian, and the statement applies to others working in the same tradition.

One might say that Transcendentalists as a type—if such a type exists—are most at home in essays and poetry. If they turn to fiction, as Wilder did, they write novels dealing with morals rather than manners. Manners are the expression of standards prevailing in a group, and Transcendentalism denies the existence of groups except as arithmetical sums of separate persons: one plus one plus one. Only the individual is real and bears within himself a portion of the Over-Soul. That is the other doctrine omitted from Hart's admirable paragraph, and it explains why the Transcendental cast of mind is skeptical about political science and usually contemptuous of politicians. Aiken, for example, says of himself in *Ushant:* "... he had never found it possible to take more than a casual and superficial interest in practical politics, viewing it, as he did, as inevitably a passing phase, and probably a pretty primitive one, and something, again, that the evolution of consciousness would in its own good season take care of."

Is consciousness, for Aiken—the consciousness of mankind as shared by each individual—close to being an equivalent of the Over-Soul? That might be stretching a point, and indeed, I should be far from saying that, among twentieth-century New England writers, there is any complete Transcendentalist in a sense that might be accepted, for instance, by Margaret Fuller. It is clear, however, that there are several New England writers, most of them among the best, whose work embodies aspects of the Transcendental system (though seldom its "absolute optimism"). The aspects are usually different in each case, but two of them, at least, are shared by all the writers I mentioned. All are fiercely individual, in theory and practice, and all are moralists or ethicists, even or most of all when defying an accepted system of ethics. Why this revival of the Transcendental spirit should be particularly evident in New England is hard to say. One is tempted to speak of something in the blood, or in the climate, or more realistically of a tradition handed down by a father or a favorite schoolteacher, rejected in the poet's youth, then reaccepted in middle age. Usually there is not much evidence of a literary derivation: for instance, Cummings and Millay were not at all interested in the earlier Transcendentalists. Aiken might be an exception here. Boldest of all in his development of certain Transcendental notions, he also, rather late in life, found them confirmed by ancestral piety and especially by the writings and career of his maternal grandfather.

William James Potter was a birthright Quaker who became a Unitarian because he felt that the doctrines of the Friends were too confining. In 1859 he was called to the Unitarian church in New Bedford, where he soon began to feel that Unitarianism was confining too. In 1866 he refused to administer the rite of communion; following the example of Emerson, he told his congregation that he could no longer do so in good conscience. In 1867 he refused to call himself a Christian and was thereupon dropped from the roll of Unitarian ministers. He was so admired, however, for being upright and unselfish and a good preacher that his congregation gave him a unanimous vote of confidence. With Emerson, Colonel Higginson, and others, he then founded the Free Religious Association, which was intended to unite all the religions of the world by rejecting their dogmas and retaining from each faith only its ethical core. Dogmas were what he abhorred.

When the poet came to read Grandfather Potter's published sermons, he was impressed by their bold speculations about the divine element in men. He wrote an admiring poem about his grandfather, "Halloween," in which he quoted from the journal that Potter had kept during his early travels in Europe. A quoted phrase was "... so man may make the god finite and viable, make conscious god's power in action and being." That sounds the

Transcendental note, and it is also close to phrases that Aiken himself had written: for example, in the 1949 preface to one of his Symphonies, where he says that man, in becoming completely aware of himself, "can, if he only will, become divine."

There is another point, apparently not connected with Grandfather Potter, at which Aiken comes even closer to Transcendentalism. Once more I quote from that convenient definition by James Hart: "...everything in the world is a microcosm containing within itself all the laws and meaning of existence. Likewise, the soul of each individual is identical with the soul of the world, and latently contains all that the world contains.... Thus occurs the doctrine of correspondence between the tangible world and the human mind." Aiken, with his senses open to the tangible world, often speaks of this correspondence, which sometimes becomes for him an identity. Thus, he says in "A Letter from Li Po":

> We are the tree, yet sit beneath the tree,
> among the leaves we are the hidden bird,
> we are the singer and are what is heard.

Reading those lines, one can scarcely fail to think of Emerson's "Brahma":

> They reckon ill who leave me out;
> When me they fly, I am the wings;
> I am the doubter and the doubt,
> And I the hymn the Brahmin sings.

Aiken is still more clearly Emersonian, however, in what is almost the last of his poems, *THEE*, written when he was seventy-seven. Though comparatively short—only 250 lines, some consisting of a single word—it appeared as a handsome book, with lithographs by Leonard Baskin, and it is indeed one of his major works. First one notes that the poet has changed his style and that here—as, to a lesser extent, in some of the other late poems —he has abandoned the subtle variations and dying falls of his earlier work. *THEE* is written in short, galloping lines with rhymes like hoofbeats:

*Who is that splendid THEE*
*who makes a symphony*
*of the one word*
*be*
*admitting us to see*
*all things but THEE?*

Obviously THEE is being used here as the Quaker pronoun: "Thee makes," not "You make" or "Thou makest." Aiken may well have learned that usage from the Potter family. As for his question "Who?" it sends us back once more to Emerson. Just as Aiken's "consciousness" at times come close to being the Emersonian Over-Soul, so THEE is the spirit of Nature as defined in Emerson's essay. "Strictly speaking," the essay says, "...all that is separate from us, all which Philosophy distinguishes as the NOT ME, that is, both nature and art, all other men and my own body, must be ranked under this name, NATURE." Aiken's name is THEE, but it has a different connotation. Whereas Emerson's Nature is admired for revealing in each of its parts the universal laws that wise men obey, Aiken's THEE is a pitiless force that nourishes and destroys with the divine indifference of the goddess Kali. Also and paradoxically, it is a force evolving with the human spirit—

*as if perhaps in our slow growing*
*and the beginnings of our knowing*
*as if perhaps*
*o could this be*
*that we*
*be*
*THEE?*
*THEE still learning*
*or first learning*
*through us*
*to be*
*THY THEE?*

*Self-praise were then our praise of THEE*
*unless we say divinity*

*cries in us both as we draw breath*
*cry death cry death*
*and all our hate*
*we must abate*
*and THEE must with us meet and mate*
*give birth give suck be sick and die*
*and close the All-God-Giving-Eye*
*for the last time to sky.*

When I first read *THEE*, it reminded me strongly of an untitled poem by Emerson, one that Aiken, so he told me, had never read—and no wonder he had missed it, since it does not appear in the *Complete Works*, even buried with other fragments in an appendix. One finds it in Volume II of the *Journals*, a volume including the period of spiritual crisis that followed the death of Emerson's beloved first wife, Ellen. She died February 8, 1831, and the poem was written July 6—at night? it must have been at night—immediately after a tribute to Ellen and thoughts of rejoining her in death. The poem, however, seems to announce the end of the crisis, since it is the entranced statement of a new faith. Here are two of the stanzas:

*If thou canst bear*
*Strong meat of simple truth,*
*If thou durst my words compare*
*With what thou thinkest in the soul's free youth,*
*Then take this fact unto thy soul,—*
*God dwells in thee.*
*It is no metaphor nor parable,*
*It is unknown to thousands, and to thee;*
*Yet there is God.*

. . . . . . . . . .

*Who approves thee doing right?*
*God in thee.*
*Who condemns thee doing wrong?*
*God in thee.*
*Who punishes thine evil deed?*
*God in thee.*

*What is thine evil need?*
*Thy worse mind, with error blind*
*And more prone to evil*
*That is, the greater hiding of the God within. . . .*

Emerson never went back to polish or even finish the poem, so that it remains a broken rhapsody—rather than an artifact like THEE—and yet it states bluntly the seminal idea that he would develop in his essays of the dozen years that followed. What made me think of the poem when reading *THEE* is something in the style, in the irregular lines—not all of them rhymed —and in the message, too, with its identification of outer and inner worlds and its assertion that men are potentially divine. Of course where Emerson celebrates the power of the indwelling spirit, Aiken gives a twist to Transcendental doctrine by stressing, first, the indifferent power of THEE, and then the dependence of THEE on the individual consciousness—with which it must "meet and mate," from which it learns to become more truly itself, and with which, perhaps, it must die. The speculation seems more imaginative than philosophical, and yet one feels that—with the whole religion of consciousness—it finds a place in the Transcendental line.

In Aiken's beginnings, he had been poles apart from Emerson. He had been atheistic and pessimistic, not optimistic and Unitarian. He had never been impressed by the German Romantic philosophers or by the Neoplatonists, let alone by Sufism and Brahmanism; instead his intellectual models had been Poe first of all, then Santayana, Freud, and Henry James. He would have been out of place in Emerson's Concord, since he continued all his life to be fond of women, mischief, bawdy limericks, and martinis. Nevertheless, at the end of his long career, he had worked round to a position reminiscent of that which Emerson had reached in 1831, before he had published anything. That seems to me an intellectual event of some interest, especially since it was announced in a memorable poem. But *THEE* aroused little attention when it appeared in 1967, and later it seems to have been almost forgotten.

In August 1972 I wrote Aiken to say that we had celebrated his eighty-third birthday with a little party and that I had read *THEE* to the guests. He answered wryly. My letter had arrived in the same mail as another announcing that the unsold copies of *THEE*—most of the copies, that is—had been remaindered.


4 ⚚ For the neglect of his work by the public, one can give several explanations, though none of them seems adequate. In the early days when he was writing a book-length poem every year, Aiken's poetry was too modern and experimental for him to share in what was then the enormous popularity of Amy Lowell and Vachel Lindsay. Later, in the 1920s, it seemed not experimental enough, or at least not eccentric enough. In the 1930s it was condemned as having no social or revolutionary meaning; in the 1940s it wasn't rich enough in images (most of his work is musical rather than visual, and music was becoming the lost side of poetry); in the 1950s it was condemned again as not being "close enough in texture" to suit the intensive reading methods of the new critics (but what should one say of the *Preludes?*); and in the 1960s it was disregarded as being written mostly in iambic pentameters, a measure that had fallen out of fashion. Aiken followed his own fashion, and his work developed by an inner logic which was not that of the poetry-reading public.

But what about the admirable prose of his novels and stories and of his great autobiography? Two or three of the stories, including "Silent Snow, Secret Snow," have appeared in dozens of anthologies, but in general the prose, too, has failed to capture the public imagination.

I suspect that the long neglect of Aiken's work is due in large part to policies more or less deliberately adopted by the author. In his heart he didn't want to become a celebrity. Not only did he never appear on a public platform, but also he refused to cultivate the literary powers, if such persons exist; instead he went out of his way to offend them. Always for the best of reasons, he bickered with editors, jeered at anthologists, rejected his own disciples one after another, and made cruelly true remarks about fellow poets, who would soon take their revenge by reviewing his books. He must have expected those reviews, familiar as he was with literary folkways. They made him angry, they wounded his pride—but did they also give him a somehow comfortable assurance that he would continue to live *"off-stage, behind the scenes, out of view"?* Was it all part of the same pattern as his resigning from Harvard in preference to writing and publicly reading the class poem?

I last saw him in January 1972. By then he had made the great circle and was living in Savannah, only a few doors from the now gutted house where he had spent his childhood. Old Bonaventure Cemetery, where his parents lay buried, also was quite near. Conrad himself was suffering from the ills of human flesh, including some rare ones whose name I heard that day for the first time, but he still made puns while his beloved wife mixed martinis. We talked about the literary world, not so excitedly as at our first meeting half a century before and with more bitterness on Conrad's part. Still, he had done his work and knew it was good. He had proclaimed his religion of consciousness and had lived by its tenets. He had never compromised—as he was to say on his deathbed—and he could feel certain that, for all his hatred of intruders, the great world would some day come round to him.

# XVI REBELS, ARTISTS, AND SCOUNDRELS

1 ✍ These chapters of literary history are drawing to a close. I thought of ending them with a brief discussion of ethics in relation to the literary life, hardly more than a footnote to a continuing argument, but meanwhile I note a gap in the narrative: not much has been said about the new generation of the 1960s. There is, in my case, a reason for the oversight. I like to deal with situations that I have known at first hand, as in the preceding chapters, whereas from 1963 to 1973, the years when the Love Generation flowered and faded, I was chiefly a detached observer. More or less I had withdrawn from the literary life: I was a deaf man gardening in the country and writing about books. Of course I saw the youngsters on my travels to universities, but, while liking most of them as individuals, I could only take note of their various idealisms, not always with a receptive ear.

As a detached observer I concluded that theirs was indeed a new generation with its own leaders and spokesmen. It had rebelled against existing society ("the establishment") and was manifesting its own sense of life, which was called "the new consciousness." On the basis of that consciousness it was determined to build a counterculture—that was the new term—and impose it on the nation and the world. The age group of the 1960s was outward-turning, "sharing," and politicized. In spite of its praise for those who "did their own thing," what it really enjoyed was coming together in communes, communities, encounter groups, student rebellions, and mass demonstrations, all designed to change the world after changing the hearts of individuals. Thus, it was taking its place in a pattern I mentioned in earlier chapters, an alternation of expansive and contractive moods as age groups succeeded each other; this I compared to an immensely slow heartbeat rhythm of diastole and systole, and I said that the cycle might take thirty years or more to complete. Clearly the 1950s had been a systolic or contractive period that placed its general emphasis on personal security, good form in life and literature, and the nuclear family. The 1960s were just as clearly expansive. In some respects they replayed the 1930s after thirty years, with the same wild optimism, the same adherence to the Movement, the same faith in the Coming Revolution. The New Left had taken the place of the Old Left, and I noted with interest that several leaders of campus rebellions were the sons or daughters of old-style radicals.

In other respects the age was vastly different from the 1930s. It had, for instance, a greater variety of ideals and slogans, many of which were confused or conflicting, with the result that they offered an implausible mixture of Marx, Bakunin, and Mahatma Gandhi, of Wilhelm Reich (the orgasm man) and Che Guevara. I am speaking here in historical terms, since hardly anyone read those philosophers. Nobody even tried to read *Das Kapital*; what the rebels accepted from Marx at second hand was chiefly his early humanism and his revolutionary fervor. Never having lived in a depression or suffered want except from deliberate choice, they took no interest in economics. They did not talk about the proletariat, which Marx exhorted to seize the factories and run them in everybody's best interest; instead they wanted to smash the factories and start over again, close to nature. They worshiped a vague entity, the People, which would rise to a man and woman—except for the bankers and policemen, or pigs— if rebellious students convinced them of the truth.

Much later, when reading Sara Davidson's *Loose Change* (1977), which is the liveliest account of the era, I found a quotation from a speech delivered by a student leader at Berkeley. He was speaking in 1966, a hopeful year for the rebels. "We don't need the Old Left," he said. "We don't need their ideology or the working class, those mythical masses who are supposed to rise up and break their chains. The working class in this country is turning to the right. Students are going to be the revolutionary force in this country. Students are going to make a revolution because we have the will!" One weakness of a revolution made by students is that—lacking a permanent social base—its momentum is hard to maintain. There are yearly changes in the student body and after four years it has been completely refashioned. New leaders keep rising to address a new constituency, but each in turn will vanish into the workaday world. Those confident leaders of 1966, addressing the crowd from under a twenty-foot banner that read "Happiness Is Student Power"—how could they predict what students even at Berkeley would be saying or doing in a very few years?

The era as a whole might be divided into three shorter periods. Morris Dickstein has done this in his generally illuminating book, *The Gates of Eden* (1977), but his names and dates are somewhat different from mine. First, I should say, came the years of hope from 1963 to 1966, a time of jubilant beginnings: linked arms, freedom marches, interracial solidarity, the Free Speech Movement at Berkeley, folk music (which was rather suddenly replaced by rock, with Joan Baez giving way to Bob Dylan), sexual liberation ("If it feels right, do it"), and the spread of the drug culture ("Turn on, tune in, drop out"). Next came the years of confrontation, 1967–70, which were marked by immense rallies and riots, with the inner cities erupting in separate revolts that had nothing to do with the students, but which spread among them a mood of anger and violence. Those were the years of the March on the Pentagon, the Siege of Chicago, the Days of Rage—but they also included the Summer of Love in Haight-Ashbury and the East Village and the Woodstock Festival of Joy (this followed too soon by another rock festival, at Altamont, that ended in disaster). More and more older people, including faculty members, were becoming involved in the Movement. It reached a climax in 1970, after the bombing of Cambodia and the Kent State massacre, when there were campus revolts and demonstrations almost everywhere in the country.

Then came a third period, the time of dispersion, 1970–73, starting before the time of confrontation had ended. One of the popular slogans was now "Back to earth!" On almost any highway, in 1970, college dropouts were moving singly or in couples, thumbs extended; they were easy to recognize by their long, unwashed hair, their faded jeans, their sleeping bags, and their boots, a sort of intersexual uniform. Some of the women had babies on their backs. Their destination was likely to be some commune or campground or community where they would be welcomed by others of their kind—most often in northern California or New Mexico or the Ozarks or Vermont. After settling down, many of them would open little shops to sell health foods or psychedelic posters or leather goods or home-fired pottery; they were developing an economy of their own based on food stamps and small enterprises.

Another manifestation of the period was the yearning for instant salvation, usually to be sought by adopting the doctrines of some sect or guru; after Zen Buddhism came Hare Krishna, Baba Ram Das, the Sufi dancers, the Moonies, and the Jesus Freaks. People in Berkeley said, "The youth movement is turning inwards." The public issue on which all the youngsters agreed had been the Vietnam war. As this dragged on toward its last shameful days, the public movements that continued to flourish were Women's Liberation (soon to be followed by Gay Liberation) and, in its various manifestations, Black Power. Women and blacks each had biological reasons for asserting their mass identity. Others who maintained their revolutionary fervor had joined the Weathermen (or Weatherpersons) and had gone underground to lay plots for urban guerrilla actions which, if carried out, would further alienate them from the People they devoutly hoped to save.

Skeptical as I was of instant salvation and hostile to urban guerrillas, those crazies, I followed the last years of the youth movement with restrained interest. Much later, however, I read about those years in *Loose Change,* where the mood of the times is vividly suggested. Sara Davidson's plan is to follow the adventures of herself and two friends, all 1964 graduates at Berkeley. Since the three women traveled widely over the country —Miss Davidson as a journalist, "Tasha" as an art dealer, and "Susie Berman" as a committed radical (those last two names are fictitious)—one or another witnessed or took part in almost all the public manifestations of the youth rebellion. To me their lives become even more interesting after the shouting had died away. Susie Berman, for example, joined a hippie settlement in Taos, traveled round the world on a stolen airplane ticket, then came back to Berkeley in 1972. There, she found that her neighbors were women, veterans of the Movement living alone with their small children. As she later reported to Miss Davidson:

"The culture they had built was, it turned out, a matriarchy. Where were all the men? Many of them had not been able to cut themselves loose from ideology and had gone down with the ideas. A few were in mental hospitals. Rennie Davis was following the Guru Maharaj Ji. Jerry Rubin was starting his life over with yoga. Jeff had joined the Communist Party. Marvin Garson had transported himself barefoot and penniless to Israel as an immigrant to be cared for by the state."

That is a revealing comment on the course of the youth revolution. In the beginning almost all its paladins had been men. By 1972 the survivors were women living alone with their one or two children of the storm. Perhaps that was because simple biology forces women to be more earthy and durable; but the women, too, were now planning to marry for good or to settle down in respectable careers. They all looked back with nostalgia to the great days and wondered what had gone wrong. They said, "All these bright, idealistic, committed people—how could they have miscalculated so badly?" Sometimes they comforted themselves by thinking of the many changes they had accomplished in ten years; as Sara Davidson lists those achievements of the Movement, they were "the end of the draft; the profound revolution in sexual relationships; the granting of the right to vote to eighteen-year-olds and the right to abortion to women." She might have mentioned still other changes affecting the fabric of American society, as notably the progress of civil rights for Negroes and, on another level, the tolerance of pornography and of deviant conduct. The youth rebellion did not bring about those changes, which were largely owed to court decisions, but it had an undetermined share in creating the atmosphere that made them acceptable.

It had a more definite share in the continuing process of changing the spoken language. That process seldom receives as much attention as it deserves. Since we think mostly in words, our vocabularies help to shape our sense of life and hence our social ideals. During the sixties American speech was enriched—and in some ways impoverished—by new words borrowed from many different sources. A principal source was the youth culture itself as it flourished on campuses and in the streets. Among many other sources were the drug culture, the gay culture (*gay* itself was a new term in common speech), Yiddish (with many turns of phrase and with words such as *chutzpah, goniff, schmuck*), women's lib (which insisted on words of common gender, *person, they* instead of *man, he*), Eastern religions (*guru, dharma, mantra, satori*), black slang (an always changing idiom from which the sixties borrowed some of the older words: *jive, funky, cat,* and *man* as a universal term of address), male obscenities (which spread from the barracks into the living room), and finally the dreadful jargons of bureaucrats, educationists, and sociologists.

Words from the drug culture were, among others, *trip, high, downers, joint, speed, acid* ("dropping acid"), *stoned, freak out,* and *psychedelic.* From the youth culture in a broader sense came *uptight, putdown, dropout, ripoff, with it, into* (for "mad about"), *kooky, groovy, big* (for "widely displayed or discussed": "Sex was big"), *off* as a verb ("Off the pigs!"), *trash* as a verb (meaning "to vandalize"), *dig* (for either "like" or "under-stand"), *rap, ball, split* (also as verbs, the last meaning "to go away"), and dozens of other compounds or words from Basic English twisted into new meanings. Most of the words have made their way into the written language. Some have already lost favor, either from being used too often or else with the decline of customs that had given rise to them, while others have become a permanent resource of American English. There should be a glossary of all the words, with derivations and connotations, but I have no leisure to compile it.

And what about American literature, my own field? Here, even as a detached observer, I cannot avoid a feeling of disappoint-ment. After so many adventures and misadventures, so much shared emotion, the Love Generation of the 1960s has still produced no monuments of the literary art. Important work was published during the period when the generation flourished, but the work was done by others. Dickstein says in *Gates of Eden* that the sixties "are as likely to be remembered through novels as through anything else they left behind." The novels he eulo-gizes are *Catch 22, The Sot-Weed Factor, V.*, and *Slaughterhouse-Five*, by, respectively, Joseph Heller, John Barth, Thomas Pyn-chon, and Kurt Vonnegut; these authors, he says, expressed or foreshadowed the sensibility of the decade. He has more restrained praise for the experimental work of Donald Barthelme, William H. Gass, Robert Coover, and other practitioners of metafiction and the anti-story. He says that their underground prose, as it might be called by virtue of its alienation from the broader public, appeared in the same years as the Weather Underground and offers an exact parallel to the tactics of those urban guerrillas. At this point he is making the common error of confusing two age groups. Not one of the authors he praises—not even Pynchon, born in 1937, who is by far the youngest—can be called a mem-ber of the Love Generation. Not one of them took part in its political activities. All are older men, veterans of the 1950s who belong to the straight world, and it would be easy to demonstrate that what they express, if in a dissident form, is the sensibility of that other era.

The actual leaders and spokesmen of the Love Generation were not men or women of letters. Most of their followers rapped about books without reading them; they watched the news on TV. Some of the leaders had once dreamed of becoming writers, but they had traded in the dream for another, that of remaking the world and their own lives. They expressed themselves eloquently at moments, but usually in speeches or manifestos or articles hastily written for the underground press. They had no time for writing masterpieces—until 1971, that is, and afterward most of them were too discouraged to write at all.[1] For a time hardly anyone under thirty entertained the notion that writing is a priestly vocation with its own strict ethical code.

2 ✍ Some friends were arguing about whether there is any correlation between character and art. The conclusion they reported to me later is that there is no correlation: a scoundrel can produce a masterpiece and so can a saint. I brooded over that statement. Isn't it much too simple and isn't there more to be said?

That a saint can produce a masterpiece I know from having read St. John of the Cross. I haven't met any saints in the literary world of today and yesterday, but I have met some truly good men and women (Van Wyck Brooks, Marianne Moore, and Heywood Broun among others). I have met my share of scoundrels in that same world. For instance there was Henri the dancer, who liked to boast that there wasn't a man in New York he hadn't lied to, stolen from, or sodomized—"Maybe you're the exception," he conceded disarmingly. Henri went on to Berlin,

---

1. That statement applies chiefly to the men of the generation. Some of the women showed powers of survival in literature as in life. Joan Didion being a little too old to be mentioned here, I should guess that in fiction Ann Tyler and Joyce Carol Oates have been the clearest voices of that particular age group. Sara Davidson has been its candid historian.

which, under the Weimar Republic, was a happy setting for scoundrels and for artists too. When he died suddenly, the whole artistic community attended his funeral. Also I remember Lancelot the poet—that isn't his name—who supported himself for almost a year by collecting funds for his friend Erica to have an abortion (she wasn't pregnant). One morning we left him and Erica sleeping in our apartment while we went to our respective offices. They were gone when we came back and there was a gap in our bookshelves: Sandburg, Sappho, Shaw, Shelley, Sophocles, Spenser, and Swinburne were missing. Both Henri and Lancelot were charming and rather gifted persons, scoundrels with a touch of roguery, but I note that neither of them produced a masterpiece.

Perhaps my hesitation in the argument is due to the blunt word "scoundrel." Max Perkins of Scribners, an upright editor, used to tell his colleagues, "The trouble with American writing today is that there aren't enough rascals." He might have been defending his young friend Thomas Wolfe, who was in truth something of a rogue (as Max would learn to his cost, but without losing his affection for Wolfe). Both "rogue" and "rascal" are words often used with an undertone of playful or even admiring disapproval. There is no such undertone in the use of "scoundrel," which my big old Webster's defines as "a mean, worthless fellow; a rascal; a villain; a man without honor or virtue." The suggestion here is of barefaced fraud and swindling. Real scoundrelism is a career in itself, like writing or painting, and it would take a man or woman of unflagging genius to succeed in both professions.

Artists who succeed are strong characters, which is something different from saying they are saintly. Some of them—most of them?—do scandalous and even scoundrelly things, as we keep learning from new biographies of famous writers; all their secret sins are being put on display. Ranged as it were in museum cases, the sins have lost their scarlet radiance. "So it's true that Byron committed incest," we say without wagging our heads. "After all, Lady Augusta was only his half-sister." That his adored Maid of Athens was really a boy seems rather less shocking than the fact that John Ruskin died a virgin. And George Sand: should we condemn her for taking many lovers, including a woman, or merely for having treated them badly? The 1960s have wrought so much confusion in our moral standards that we try not to pass judgment.

One learns in the course of years that artists and writers, as a tribal group, have certain defects of character. To be quite simple, they drink too much; all the older ones drink except the reformed alcoholics. The younger ones drink less, but most of them smoke reefers or pop pills in the effort to stimulate their imaginations. Their sexual drives are probably stronger than those of the population as a whole and their inhibitions are weaker; I am far from being the first to suspect that there is a connection between literature and libido. They may or may not be loyal husbands or wives—though I have known artists' marriages that lasted for fifty years of complete fidelity—and they are often neglectful parents. They may be the best of neighbors, at any rate the most amusing, but they are seldom loyal adherents of a government or a party, as the Communists were pained to discover in the 1930s. Financially the younger ones are not very responsible—how could they be?—and sometimes they wreck the furniture of rented houses.

Is there any psychological or professional basis for this pattern of conduct? Perhaps there is; perhaps artists are more inclined than others to be egocentric and hence unfeeling in their personal relations. They need strong egos to do good work. It may be that their working habits, if nothing else, often lead them into a manic-depressive cycle. During the manic phase they write or paint furiously, but then the words and visions stop coming and they fall into a depressed phase of guilt and self-questioning. A special weakness of imaginative novelists and poets is that they often project fantasies with themselves as heroes. Some of them boast and lie, to put it bluntly, and by so doing they create immense difficulties for their biographers (as I have noted in the case of Erskine Caldwell, while mentioning several other names). That doesn't make them scoundrels. A scoundrel also boasts and lies, but he does it for profit, in the course of a swindle. There is something innocent, I find, in the stories that many imaginative writers tell about themselves; something connected with the quality of the image they project and hence ultimately with their work.

"An artist is a creature driven by demons," Faulkner said in a famous interview. "... He is completely amoral in that he will rob, borrow, beg, or steal from anybody and everybody to get the work done.... He has no peace till then. Everything goes by the board: honor, pride, decency, security, happiness, all, to get the book written. If a writer has to rob his mother, he will not hesitate; the 'Ode on a Grecian Urn' is worth any number of old ladies." Here as in other instances Faulkner was romanticizing his public image, for he ended, in fact, as a dutiful son and a responsible member of the community. He spent the first thirty years of his life piling up debts and the last thirty years paying them back to the last penny and the last returned favor. The writing of more than one book had been postponed while he slaved in Hollywood to support his family. Moreover, he was mistaken in what he said about the complete amorality of artists in general. Many of them beg and a few of them steal, but the good ones try—not always successfully—to live and work by a harsh code that the public fails to recognize because, at many points, it runs counter to ordinary moral judgments.

Thus, I have heard more than one poet condemned for being a good citizen, on the ground that by living respectably he was putting blinders on his imagination. As for family responsibilities, "One has no business to have any children," we read in Henry James's "The Lesson of the Master." "I mean, of course," the Master explains to a new disciple, "if one wants to do anything good." Children, he says, are "an incentive to damnation." James's version of the code was too uncompromising for most artists to accept, but still one hears echoes of his judgments. When a gifted novelist fell short of his mark, one of his rivals explained to me why he had failed: it was the result of his having stayed married to a saintly woman. "Why didn't he leave her," the other novelist said, "as soon as he found out that she was interfering with his work?" In the artist's code of morals, "work" is always a verb in the imperative mood, even when it seems to be a noun. A merely human relationship should be broken off if it keeps one from working.

On the other hand—to choose an example from the past —Hawthorne is thought to have shown moral courage when he refrained from working because he felt that his mind had lost its temper and its fine edge. "I have an instinct," he said in a letter to his publisher, "that I had better keep quiet. Perhaps I shall have a new spirit of vigor if I wait quietly for it; perhaps not." Shortly before writing the letter, Hawthorne had lost his little fortune through entrusting it to a friend. He wanted to provide for his family. That shouldn't have been an insoluble problem, since he had already earned his reputation and since any new novel of his, good or bad, would have had a wide sale. Lately he had started three different novels and the last start had been promising; he had only to continue as best he could and publish the result. But he stopped, feeling that however profitable the result might be and however much it might help his wife and children, it would not be up to his own standard of excellence. That was an artist's decision, for which he is respected by other artists.

Then what shall we say about the very different example of Anthony Trollope? Week in, week out, in the midst of other exacting duties, he produced forty pages of fiction, even when the week was spent in stage coaches or at sea. "As I journeyed across France to Marseilles," he says in his *Autobiography*, "and made thence a terribly rough voyage to Alexandria, I wrote my allotted number of pages every day. On this occasion more than once I left my paper on the cabin table, rushing away to be sick in the privacy of my state-room. It was February, and the weather was terrible, but still I did my work." He does not say whether it was good work or whether it had the taste of bile; quite simply it was work performed on schedule. Yet Trollope as well as Hawthorne is now admired by other writers (after a period of hesitation, it is true) and is felt to have carried out a moral choice.

There is no real conflict in this judgment about the two men. Both Hawthorne and Trollope were devoted to their craft, to their vocation, and were willing to make sacrifices for it—in one case a financial and family sacrifice, in the other a sacrifice of comfort. Therefore both were observing the artist's particular code of morality.

3 ❧ Not often formulated, sometimes jeered at for being irrelevant or elitist (as in the 1960s), but still enforced by famous examples, this code can be reduced to a very few commandments that persist today in the depths of an artist's mind.

First, he must believe in the importance of art, as well as the all-importance in his own life of the particular art to which he is devoted, whether this be fiction, poetry, painting, sculpture, or music. "O art, art," Henry James wrote in his notebook, "what difficulties are like thine, and, at the same time, what consolation and encouragements, also, are like thine? Without this, for me, the world would be, indeed, a howling wilderness."

Second, he must believe in his own talent, something deep in himself and apart from his daily life, yet having a universal validity. He must try by any means whatever to unearth this buried talent, with the conviction that, if fully expressed in works, it will be treasured by future generations. In a sense he is competing for a share in the future against every other artist in his field, with the chance of success ten thousand to one against him.

Third, he must honestly express his own vision of the world and his own personality, including his derelictions. Hawthorne, the least confessional of our great writers, said near the end of *The Scarlet Letter,* as if appending a moral to the story, "Be true! Be true! Show freely to the world, if not your worst, yet some trait by which the worst may be inferred!" In the chapter about Conrad Aiken, another devoted artist, I quote his statement that the real business of the poet was "consciously or unconsciously to give the lowdown on himself, and through himself on humanity." I also quoted from a stern letter he had sent me after reading some of my poems. "But you?" he said, "what do you think or feel which is secretly you? shamefully you? intoxicatingly you? drunkenly or soberly or lyrically you? This doesn't come out?" He accused me—I hope wrongly, but in accordance with the artist's code—of having "avoided the final business of self-betrayal."

Fourth—to continue this rather solemn list of commandments—the true artist must produce grandly, to the limit of his powers. Here again one can quote from James's notebooks. "I have my head, thank God, full of visions," he wrote for his own eyes in February 1895, a month after the catastrophic failure of his play *Guy Domville*. "Ah, just to let one's self go—at last; to surrender one's self to what through all the long years one has (quite heroically, I think) hoped for and waited for—the mere potential, and relative, increase of *quantity* in the material act— act of application and production. One has prayed and hoped and waited, in a word, to be able to work *more*. And now, toward the end, it seems, within its limits, to have come. That is all I ask. Nothing else in the world." At the mere thought of producing *more*, James felt himself to be a happy and virtuous person.

Conversely, when an author produces less, he is oppressed by guilt at having violated this fourth commandment. He may hesitate, however, before going to a psychiatrist for confession and absolution. To mention one example, Scott Fitzgerald wrote long letters to various psychiatrists who had been treating his wife Zelda. Some of them recommended that Scott should also be treated. We learn from one of his biographers, Andrew Turnbull, that "Fitzgerald balked at psychotherapy for himself, partly from pride . . . and partly from the artist's instinctive distrust of having his inner workings tampered with. He was afraid that psychiatric treatment might make him a reasoning, analytic person rather than a feeling one, and he instanced several novelists who had been psychoanalyzed and had written nothing but trash ever since." Like many other writers he regarded his neuroses, drinking included, as part of his literary equipment; perhaps that is another of the tribal weaknesses. As Louise Bogan said in her poem "Several Voices Out of a Cloud,"

*Come, drunks and drug-takers; come, perverts unnerved!*
*Receive the laurel, given, though late, on merit; to whom*
*and whenever deserved.*

*Parochial punks, trimmers, nice people, joiners true-blue,*
*Get the hell out of the way of the laurel. It's deathless.*
*And it isn't for you.*

The fifth and last commandment has to do with the deathless laurel. It is that the work of art should be so fashioned as to have an organic shape and a life of its own, derived from but apart from the life of its maker and capable of outlasting it. Only the work provides the artist's claim on the future, his hope of heaven, and it is worth almost any sacrifice of earthly comfort. Proust said at the end of *Time Recaptured*, "Let us allow our body to disintegrate, since each fresh particle that breaks off, now luminous and decipherable, comes and adds itself to our work to complete it at the cost of suffering superfluous to others more gifted and to make it more and more substantial as emotions gradually chip away our life." For Proust, and I suspect for others as well, every true artist is a sculptor chipping away at his own flesh, turning it to stone, and leaving behind him a lasting effigy.

I have said that these five commandments, this pentalogue, have seldom been formulated, but that they persist in the depths of an artist's mind. They inculcate a sense of duty that sometimes, at moments of stress, bursts forth with moral vehemence. "A *mighty will*, there is nothing but that!" James wrote in his notebook. "The integrity of one's will, purpose, faith!" Fitzgerald harangued one of Zelda's psychiatrists about the integrity that makes one writer better than another. "To have something to say," he lectured, "is a question of sleepless nights and worry and endless ratiocination of a subject—of endless trying to dig out the essential truth, the essential justice. As a first premise you have to develop a conscience and if on top of that you have talent so much the better. But if you have the talent without the conscience, you are just one of many thousand journalists."

Will, conscience, probity: the solemn words keep recurring when artists are speaking about themselves and forget to be ironical. "A writer should be of as great probity and honesty as a priest of God," Hemingway said in his introduction to *Men at War*. "He is either honest or not, as a woman is either chaste or not, and after one piece of dishonest writing he is never the same again." Later he said to me, "If you once do something shitty it spoils everything else you do, like the one bad apple in the barrel." We have learned from the record that Hemingway did many shitty or scoundrelly things, perhaps more of them than any other famous American writer except Robert Frost, our other great example of a man who produced masterpieces in spite of moral failings (or partly because of them, who knows?). Most of Hemingway's derelictions were caused by his raging desire to be first in everything. Many of them took the form of attacks with stiletto or bludgeon on persons who had helped him—Sherwood Anderson, Ford Madox Ford, Fitzgerald, Gertrude Stein—as if he were trying to obliterate the notion that he had ever accepted help. His image as an omnicompetent hero had to be preserved at any cost to his friends. As a writer, however, Hemingway tried hard to observe those five commandments, including the adjuration to give the lowdown on himself (as note "The Snows of Kilimanjaro").

Frost too was bent on being first, though not in everything; he merely wanted to be first in public esteem as a poet and a sage. He too made ruthless and sometimes childish attacks on anyone who seemed to threaten his primacy. In reviewing Lawrance Thompson's biography of Frost, James Dickey said of him, "No one who reads this book will ever again believe in the Frost Story, the Frost myth, which includes the premises that Frost the man was kindly, forbearing, energetic, hardworking, goodneighborly, or anything but the small-minded, vindictive, ill-tempered, egotistic, cruel, and unforgiving man he was until the world deigned to accept at face value his estimate of himself." Bernard DeVoto, who had worshiped him, put all that in simpler words. "You're a good poet," he said after Frost had carried jealousy to the point of setting fire to a fistful of papers in order to disrupt a poetry reading by his rival Archibald MacLeish—"You're a good poet, Robert, but you're a bad man."

Frost agreed with him in a letter to DeVoto that tried and failed to effect a reconciliation. "Look out for me," he said. "... I'm telling you something in a self conscious moment that may throw light on every page of my writing for what it is worth. I mean I am a bad bad man." No less than Hemingway, however, he observed those five commandments in his work, which was sometimes foolish—when he tried to be a pundit—but was never fraudulent. He spoke in his true voice. In his work he was the opposite of a scoundrel.

4 ✍ One feature of the artist's code is that it preaches a curious mixture of extreme self-centeredness with something close to self-abnegation. The ideal artist, according to the code, is completely absorbed in himself, or rather in the task of producing something out of himself, but he forgets himself in the task, often to the point of deliberately incurring hardship, illness, or public ridicule. A more disturbing feature of the pentalogue is that it is dangerously incomplete. Unlike the Decalogue, it is not a guide to one's daily conduct as a spouse, a parent, or a neighbor. It does not guard the artist against the seven deadly sins, except possibly sloth; for the rest he can be proud, covetous, lustful, angry, gluttonous, and bursting with envy. The code even leads him into temptation with regard to some lesser sins or defects of character, as notably selfishness, vanity, neglect of one's family, and the abuse of stimulants or depressants in the hope of releasing one's imagination. Nevertheless it *is* a moral code and one that some great artists have followed with saintlike dedication; one thinks of Flaubert, James, Mallarmé, Joyce, Thomas Mann, and of a few others, including some who literally sacrificed their lives to their work. Art has its own hagiography and its Book of Martyrs.

Marcel Proust is clearly one of the martyrs. He died at fifty, having surrendered what should have been his remaining years on earth in order to bring his novel as near as possible to completion. Living alone, except for the family housekeeper; gaunt, wasted, unshaven; barely sustaining himself on beer and ices (he had them brought round from the Ritz); refusing other nourishment because someone had foolishly told him that the brain functions best on an empty stomach, he worked night after night on his enormous manuscript. In his last months, when he took to writing in bed because he no longer had strength enough to sit at a table, the work went very slowly. One night at three o'clock he made the old housekeeper sit beside him and—now that he was too weak to hold a pencil—dictated to her for a long time. "Celeste," he said at last, "I think what I've made you take down is very good. I shall stop now. I can't go on." He died the following afternoon.

Proust was a social climber, a shameless careerist, and an invert who loved nobody after his mother died; for others his strongest feeling was jealousy. Still, there is no question about his deliberate self-martyrdom; and one can think of many others who lived and died as victims to their art. In some cases such as those of Fitzgerald, Hart Crane, and Dylan Thomas, the victimage resulted from their persisting in a course of conduct which they recognized as self-destructive, but which they thought essential to the production of masterpieces. One might call some of them rogues, but they were clearly not scoundrels or sons-of-bitches.

And so, by a long detour, we come back to the original question, whether character and art are correlated. The answer is that they are, but in a complicated fashion. Masterpieces can be produced by saints of art or of the church; they can be produced by rascals or crazies or even, at times, by accident; but I refuse to think that they can be produced by genuine scoundrels, "men without honor or virtue." The artist, no matter what his sins may be, is bent on giving himself away; the scoundrel has no choice but to hide himself as best he can. In the end he cannot help revealing his scoundrelism—not so much in his subject matter or in what he seems to be saying about it, as rather in the shape and sound, the color and rhythm of his words. False, false, the reader unconsciously feels, closing the book. Once I made in my journal a statement that needs to be qualified, but that still holds a general truth. "No complete son-of-a-bitch," I said, "ever wrote a good sentence."

# Index

Hillyer, Robert, 37, 39
*Histoire de la Littérature Française*
(Jasinski), 18
*Histoire de la Révolution* (Michelet), 4
History, rejection of, 240–41
Hitler, Adolf, 100, 110, 127, 134, 135, 136, 147, 149–54 *passim,* 157, 158, 160
Holland, 59
Holmes, Oliver Wendell, 2
Homer, Winslow, 2
*Hound & Horn,* 76
Howe, Julia Ward, 163, 166
Howells, William Dean, 2, 7, 162, 163, 165
Humes, Harold, 178
Humphries, Rolfe, 72
Huntington, Archer M., 164, 168–174 *passim*
Hyman, Stanley Edgar, 23, 24, 26, 28

*Idea of a Theatre* (Ferguson), 204n.
Imagism, 107, 167
*In Cold Blood* (Capote), 209
*In Our Time* (Hemingway), 20
*In Search of Bisco* (Caldwell), 130
Interviews with writers (*Paris Review*), 176–89 *passim*
Ionesco, Eugène, 196
Irving, Washington, 18
Irwin, John T., 215, 216, 217, 219, 220, 221, 222, 224–30 *passim;* quoted, 217, 218, 221, 225, 228, 230
Italy, 6, 237

James, Henry, 2, 5, 9, 125, 163, 178, 180, 182, 187, 246, 259, 262, 265; quoted, 5, 181, 259, 261, 262, 263
James, William, 2, 146
Jarrell, Randall, 107
Jasinski, René, 18
Jeffers, Robinson, 104, 107, 167, 175
Jefferson, Thomas, 9
Jenkins, Sue, 38
Jewett, Sarah Orne, 2
Jewish ethnic tradition, 19
*Jig of Forslin, The* (Aiken), 232
*John Brown's Body* (Benét), 167
Johnson, Robert Underwood, 162, 163–64, 166, 167, 168, 175

Jonson, Ben, 239
*Joseph Andrews* (Fielding), 19
Josephson, Matthew, 62, 90
*Journey in the Seaboard Slave States* (Olmsted), 96
*Journeyman* (Caldwell), 127
Joyce, James, 125, 127, 205, 265
*Judgment Day* (Farrell), 99

Kafka, Franz, 20, 237
Kauffman, Reginald Wright, 53
Kaye-Smith, Sheila, 55
Kazin, Alfred, 22
Keats, John, 42
Kennedy, Margaret, 204, 211
Kenner, Hugh, 195, 198, 203, 209n.; quoted, 195, 209n.
Kerouac, Jack, 15
*Kid, The* (Aiken), 239
Kierkegaard, Sören, 20
Kipling, Rudyard, 190; quoted, 190
Kirkland, Jack, 115, 116
Koestler, Arthur, 110
Kreymborg, Alfred, 118
Krivitsky, Walter, 154

La Farge, John, 2, 163
Laforgue, Jules, 35, 36, 45, 70–81 *passim*
*Land of Plenty, The* (Cantwell), 98–99, 105
Language, changes in, during 1960s, 254–55
Lannigan, Helen, 118
Lardner, Ring, 3, 209
*Last Tycoon, The* (Fitzgerald), 102
League of American Writers, 138
Legouis, Emile, 13
Lenin, Vladimir, 145, 146, 156, 157
Lessing, Doris, 137
*Lesson of the Masters, The,* 200
*Let Us Now Praise Famous Men* (Agee), 98, 106
*Letters on Literature and Politics* (Wilson), 154n.
Lewis, Sinclair, 3, 166, 167, 168
Li Po, 239, 243
Liberals, guilt feelings of, 136
Lieber, Maxim, 115
Light, Jimmy, 38
Lindsay, Vachel, 247
Literary Guild, 84
*Literary History of the United States* (Spiller et al.), 17

810.9
COW    Cowley, Malcolm
       -and I worked at
       the writer's trade

810.9
COW    Cowley, Malcolm
       -and I worked at
       the writer's trade

## The Helen Kate Furness
## Free Library
Wallingford, Pennsylvania  19086